Human Rights and Social Movements

NEIL STAMMERS

PLUTO PRESS
www.plutobooks.com

First published 2009 by Pluto Press
345 Archway Road, London N6 5AA
175 Fifth Avenue, New York, NY 10010

www.plutobooks.com

Distributed in the United States of America exclusively by
Palgrave Macmillan, a division of St. Martin's Press LLC,
175 Fifth Avenue, New York, NY 10010

British Library Cataloguing in Publication Data
A catalogue record for this book is available from the British Library

ISBN   978 0 7453 2912 3   Hardback
ISBN   978 0 7453 2911 6   Paperback

Library of Congress Cataloging in Publication Data applied for

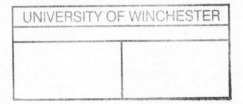

This book is printed on paper suitable for recycling and made from
fully managed and sustained forest sources. Logging, pulping and
manufacturing processes are expected to conform to the environmental
standards of the country of origin. The paper may contain up to
70 per cent post-consumer waste.

10   9   8   7   6   5   4   3   2   1

Designed and produced for Pluto Press by
Chase Publishing Services Ltd, Sidmouth, England
Typeset from disk by Stanford DTP Services, Northampton, England
Printed and bound in the European Union by
CPI Antony Rowe, Chippenham and Eastbourne

CONTENTS

LIST OF FIGURES

ACKNOWLEDGEMENTS

This book has been a long time in the making and draws much from experiences outside and beyond an academic environment. In particular, many years of working in, and helping to manage, a range of non-governmental organisations concerned with rights, homelessness, welfare and housing in my home town have importantly informed this study. So it is right to begin these acknowledgements with a big thank you to users and colleagues of Brighton Housing Trust, Brighton Law Centre and Brighton Rights Advice Centre.

Though seemingly an age away now, my doctoral research was on civil liberties in Britain during the Second World War and I now realise that the seeds for this study were in some ways sown then, when I was unable to find satisfactory pre-existing theoretical frameworks through which my research could be adequately presented. So thanks to Bob Benewick and John Dearlove for all their support in those early years and subsequently. From 1989 to 2005 I worked in the Politics Department at the University of Sussex. Innumerable discussions with students, friends and colleagues both in the department and the School of Social Sciences and Cultural Studies have helped to shape important aspects of this project. Particular thanks go to students and faculty involved with the graduate programmes in Human Rights and in Social and Political Thought.

While work on this book was under way I was also lucky enough to be involved with the Development Research Centre on Citizenship, Participation and Accountability at the Institute of Development Studies led by John Gaventa. I gained some important insights and met some great people through my involvement with this Centre. Special thanks go to Celestine Nyamu-Musembi, Research Fellow at the Institute, for her consistent encouragement and support for this project. Many others have also offered me inspiration, support and encouragement for this project over the years. Amongst these, Christien van den Anker, Amy Bartholomew, Gurminder Bhambra, Jane Cowan, Marie Dembour, Tony Evans, Anna Grear, Beate Jahn, Zdenek Kavan, Jenneth Parker and Justin Rosenberg all have a special place.

I was also very lucky to have a group of friends and colleagues who were willing to comment on my work as it was going along. Marie Dembour and Zdenek Kavan both unflinchingly waded through draft chapters offering the constructive criticism that is so invaluable and necessary to anyone endeavouring to write. Then Gurminder Bhambra, Emily Haslam, Jenneth Parker, Rob Raeburn, and Zdenek Kavan all went through the completed manuscript providing vital feedback on a range of issues great and small. I must say another word or two about Zdenek Kavan here. With remarkable patience and good grace, especially when I refused to heed his advice, he has sustained his interest and engagement throughout. Truly help beyond words.

Clearly, this book is much better for all the help, comments and advice I have received, but the usual indemnity applies: weaknesses, mistakes and failures are my responsibility alone.

My partner Teresa Harris has seen the process from beginning to end, putting up with some of those strange habits writers engage in – in my case, for example, jumping out of bed at an unearthly hour to make a note about some point which seemed so crucial at the time. Despite such habits, she has offered me unswerving support and helped to keep me grounded in the world. The importance of this latter point can hardly be overestimated.

LIST OF ACRONYMS
AND ABBREVIATIONS

CRC   Convention on the Rights of the Child
DFID   Department for International Development
GA   Globalisation from above
GB   Globalisation from below
FoEI   Friends of the Earth International
INGO   International non-governmental organisation
(I)NGO   This acronym is used to mean international non-governmental organisation *and/or* non-governmental organisation. I use the more familiar acronyms NGO or INGO where I want to be more specific
LGBT   Lesbian, Gay, Bisexual and Transgender
OHCHR   Office of the High Commissioner for Human Rights
MAI   Multilateral Agreement on Investment
NGO   Non governmental organisation
NSM   New Social Movement
TSMO   Transnational social movement organisation
UNDHR   United Nations Declaration of Human Rights, 1948
WSF   World Social Forum
WTO   World Trade Organisation

INTRODUCTION

This book explores the analytical significance of the historical link between human rights and social movements, arguing that ordinary people – working together in social movements – have always been a key originating source of human rights. The approach taken here contrasts starkly with other approaches that claim the meaningful origins of human rights are to be found in philosophy or law. As a consequence, this book also tries to identify the contours of a framework through which the potentials and limits of human rights might be better and more effectively assessed.

Given the millions of words written about human rights worldwide each year, the first instinct of many readers might be to wonder whether anything novel could possibly be said on the subject. Yet, because the significance of the link between human rights and social movements remains largely unexplored in the specialist academic literature on human rights, such an investigation is sorely needed – not only for understanding human rights in the world today but also for interrogating other key areas, for example, around power, globalisation, democracy, participation and, last but not least, contemporary forms of institutions and institutionalisation.

Prior to the mid-1990s, any reference at all to a connection between human rights and social movements was a rarity. One exception was Stuart Scheingold's (2005) *The Politics of Rights*, first published in 1974. Occasionally the odd comment might be made (for example, Weston, 1992), but generally the literature on human rights ignored social movements altogether. The last decade has witnessed the beginnings of a shift, with some well-known scholars at least acknowledging a historical connection between social movements and human rights. From positions avowedly rooted in the liberal tradition, Michael Ignatieff (2001) has brought social movements close to centre stage in his recent account of *Human Rights as Politics and Idolatry* and the second edition of Jack Donnelly's (2003) *Universal Human Rights in Theory and Practice* gives significantly more attention to social movement struggles than did the first edition of that work. Coming from the field of legal scholarship, Steiner and Alston's (2000) encyclopaedic volume *International Human Rights in Context* makes what they call the 'human rights movement' a central focus of their work. Attention to social movements has also been paid by more critical voices. Both Costas Douzinas (2000) and Boaventura de Sousa Santos (1995, 1999) have called for the understanding of human rights to be reconstructed through grasping their connections to social movement struggles, while Upendra Baxi has argued that over the last 60 years it has been the oppressed of the world – mobilised in and through social movements – who have been the hidden authors of contemporary developments in human rights (Baxi 2002). Balakrishnan Rajagopal (2003) puts social movements at the centre of 'third world resistance' in his focus on the possibilities for the development of 'international law from below'. Finally, Brooke Ackerly (2008) has attempted to reconstruct a political theory of human rights from insights and analyses drawn from feminist activism. Yet, despite these beginnings, the connection between human rights and social movements is still generally ignored and certainly no systematic attempt has been made to examine its analytic significance. As Baxi put it a few years ago, 'we have as yet no historiography, nor an adequate social theory of human rights' (Baxi 2002: xi). This book attempts to address Baxi's concerns, though in an indicative rather than conclusive way.

A central theme that runs throughout this book is that the historical emergence and development of human rights needs to be understood and analysed in the context of social movement struggles against extant relations and structures of power. In other words, this is an important element of the answer to the question 'where do human rights come from?' By itself, this answer can be interpreted in a way that avoids disturbing many assumptions that dominate the human rights literature. But when its implications are fully integrated into attempts to answer the question 'what are human rights?', then the consequences are much more far-reaching. For example, to the extent that human rights initially emerge as 'struggle concepts' to support social movement challenges to power, the question of what happens to them when they are institutionalised is then necessarily brought into focus. The trajectory of my analysis suggests that – once institutionalised – human rights come to stand in a much more ambiguous relation to power. While they can still be used to challenge power, their origins and meanings as 'struggle concepts' can get lost or be switched in ways that result in human rights becoming a tool of power, not a challenge to it. While many critics of human rights have made this latter point and explained it in a variety of ways, they have rarely sought to focus their attention on the nature of institutions and processes of institutionalisation as such. What I will call the paradox of institutionalisation leads us into areas of analysis rarely touched upon in the human rights literature.

Most obviously it poses the question of what can be done about this paradox. Can it be resolved? Or does it need to be recognised as a necessary and perennial problem, perhaps requiring the reconstruction of ideas and practices of human rights? Because it is a paradox of *institutionalisation* it also leads us towards a broader consideration of the relations between institutionalised forms of human rights and non-institutionalised or pre-institutionalised expressions of human rights. What are these latter forms and what is their relevance to our understandings of human rights? Such questions then point, in turn, to a consideration of the relationship between human rights and other forms and aspects of historical social movement struggles which have not generated expressions of human rights. Should we, for example, locate human rights as one expression of that broader pantheon that is the history of struggles against oppression and domination? I will argue that claims for human rights have sought to challenge 'old wrongs' organised through five sites of power that have trans-historical and trans-cultural reach and impact.

This brings me to a point where it is important to spell out what this study is *not* about, or rather, to anticipate possible misunderstandings of underlying assumptions. Firstly, I am not claiming that ideas and practices in respect of human rights are only or solely constructed by social movements. I am simply making the case that social movements are an important source of human rights praxis and should not be ignored. Secondly, as indicated above, neither am I arguing that human rights are in any way the dominant form of social movement praxis. Social movements generate all sorts of ideas and practices, only some of which relate to human rights. Thirdly, while I believe that social movements have been an important source of change and transformation in human history, I do not believe that they are the sole source of such change and transformation. In other words, I do not privilege social movements as *the* agents of historical change. Finally, let me stress that I do not believe that social movements are necessarily forces for good. Both history and the contemporary world are full of examples of deeply regressive and xenophobic social movements. That said, I do believe that the historical record shows that the creative praxis of social movements has been an important source of positive developments in human history. Whether human rights should be regarded as one of those positive developments is one of the fundamental questions to be tackled here.

It is important to spell out the approach I have taken in researching this book and how I have chosen to present it. This study is not based on primary research. I neither delved into historical archives, nor did I undertake research on contemporary documents or interview human rights activists in social movements. Given the necessary breadth of this study, any pretensions to conduct systematic primary research would have quickly collapsed under its own weight. So, instead, this study takes a synthetic approach. Having been engaged with the specialist literature on human rights over the last 20 years and found it wanting, I have drawn much of my material from work and scholarship in a range of cognate disciplines and intellectual traditions which intersect with the study of human rights.

As I shall argue in Chapter 1, dominant assumptions in the human rights literature amount to a set of orthodoxies which are rarely challenged but which seriously distort understandings of human rights by obscuring sight of the links to social movements. To examine and challenge those orthodoxies I have drawn from substantial and authoritative work in what I hope is an effective interdisciplinary way. For example, in exploring the place of human rights in the American and French revolutions, I began by trying to identify authoritative reviews of the historical scholarship by historians specialising in a specific topic. Thus, I was able to locate historical arguments relating to social movements and human rights in the wider trajectories and traditions that comprise historical scholarship on a specific subject matter. From there, I then tried to engage with the commonalities and differences across various sets of specialist literatures in order to reflect critically on the assumptions found in the dominant human rights literature. In later chapters, when I engage with topics such as institutionalisation, 'new social movements' and globalisation, I have likewise sought to access substantive and authoritative scholarship from social theory, social movement studies, international relations and politics. My underlying claim is that, through accessing quality scholarship in these disciplines and traditions, the limits and distortions of much of the existing human rights literature quickly comes to light and the possibilities for reassessment and reinterpretation are suggestively opened up. Yet, given the paucity of present work on human rights and social movements, this volume can only be a beginning not an endpoint, which is why it is offered as indicative rather than in any way a conclusive study.

In developing this work, I have intentionally tried to interweave chronological and analytical themes in a way that generates coherence in the development of the narrative. However, a certain unevenness remains which I hope the reader will not find too disruptive. The chronological theme is clear enough to begin with. Chapter 2 focuses on the seventeenth and eighteenth centuries and Chapter 3 on the nineteenth century. In Chapter 4, the chronological theme takes a back seat, but is still there in so far as its historical focus is on the establishment of the international human rights system from the end of the Second World War. Chapter 5 is historically grounded by the so-called New Social Movements, which are widely assumed to have emerged from the 1960s onwards. Chapter 6 is something of a chronological pause, although the historical connections remain in so far as it engages with work that emerged subsequent to the rise of the so-called new social movements. Chapter 7 brings us to the recent past by looking at developments and analyses from the 1990s onwards. Chapter 8 explores specific key contemporary issues with one eye on the future.

A key range of analytical themes that ground and inform the study are presented in Chapter 1. The first half of that chapter introduces a range of critiques of the dominant human rights literature summed up by my use of the metaphor of a hall of mirrors. The second half begins by setting out my stall, clarifying underlying assumptions and orientations towards key issues in social analysis. I then offer a conceptualisation of social movements and look at their capacity to generate creative social praxis. The analytical themes of Chapters 2 and 3 develop my critique of the dominant literature through engagement with historical evidence and interpretation. Chapter 4 is a key analytical chapter, introducing and developing the notion of the paradox of institutionalisation. It does so in relation both to the histories of the two previous chapters and in relation to the establishment of the international human rights system. Chapter 5 begins to develop some reconstructive proposals relating to the identification of 'old wrongs' and recognition of the persistence of trans-historical and trans-cultural sites of power. It is argued that, historically, a creative praxis of human rights has been constructed as a challenge to the legitimacy of such power. Chapter 6 then examines the importance of expressive and instrumental dimensions of human rights activism, arguing that this specific terminology enables us to transcend the limitations of debates about human rights focused on interests, identities and recognition. Chapter 7 engages with a wide range of arguments about globalisation and whether any meaningful 'globalisation from below' is possible. Finally, in Chapter 8, these various analytical threads are brought together in an assessment of the contemporary crises of human rights, consideration of what might constitute creative human rights praxis in the future and some exploration of the relationship between human rights and possibilities for institutional democratisation.

1

GETTING BEYOND THE HALL
OF MIRRORS

To explore the significance of the relationship between social movements and human rights it is necessary to embark on a journey that traverses territory perhaps unfamiliar to some working in the field of human rights. It takes us beyond the specialist literature to draw from a range of academic disciplines and to re-examine some fundamental questions underpinning all forms of social analysis. The journey also requires some willingness to acknowledge and engage with complexity and ambiguity. The regurgitation of familiar assumptions and arguments – no matter how authoritative, established or theoretically well-honed – will not do. In particular, simplistic claims that human rights are necessarily and entirely either 'good' or 'bad' only serve to confuse and distort the debate about the origins, potential and limits of human rights. Yet much work that specifically focuses on human rights implicitly or explicitly tends towards one of these polar positions. I will use the terms 'uncritical proponents' and 'uncritical critics', sometimes shortened simply to 'proponents' and 'critics', as a way of referring to work that exhibits such tendencies. To understand why the literature on human rights is shaped in the way it is, we have to examine the ways in which assumptions and positions underlying much of that work are themselves patterned. To do this, I employ the metaphor of a hall of mirrors. My argument is that this underlying patterning has effectively hidden the link between human rights and social movements, so much so that understandings of human rights drawn from this literature are typically and systematically distorted.

While it may be relatively easy to demonstrate how the link between human rights and social movements has been obscured, to then go on to assess this link requires us to engage with specific approaches to social analysis. While these approaches are now well-recognised and well-respected within the social sciences generally, they have rarely been applied to the study of human rights. Thus to make these explicit and transparent, the second part of this chapter begins by looking at three of them: the relationship between actors, structures, agency and power; the nature of social change and social transformation, and the configuration of the relations between the social, the political, the economic and the cultural. Having set out my stall on these topics, I then look at the concept of social movements and explore how social movements impact on historical and social change. My argument here is that social movements can be innovative and creative and that, historically, ideas and practices in respect of human rights have been persistent and important constructions arising from the creative praxis of social movements.

The Hall of Mirrors

By suggesting that we can get beyond the hall of mirrors, I am not claiming that *the* authentic version of human rights will then somehow be magically revealed. Clearly, ideas and practices in respect of human rights do not just emanate from social movements praxis and there is no doubting that the scholarly literature has provided and developed many crucial insights in our understandings of human rights. Nevertheless, I am suggesting that we will find another story of human rights: one that is no less authentic and one which, moreover, provides us with ways to develop a new analytic framework through which the potentials and limits of human rights can be critically reassessed.

The sort of hall of mirrors I am talking about here is the type found at funfairs and carnivals: those that produce distorted, often grotesque, reflections of their subject matter. By the hall, I mean the entire range of contemporary social praxis around human rights worldwide. That includes all those ideas and practices connected to human rights whether these come from academic scholarship, non-governmental organisations, states, international institutions or social movements. The mirrors in the hall refer to that specialist scholarly literature whose specific and central focus is on human rights. This is the sort of literature that most human rights scholars would see as being 'within the field' and which is likely to appear on reading lists for undergraduate and postgraduate courses on human rights. Below I identify two ways in which those mirrors have been shaped and polished, firstly through academic disciplinarity and secondly through the ideological predispositions and commitments of authors and the institutions they are involved with. As will become clear, there are strong links between them but there are also important distinctions, not least because it is through academic disciplinarity that claims to intellectual rigour, objectivity and truth are often made.

My various discussions of the human rights literature throughout this book could quite properly be seen as an analysis of discourse. So it is worth briefly explaining why I have chosen not to present it through the methods of discourse analysis. As my above references to mirrors and distortion indicate, there is – in part – a 'realist' underpinning to my approach to social enquiry. This contrasts with 'idealist' trajectories often found in post-structuralist approaches to discourse analysis derived, for example, from the work of Michel Foucault or as developed by Ernesto Laclau and Chantal Mouffe.[1] So, while I insist that human rights are and can only be socially constructed, the whole point of this book is to argue that there are nevertheless 'realities' to human rights that are not properly recognised or given appropriate signification in the 'rhetoric' that is the specialist scholarly literature on human rights. Linked to the above are two further specific reasons why I have chosen to work outside a 'discourse analytic' framework. Firstly, influential theorists such as Laclau and Mouffe (1985) have expanded their use of the term discourse to cover the whole of what I call here social praxis (see also Howarth 2000:Ch.6) thus threatening to obliterate any analytical distinction between 'rhetoric' and 'reality'. Secondly, key approaches to discourse analysis are rooted in what, in my view, is an untenable epistemological assumption that models and approaches drawn from structural linguistics and its various derivatives can be usefully and meaningfully applied to the study of social relations in general (for example, Howarth 2000:13).

Academic Disciplines

Let me start with the apparently obscure point that there are strong 'imperialist' tendencies in academic disciplines. Practitioners often regard their own discipline as the 'master' discipline; the discipline through which all other academic disciplines should be understood. There are frequent attempts by one discipline to subordinate or colonise another. Additionally, practitioners in disciplines perceived as 'subordinate' often try to ape supposedly 'superior' disciplines in attempts to demonstrate the virility of their own work. As the terminology suggests academic disciplines are also highly disciplinary, their boundaries policed and their subject matter and methodologies vetted in their disciplinary associations and through the process of peer review for the top academic journals (Sayer 2003; Moran 2006). The importance and impact of these two tendencies ought to be clear enough within academic scholarship itself (although often they are not) but the fact that practitioners outside the academy have been trained within particular disciplines means that they are also likely to take the assumptions of 'their' discipline out into the wider world if, for example, they are employed as a researcher by an international institution or non-governmental organisation.

While territorial claims and arguments over legitimacy are familiar themes of academic debate, disciplines are neither monolithic nor homogeneous. Indeed, historically it has often been the work of disciplinary dissidents that has proved the most interesting and innovative. One straightforward explanation for this relates to the gaps or spaces that can exist between different disciplinary boundaries, meaning that potentially important aspects of a particular topic will be ignored except by those willing to step outside of their disciplinary boundaries. As Susan Buck-Morss puts it in a fascinating article on 'Hegel and Haiti', '[d]isciplinary boundaries allow counterevidence to belong to someone else's story' (Buck-Morss 2000:822).

Human rights is an unusual field of study. It is not a discipline in its own right and neither can it be confined within one academic discipline. That said, just a few disciplines have historically dominated the scholarship on human rights. By far the most important are philosophy and law, each claiming the centre of gravity of human rights within their own traditions. Somewhat less central but of increasing importance in the last few decades have been the disciplines of international relations and political science.[2] So what are the key characteristics involved in these various disciplines? Firstly, philosophical approaches to human rights typically focus on the internal logic and/or analytical rigour of a canon of celebrated texts. In many university departments and programmes, this canon exclusively comprises the work of male thinkers of European descent. More fundamentally, there is often no attempt to examine human activity beyond the realm of thought.[3] Indeed, what many people do when they theorise from such perspectives is intentionally ignore the real world in an attempt to grasp a cleaner, more pure, truth or logic. In other words, they try to 'get beyond the fray' so as to access some deeper truth or meaning. While an admirable ambition, one manifest consequence is that social activism and social struggles are usually ignored, except in so far as they can be reduced to philosophical ideas found in those canonical texts. Switching attention to law, human activity does come back into the picture. But most evidently this is activity in judicial institutions and the interpretation of legislation by lawyers, judges and legal scholars. At the heart of the study of law are, once again, the study and interpretation of texts and another canon, this time 'the law' as it stands at any particular point in time within a specified jurisdiction. While institutional structures of legal systems are studied, all other forms of social activism and social struggles are typically ignored except in so far as they intersect with the law or related legal processes. In international relations and political science there has been a strong tendency towards state-centric approaches. In the case of international relations this has traditionally meant looking at the 'outside' of state activity, that is, what states do in the inter-state system (see Walker 1993; Bayliss and Smith 2005). In the case of political science this has meant looking at the 'inside' of state activity, that is, what goes on within a particular state (or in a number of states that are being compared with one another). Despite this important distinction, both disciplines strongly reinforce the view that human rights are, or should be, understood through the analyses of states, state policies and/or the inter-state system. Now there are critical traditions in all these disciplines. Indeed, it has often been scholars from those critical traditions who have posed questions about the link between social movements and human rights. Nevertheless, it remains clear that neither the orientations nor the perceived boundaries of these disciplines are hospitable to any sort of analytical focus on the relation between human rights and social movements. In the last decade or two an increasing number of anthropologists and sociologists have begun working on human rights, with some suggestions that an 'anthropology of human rights' or a 'sociology of human rights' would add new and significant understandings to the field (Wilson 1997; Cowan, Dembour and Wilson 2001; Turner 2006). In addition, interesting and significant work is emerging from crossovers and encounters between anthropologists and lawyers (Riles 2006; Dembour 2006; Cowan, 2006). While, clearly, anthropology and sociology also have their own disciplinary orientations and boundaries, their broader focus on 'the cultural' and 'the social' suggest that they ought to be more open to examining the link between social movements and human rights.[4]

One curious but important point to note here is the general absence of history as a discipline within the specialist academic scholarship on human rights. While some historians have worked on or around the subject (for example, Hunt 1996), histories of human rights are more likely to be written by scholars from the disciplines already discussed (see Ishay 2004). This absence of history as a discipline is particularly significant. Firstly, the relationship between human rights and social movements can only be fully grasped through historical, as well as social, analysis. Secondly, as we shall see below, especially in Chapter 2, there is a strong tendency by both proponents and critics to 'read history backwards' – that is, to confuse outcomes with processes and assume that history 'is' what history 'became'. While, of course, there are enormous historiographical debates involved here,[5] the significant involvement of historians in the field of human rights could sensitise scholars from other disciplines to the importance of such issues.

In summary, while the field of human rights demands interdisciplinary scholarship, the mainstream literature on human rights has instead been dominated by the orientations and proclivities of particular disciplines largely inhospitable to the possibility of exploring the link between social movements and human rights.

Political Ideologies

The impact of ideological factors on the specialist scholarship on human rights can hardly be overestimated. Here I deal with political ideologies understood as 'world-views' or *weltanshauung*.[6] It is important to stress that, in specifying the ideological groupings below, it is not my intention to homogenise them. Ideologies are typically diverse, sometimes contradictory, sometimes crosscutting and sometimes overlapping. Nonetheless, it is clear that each of these ideological groupings have had a substantive impact on the way in which ideas and practices around human rights are understood and regarded. Without going into detail, it is important briefly to sketch out key themes as they bear on human rights.[7]

'Classical Liberalism'/Neo-liberalism

A foundational feature is a commitment to stark forms of individualism. Flowing from this is a privileging of an atomised individual pursuing her/his material interests which lies at the centre of a particular understanding of social relations. Freedom in 'the market' is taken to be the archetypal expression of freedom in general. Classical liberals/neo-liberals are not anarchists, they believe in a small but strong state. In other words, state power is regarded as both necessary but an ever present danger. Hence the almost exclusive focus on negative liberties and rights (that is, rights which protect the individual from state power). For classical liberals, only political power (in modern terms, state power) is identified as a problematic and dangerous form of power. There is little or no commitment to ideas and values of equality and solidarity

'Social Liberalism'/Social Democracy

Social liberalism/social democracy appears to make a significant break with the foundational individualism of classical liberalism and, in this sense, appears to work from a very different set of assumptions. Most importantly, the individual is recognised as a social individual not an atomised one. While the extent and depth of this recognition can be questioned (see Stammers 1995) it does lead to accounts of human rights that appear distinct from classical/neo-liberal versions. While social liberalism/social democracy remains committed to the capitalist market as a site of innovation, growth and allocation, it recognises the potential for markets to produce inequalities which can have serious adverse social consequences. Thus, rather than seeing markets as an expression of freedom, markets are seen as necessary but problematic. Social liberalism/social democracy thus emphasises some form of management of markets to ameliorate inequalities. Social liberalism/social democracy embraces notions of positive as well as negative liberties and rights but can be highly state-centric in its orientation to them. Social liberalism/social democracy is also much more sensitive and accommodating to issues around equality and solidarity but again state-centric, in most guises committed to elite rule and 'technocratic governance' (Stammers 2001a).

Reductionist Marxism

Here I am talking about a series of positions and assumptions that have been articulated by dominant forms of Marxism in the world over the last 100 years or so. But there are also important currents in Marxism that would firmly reject the positions and assumptions of 'reductionist Marxism'. Indeed, below I often use the work of Marxist scholars, especially the 'English Marxist Historians', to develop some of my arguments. What I am calling reductionist Marxism assumes both a historical teleology and a form of economic determinism which leads to seeing systems of ideas as superstructural epiphenomena produced by, and merely reflecting, the deeper economic and historical logic of the particular mode of production within which it is situated. Similarly, it is understood that social change is driven by contradictions in deep structures and that the agency of social actors is derivative of those structures and subordinate to them. In terms of political strategy, reductionist Marxism relies on a binary polarity between reform and revolution so that all reform is assumed to reinforce the existing status quo whereas revolution is assumed to overthrow it. Any possibility of transformative change being achieved anywhere along a continuum between these binary polarities is typically obscured.

Feminism

While reductionist forms of Marxism have been historically dominant within the broader Marxist tradition, in the case of feminism it is not possible to argue that there are either dominant or marginalised attitudes towards human rights. Feminism has been persistently and deeply split over the question in complex ways that cannot be easily captured by looking at, for example, distinctions between liberal, socialist, radical and poststructuralist feminists. That said, what feminism brings to debates about human rights is a recognition that ideas and practices of human rights have been significantly gendered. This takes a variety of forms, from exploring the extent to which concepts of human rights are necessarily 'malestream' and need to be abandoned, to subjecting the relationship between human rights and women's rights to close forensic examination – for example the incisive work of Catherine Mackinnon (1993) on the role of rape in war – to struggling for the non-discriminatory implementation of existing human rights. What unites all forms of feminism and is also central to this study is the crucial recognition that power has been fundamentally organised around sex and gender across histories and cultures.

Post-structuralism/Post-modernism/Post-colonialism

Despite the treacherous waters of trying to untangle various forms of 'post-isms', perspectives on human rights from these sorts of positions will likely focus on the extent to which human rights are a universalising metanarrative of the Enlightenment, a touchstone of Enlightenment and modernist thinking. Underpinning this is likely to be incredulity towards the idea of a coherent or unified subject who can be the bearer of human rights. A particularly important slant that post-colonialism adds to this mix is a critique of Eurocentric assumptions and western bias in many under-standings of human rights. Post-colonialist insights lead us to the key point that the history of human rights cannot be separated historically from the conquest, genocide, slavery and forms of colonialism perpetrated by European powers and their colonists in other lands. However, curiously, what constitutes Europe and Eurocentrism are then themselves sometimes homogenised and essentialised to the extent that recognition of the impact of resistance and struggle on European ideas and practices 'is lost in the timelessness of colonial modernity' (Cooper 2005:16). The relationship between knowledge and power has been subjected to careful analysis and the concept of power itself significantly problematised, especially through the works of Michel Foucault. However, as mentioned above, we also need to note the strong tendency in many 'post-isms' towards understanding social relations through the analysis of discourse which can lead to forms of 'discourse reductionism'. Of particular concern is the extent to which the turn to discourse brings with it a return to forms of (albeit complex) structural determinism and the elimination of the possibility of social actors being able to engage in any form of meaningful agency.

Strong Communitarianisms

I am stretching my terminology here because strong communitarianisms encompass an even wider and heterogeneous set of ideas than those groupings discussed above. By using the term I am trying to cover a range of belief systems which both seek to identify and privilege some sort of authentic, holistic, 'uncontaminated' community as the basic unit of social life and are driven by assumptions of ontological, epistemological and methodological holism through which individual human beings are seen as part of a greater whole to which they are (or should be) subservient. Both the strength and weakness of this term is that it can encompass political and religious ideologies and demonstrates ideational linkages that connect forms of conservatism, fascism and Marxism in the west with a wide range of other communitarian perspectives worldwide which have produced – for example – Islamic and Asian critiques of human rights. More broadly, the strong cultural relativist critique of human rights (Brems 1997) is usually derived from strong communitarian positions.

A Contestation of Mirrors

This disciplinary and ideological shaping and polishing means that the mirrors in my metaphorical hall reflect their surroundings and each other in a myriad of crosscutting and intersecting ways. In previous work (Stammers 1999a) I identified four particularly important ways in which these mirrors have been fashioned which I labelled 'metaphysical abstraction', 'legal positivism', 'strong particularism' and 'structuralism'. The first two of these deeply impact on the literature from proponents of human rights, while the latter two often underpin the work of critics of human rights.

The problem with metaphysical abstraction lies quite simply in attempts to construct supposedly timeless and universal understandings of human rights that are entirely independent of social context. Although most obviously associated in disciplinary terms with political philosophy and normative political theory, it has wider purchase. For example, it lies at the heart of virtually all liberal and social democratic attempts to justify and ground the concept of human rights theoretically. Without denying that metaphysical abstraction can provide important insights into the human condition, there is a real problem in so far as the analytic categories generated and deployed by this method can dangerously obscure, rather than clarify, our understanding of the social world.

The term 'legal positivism' is not to be understood here in its technical sense. Rather, it signals the intent and ambition of what might be termed 'the global human rights industry'. There is an enormous literature arising from this industry, a literature over-whelmingly concerned with the establishment, implementation and enforcement of human rights as state and international public law. Here the problem is not that social movement struggles are unrecognised. They would probably be acknowledged as having provoked important recent debates on human rights. But these approaches are tightly focused on the processes of institutionali-sation and legal codification and thus the connection between social movements and human rights is not given any analytic weight. While obviously intimately connected with the discipline of law, such approaches also represent the 'realist'[8] orientation of those state and non-state actors: those international agencies and organisations in the business of 'doing' human rights in an institutionalised context. It is also this perspective which strongly reinforces state-centric assumptions – that the state is the maker and breaker of human rights.

Approaches grouped under the heading of 'strong particularism' emphasise the particularities of the social construction of human rights. But they do so in an overly homogenised way. Typically, they deny the possibility of human rights being universal, seeing any claims in that direction as attempts to impose one form of particularism on others. Such perspectives fail to grasp the full extent to which relations and structures of power are multifaceted and have necessarily permeated what are assumed to be (or assumed that they ought to be) sealed and homogenised cultural formations and political communities. Although traditionally associated with the discipline of anthropology (though see Cowan 2006), strong particularist perspectives sometimes arise through curious intersections between strong communitarian approaches and elements of post-structuralist, post-modernist and post-colonialist thought, emphasising fragmentation and difference and denying the legitimacy of any metanarrative of human rights.

Structuralist approaches see human rights as a determined 'product' or 'effect' of more fundamental structural dynamics within social relations. But while rightly grasping the importance of social structures in shaping social relations, these approaches typically rely on overly simplistic, often monocausal, models of structural determination both to explain social change and to deny the possibility that human action can constitute meaningful agency. Unsurprisingly, advocates of such perspectives see little or no positive potential in social movement struggles for human rights. Structuralist explanations can be found in a range of academic disciplines and were once dominant in sociology (Turner 2006). Here they are probably more usefully understood as specific strands within broader schools of social and political thought such as Marxism, post-structuralism, post-modernism and post-colonialism.

Despite their very significant differences, these four approaches share an important characteristic. Each for their own reasons fails to take proper account of historical praxis and processes. In each case, *a priori* assumptions (ontological, epistemological and methodological) take the place of concrete historical and social analysis. It is this shared characteristic which, above all, has shaped the mirrors in the hall in such a way that key social dimensions of human rights disappear altogether. By effectively erasing the possibility that the link to social movements is important for understanding the potentials and limits of human rights, those uncritical proponents and uncritical critics who have often dominated the scholarly literature on human rights over the last 60 years can be seen as trapped in a futile contestation of the mirrors.

Key Distortions of the Mirrors: Three Clusters

In my view we can identify three key clusters of distortions introduced by the mirrors in the hall and each of them goes to the heart of contemporary debates about human rights.

What are Human Rights?

The first cluster relates to this basic question and it is crucial to grasp that many proponents and critics actually share a range of fundamental assumptions about the nature of human rights. Compare, for example, the 'classical liberal' and 'reductionist marxist' accounts. They share the assumptions that:

- human rights are the rights of 'separated' individuals, allowing 'freedom' to pursue self-interest;
- collective rights are not 'real' human rights;
- civil and political rights are privileged over economic and social rights;
- human rights are intimately related to the rise of capitalism as an economic system.

While many commentators would now reject at least one of these assumptions and, in this sense, debates about human rights have become more nuanced, these shared assumptions held centre stage for much of the latter half of the twentieth century. Indeed, their strength was buttressed by aspects of key global geopolitical realities from the end of the Second World War. Especially during the Cold War period, this was the 'stuff of debate' both intellectually and ideologically as these shared assumptions were batted backwards and forwards between the then two superpowers and their Cold War allies. Yet, even in their heyday, these assumptions only connected to one aspect of the story of human rights post-1945. As we shall see in later chapters there were many more radical and creative aspects to developments around human rights in that period. What needs to be emphasised here, though, is that assumptions derived from studies of this period should not have been simply projected backwards in time and assumed to apply to the entire history of human rights. Yet many proponents and critics fell into that trap. This is an example of where the absence of history as a discipline – with issues about how to understand and interpret the past at its very heart – is telling.

The Fetishism of Institutional and Legal Domains

While, historically, a key trajectory of human rights claims has been to seek their institutionalisation as constitutional provision and law, many accounts of human rights are often fixated upon existing institutional and legal frameworks rather than on the social processes leading to, and involved in, such institution- alisation. For example, human rights are often assumed to be nothing other than potential or actual law. This assumption is then sometimes stitched together with a view that human rights were only meaningfully 'born' in 1948 and that there is nothing worth exploring or thinking about prior to that date. Then there are those accounts that focus exclusively and in detail on the international human rights institutions. The 50th anniversary of the United Nations Declaration of Human Rights in 1998 produced a rash of uncritical celebrations of the international human rights system although some more measured and critical assessments have re-surfaced since then (for example, Mertus 2005; Meckled-Garcia and Cali 2006). Finally, state-centrism is held in tight focus through those analyses of international covenants and conventions which are agreements and treaties between 'states parties' and through the overwhelming assumption that correlative duties with respect to human rights rest with states, in particular one's own state. The logic of this approach is summed up neatly by Jack Donnelly (2003:Ch.7) when he argues that human rights are a fundamentally national issue.

This fetishisation of the legal and institutional aspects of human rights leads in opposing directions. For proponents, their commitment to these domains means that they typically fail to recognise that – in their legalised and institutionalised form – human rights can have a highly ambiguous relationship to power.

In its most extreme form, and when wedded to an elitist, top-down view of politics, human rights are sometimes seen as part of a top-down, 'civilising' process which can be legitimately imposed on the world, if necessary by military force (Bartholomew 2006: Ch.9). In contrast, for many critics, the legal and institutional practices in respect of human rights since 1948 contain so many elements and moments of negativity – for example, so many instances of states using and abusing human rights to serve their foreign policy interests – that this is taken as proof positive that human rights necessarily are, and can only be, an instrument of power. While I share many of the concerns of the critics, their focus on the institutionalised and legal aspects of human rights means they are unable to recognise important parts of the story of human rights both in the past and the present.

Beyond that, as I will argue in Chapter 4 below, in a longer historical timeframe the period after 1948 can be seen as something of an anomaly in terms of the history of human rights. While a very important anomaly to be sure, and arguably one presaging a fundamental shift in the development of human rights, the privileging of the present in this view combined with the fetishisation of the legal and institutional aspects of human rights obscures other key dimensions of human rights.

Historical and Social Practices Obscured

This brings me to the third cluster of distortions. To assume that the meaningful history of human rights only begins in 1948 means that 350 years of western history, let alone other histories, are ignored. The absence of a proper historical perspective has led to a range of very serious gaps and limitations. Quite remarkably, in many accounts of the development of human rights, the nineteenth century largely disappears in terms of making any analytically significant contribution. This, in turn, helps to erase what I call below the 'sociality' of natural rights, for example, the extent to which understandings of collective rights had a degree of historical continuity from the seventeenth century onwards. This process continues today in so far as the social struggles generating apparently 'new' claims to human rights (for example, the right to a healthy environment) remain largely invisible up until they generate recognisably philosophical and legal expressions.

Sustained and concrete socio-historical analysis would also help to throw light on the dynamics of what I term the paradox of institutionalisation and the relevance of pre-legal and non-legal dimensions of human rights. This would then open up the possibility of examining what I shall term the expressive dimension of human rights activism. Here we are necessarily relating human rights back to a more open ended general exploration of social relations which cannot simply be captured through the confines of a particular academic discipline such as philosophy or law.

Rediscovering Creative Movement Praxis

To get beyond the hall of mirrors implies that we can somehow escape the distorted images they produce. But, to continue the metaphor, given that mirrors are a necessary and important aid to our reflection on the world, how can we do this? Interestingly, many of the tools necessary for refashioning the mirrors already exist. In fact they are relatively uncontentious and routinely deployed in broader fields of social enquiry. However, since they are rarely central to debates about human rights, some discussion of them is required here before we can move on to consider the creative praxis of social movements. For instance, the very idea that social movements can use human rights to challenge power implies both that social movements have agency and that some degree of social change is possible. Underlying such a statement must also be some conception of 'the social' and how that relates to 'the political', 'the economic' and 'the cultural'. Acknowledged or otherwise, answers to these sorts of questions underpin all social enquiry. Therefore, the section below briefly explores some of them in order to set out the working assumptions, the refashioned mirrors, which underpin this study.

Working Assumptions

Actors–Agency–Structures ... and Power

I begin with what is often termed 'the agency–structure problem'.[9] In the very naming of the issue, we can see the first difficulty. Describing the problem as being one of the relations between agency and structure reflects a strong tendency to conflate actors and agency and assume that agency is solely a property of social actors not social structures (Lukes 1977, 2005). Moreover, the concept of agency is then often further narrowed by being considered as solely a property of individual actors. Thus, in such formulations, neither social structures nor collective actors are credited with any agency. In contrast, my conceptualisation of these relations is initially triadic (see Figure 1.1) with both actors (individual and collective) and social structures potentially having agency, that is, the capacity to influence actions and outcomes.

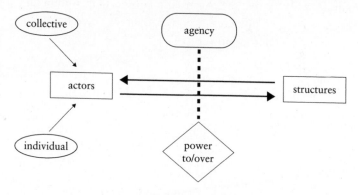

Figure 1.1   Actors, agency, structures ... and power

But as soon as we say this it becomes clear that the term agency is another way of talking about power, that is, the capacity – the 'power to'– change things. That then raises the question of the relation of 'power to' and 'power over'. Most people mean 'power over' when they talk about power and I will sometimes do the same. So, for example when I talk about social movements challenging power, I am using a form of shorthand to talk about challenging 'power over'. Yet the concept of 'power to' is vital too. Curiously, it has only been in recent years that the relations between 'power over' and 'power to' have become central to the analysis of power, despite the fact that it is precisely these relations that reveal the necessary complexity and ambiguity of power. People come together, work with one another, create movements and create organisations and institutions because they believe that, collectively, they will have more 'power to' than if they acted separately as individuals. Yet at the same time, it is clear that – once established – such social structures then carry significant capacity for 'power over', reaching huge proportions in the case of powerful states and transnational corporations. In my view, the best way to think about the relationship between 'power over' and 'power to' is to see 'power over' as a particular form or manifestation of 'power to'. Understood in this way, the ambiguities and complexities of power become much clearer. We can more easily see that the construction of social institutions and structures designed to increase 'power to' are very likely to carry the threat of increasing 'power over'.[10]

That the 'agency–structure problem' has often been set up as a binary opposition between agency and structure illustrates direct connections back to some of the specific mirrors discussed above. As an ideological framework, 'classical' liberalism/neo-liberalism typically assumes that it is only individual actors who can exercise meaningful agency in the world and that social explanation must be rooted in the analysis of the views and behaviour of individuals. Methodological individualism, strong in some academic disciplines, operates from the same assumptions (Lukes 1974; Carter 1990). In contrast, a range of disciplinary approaches and ideological positions adopt structuralist explanations of social processes and social change. In its most extreme forms, human beings are seen as merely the 'bearers' of structural determinations. (see E.P. Thompson 1978; Cheah 1997; Turner 2006) or, as some post-structuralist theorists would have it, the whole of human subjectivity is entirely constituted by discourse (Howarth, 2000).

While still very strong, such binary polarities have been substantively challenged in recent decades by a range of approaches, all of which seek to grasp the interactions between actors and structures in social processes. While there are many controversies around and between them, Alain Touraine's approach to the self-production of society (Touraine 1977; Clark and Diani 1996), Anthony Giddens' theory of structuration (Giddens 1979, 1984), the school of critical realism originating from the work of Roy Bhaskar (Collier 1994) and Margaret Archer's understanding of 'morphogenesis' (Archer 1995) all acknowledge deep interaction and complexity. From an engagement with these sorts of debates and in a very neat summary, Piotr Sztompka (1990) argues that his own model of agency is able to bridge at least three pervasive and misleading polarities of sociological theorising. For Sztompka, agency:

- is conceived neither as individualistic nor collectivistic but as a product of both actors and structures;
- is conceived neither in idealist or materialist terms, but rather links structural and natural (material) resources with human knowledge, beliefs, reasons and imagination;
- bridges the dichotomy of social stability and social dynamics. As Sztompka puts it, agency lives in the present, though looking forward to the future and shaped by the past.

While Sztompka does not make the link between agency and power as set out above, this textual formulation otherwise captures the key elements of my own orientation. It also brings us to the next issue.

Social Change and Social Transformation

Understandings of the relations between actors, agency and structure impact deeply on how one conceptualises social change and social transformation and hence on what one believes to be possible. In many accounts of change, the vast majority of human beings who have lived on the planet – ordinary people in their everyday lives – are assumed to have contributed little or nothing. Even from those positions privileging the role of actors, ordinary people often appear as little more than pawns. For example, the 'great men of history' approach emphasises the impact of individuals such as Churchill, Hitler, Stalin, Gandhi or Mandela in shaping the course of history in ways that ordinary people simply do not and cannot. Ordinary people are, in other words, the supporting cast for these 'great men'. We have already seen how the 'great philosophers of history' variant of this approach has crucially shaped understandings of human rights. Those canonical men of European descent are widely seen as the key authors of human rights. In its institutionalised and rationalised form, the 'great men' become those who occupy the peak positions in the institutionalised worlds of politics, economics and culture. Here, even when ordinary people elect these elite actors, the story of how social change takes place still leaves the mass of the people going about their daily business – outside as it were, but subject to, the world of power. As indicated earlier, in structuralist explanations of social change, actors with any meaningful agency also tend to disappear. While the emergence of structuralist explanations in the nineteenth century can probably be explained by the desire of early social scientists to emulate the success of the natural sciences in uncovering apparently universal laws, this left a difficult legacy which has yet to be overcome. This was particularly so in the emerging discipline of sociology within which many key theories of social change and transformation were developed.

Sztompka (1990) argues that, by the nineteenth century, three models of social order and social change had been elaborated. The first of these assumed what he calls 'operation without transformation', that is, order without any significant change taking place. The second identifies cyclical processes that eventually return to their starting point after a more or less intricate and prolonged sequence of changes. Sztompka describes this as 'change without novelty'. The third model sees social change as being an orderly, patterned sequence of fundamental transformations, each stage bringing the process closer to some specified ultimate standard. Describing this as 'directional transformation', Sztompka claims this was the '...image central for theories of social development, with evolutionism and historical materialism as their major nineteenth-century varieties' (Sztompka 1990:247). This third model is very important, not only because it is still alive in academic scholarship, but also because contemporary ideologies (neo-liberalism, social democracy and Marxism) all remain strongly influenced by models of 'directional transformation'.

Crook, Pakulski and Waters (1992) identify three main explanations of social change within 'modernity'. Associated with the Durkheimian, Marxist and Weberian traditions in social theory, each of these is a specific account of Sztompka's 'directional transformation' identifying processes of differentiation, commodification and rationalisation respectively. Each explanation identifies developmental processes which tend to 'unfold', taking on the appearance of historical laws, or at least having scientific 'law-like' properties. In other words, there doesn't appear to be very much that anyone can do to halt such processes or, alternatively, change their direction. Especially interesting in the light of what I term the 'paradox of institutionalisation', the rise and problematic nature of instrumental reason and formal rationality is identified in each of these explanations, albeit in different ways. It was Max Weber, though, who identified formal rationality embedded within institutional structures as being the central but problematic feature of 'modernisation'. For Weber, formal rationality not only displaces tradition, it also progressively erodes any ethical basis of commitment to general or substantive values. In sum, rationalisation involves '...the depersonalisation of social relationships, the refinement of techniques of calculation, the enhancement of the social importance of specialised knowledge, and the extension of technically rational control over both natural and social processes' (Brubaker 1984:2). Rationalisation involves extensions of control over natural and social objects. Relevant here is the emphasis on the technical rationalisation of social relationships. Put another way, human beings need to be disciplined in order to conform to the instrumental needs of centrally organised industrial and administrative systems. There are some clear and strong parallels here with Foucault's account of modernity in terms of the rise of disciplinary society (Foucault 1977, 1978; Honneth 1991: xxvi–xxviii and Ch.5; Cohen and Arato 1992:272–86).

Weber's account is often portrayed as starkly pessimistic, increasing rationalisation and the subsequent 'disenchantment of the world' being seen as a necessary but inevitably destructive historical process. But if we draw back from the assumptions of necessity and inevitability perhaps what we then have instead is a depiction of the world as it was being made in the early part of the twentieth century. In other words, a depiction of the world understood not as outcomes of immutable historical laws but rather as the systematic (intentional and unintentional) accomplishments of both powerful actors and existing institutional structures of power. Arguably, that story continues. If such accounts do indeed capture something of what the world has indeed become over the last 200 years under the domination of western powers, we can ask whether it could have turned out otherwise. How one answers that question then crucially shapes the way one understands the possibilities of future change, locally and globally. So far, none of the explanations discussed leaves much space for considering the impact of the creative praxis of social movements on historical development. So, are there any other ways of conceptualising social order and social change?

Sztompka again provides a neat summary. Rejecting teleological explanations of social change, he argues that social transformation is possible precisely through the potentialities of creative social praxis. He offers a fourth model which could be called 'contingent progress through social transformation'. It is an explanation which is consonant with the work of those historians who have focused on the construction of 'history from below' (E.P. Thompson in D. Thompson 2001:481–9) and could support contemporary arguments emphasising the importance of 'globalisation from below' (see Chapter 7). Stompka again points to recent theoretical innovations that have sought to transcend the limitations of traditional explanations of social change, this time seeking to grasp the complexity of the social via a broader understanding of creative social praxis throughout social relations. The emphasis, he points out, has turned towards real socialised individuals in their actual social and historical contexts. He argues that '[c]ommon people are brought back into the picture and acquire truly human size: as aware but not omniscient, powerful but not omnipotent, creative but not unconstrained, free but not unlimited' (Stompka 1990:250).

Such an account of agency offers us, he says, a new way of thinking about social change and social progress as possible but contingent, involving:

- potential capacity rather than ultimate achievement;
- dynamic but shifting concrete processes rather than any absolute, universal, external standard;
- historical possibilities as open options rather than necessary, inevitable, inexorable tendencies;
- social progress as a product of (intended and unintended and even unrecognised) human collective actions, rather than a result of Divine Will, the good intentions of exceptional individuals, or the operation of automatic social mechanisms. (Stompka 1990:251)

This certainly gives us a picture of both the pervasiveness of possibilities for change and a concept of progress as an open-ended, contingent, social project. But it also reminds us of the complex relationship between continuity and discontinuity in historical processes which brings me to the last point I want to make here. In common with other topics considered above, much analysis has set up continuity and discontinuity in terms of a binary opposition.

One of the most important of these when thinking about social change has been the binary polarity asserted between reform and revolution. For the last 150 years or so, the left has split into deeply hostile oppositional camps around this polarity. For revolutionaries, all attempts at reform are typically seen as futile and those engaged in it 'selling out'. For reformists, revolution is typically seen as deeply problematic because of its reliance on violence and its potential to degenerate into tyranny rather than achieve its declared objectives. Yet, as soon as one rejects the construction of this binary polarity, a whole range of other possibilities necessarily come into view. I will describe these as possibilities for social transformation. Neither continuity nor discontinuity are privileged *a priori* here, rather it becomes incumbent upon us to consider and judge what might constitute greater or lesser degrees of political, economic and cultural change.

Social, Political, Economic, Cultural

I have already used various terms relating to 'the social' so it is important to specify what is meant by 'the social' here and how it relates to those cognate phrases 'the political', 'the economic' and 'the cultural'. The relation between these terms often remains unspecified and can be a source of considerable confusion. For example, some writers use a triad of 'economic', 'political', 'social' in a way that suggests that, for them, 'social' covers phenomena that others would depict as 'cultural'. My understanding of these relations is configured as shown in Figure 1.2, with 'the social' being a superordinate category and the political, economic and cultural each being a realm or domain of the social.

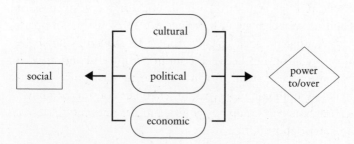

Figure 1.2   Analysing 'the social'

Within this analytic framework I assume dynamic interaction between the political, economic and cultural, again without an *a priori* privileging of one of those domains over another. The extent to which these domains interact and the extent to which – in particular circumstances – one domain might be dominant is left open to investigation and analysis. In the context of this diagram, institutions and law are embedded dimensions of 'the social' each with significant political, economic and cultural impacts. Importantly, if we now locate power in relation to this configuration, I am also assuming that, at this level of abstraction, 'power to' and 'power over' exist in all realms of the social and that there is a complex interplay between different forms of power resulting in a more complex patterning of social power than many thinkers have been willing to consider. This is not to say that when we look at concrete instances of historical development and change these forms of power will not 'cash out' in particular ways. Rather, again, I am avoiding the ontological privileging of a particular form of power in a particular realm of the social without denying the vast asymmetries of 'power over' in the world.

This approach contrasts with positions, strong in many academic disciplines and ideological traditions, that presume that the key, determinant, form of social power is to be found in one of the realms of the social – economic, political or cultural – with the consequent emphasis on that realm as being the 'driver' of social change in general. Such approaches automatically preclude the possibility of the understanding of social change being a contingent outcome of the complex interaction of political, economic and cultural factors. For much of the twentieth century, key disciplines such as economics, politics and international relations were largely dominated by approaches which privileged the economic and/or the political and in some areas this remains so, despite the significance of the cultural turn in the social sciences. Unfortunately, culturalist approaches have often simply sought to replace the economic and/or political with 'the cultural' as the central driver of social relations rather than integrate culture into a more holistic and dynamic framework for analysis. Indeed, in the hands of some theorists, the cultural turn narrowed to the linguistic turn, which viewed language or communication as the central, privileged, driver of the social.

Social Movements and Creative Social Praxis

Underpinning the argument of this book is a contention that through innovative creativity in ideas and practices (understood together as praxis) social movements contribute significantly to the shaping of historical development. While this may occur in a whole variety of ways, this volume focuses on the development of ideas and practices with respect to human rights. Below, I briefly explore evidence and arguments demonstrating the importance of the creative social praxis of social movements.

What are Social Movements?

The use of the term movement with a range of prefixes (political, cultural, religious and social) is ubiquitous. So one might imagine that how a movement is distinguished from other forms of human association is clear and unproblematic. Yet nothing could be further from the truth. Whether in common usage or in scholarly investigations, movements – social or otherwise – are defined and discussed in a wide variety of ways. In particular, movements are often confused or conflated with more formally constituted organisations or, alternatively, with broader cultural trends and shifts. Moreover, the use of the specific term 'social movements' is relatively new, developing largely in the latter half of the twentieth century and emerging largely out of the discipline of sociology. That does not mean, however, that the term cannot be meaningfully used either to look at movement activism in earlier periods of history (for example, Tilly 1986, 1993, 2004) or at movements that have been given a different prefix. Given these conceptual problems and confusions, unsurprisingly there are a range of issues and features that frequently recur in attempts to conceptualise social movements.

Firstly, the question of the relationship of social movements to organisations and institutionalised social action is of vital importance (see Stammers and Eschle 2005). Secondly, there is the extent to which the term social movement implies a degree of collective self-consciousness, a collective identity, shared by those actors comprising the movement. Thirdly, there is an issue about the purpose of social movement action, usually understood in terms of an orientation to social conflict. Fourthly, but in a somewhat different register, analytic frameworks have sought to explain social movements in terms of 'why' they occur or 'how' they occur (Melucci 1989) rather than seeking to identify shared features common to all social movements.

Having surveyed these difficulties and the whole range of approaches to understanding social movements, Mario Diani has developed what he calls a synthetic definition that draws together the common threads of different approaches. He argues that '[a] social movement is a network of informal interactions between a plurality of individuals, groups and/or organisations, engaged in political or cultural conflict, on the basis of a shared collective identity' (Diani 2000:165). Interestingly, and importantly from the point of view of this volume, he also insists that '...social movements are not organisations, not even of a peculiar kind' (Diani, 2000:166). Thus it follows that we need to maintain a clear analytic distinction between organisations and social movements. While organisations may well be part of a movement, social movements need not give rise to any formal organisations at all. One area where I would want to take issue with Diani's conceptualisation is in its implication that social movements could comprise a network of interactions linking only formal organisations. It seems to me that informal and non-institutional activism is a necessary precondition for the existence of a social movement and that, if such activism and the accompanying non-institutional articulations of collective identity entirely disappear, then a social movement ceases to exist. A network linking *only* organisations looks much more like what Keck and Sikkink (1998) have usefully identified in a transnational context as an 'advocacy network'.

An important aspect of Diani's conceptualisation is its relation to my configuration of the social depicted above. Firstly, while Diani makes it clear that social movements can have political and cultural dimensions, he doesn't mention 'the economic' at all. Yet, recognising that social movements can have economic dimensions serves to strengthen rather than weaken his conceptualisation. Secondly, his definition enables us to think about how social movements may straddle the institutional and everyday worlds. Distinguishing between organisations and institutional activism on the one hand and informal networks and non-institutionalised activism on the other allows us to recognise that organisations often emerge from social movements, offering us the possibility of exploring how social movement activism can straddle the porous boundaries between the institutional and everyday worlds (see Figure 1.3).

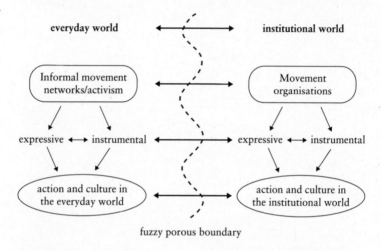

Figure 1.3 Movements straddling the institutional and everyday worlds

As Darnovsky, Epstein and Flacks (1995:vii) put it '...collective action becomes a 'movement' when participants refuse to accept the boundaries of established institutionalised rules and routinized roles'. Yet, at the same time and typically, social movements generate organisations that both engage with the institutional world and often themselves become institutions. As I shall argue in Chapter 4, movement organisations then necessarily become enmeshed in what I call the paradox of institutionalisation. Yet this capacity of social movements and their organisations to straddle the institutional and everyday worlds in the particular and distinctive ways they do raises interesting questions and possibilities relating to the future of participation and democracy. I come back to these issues later, especially in Chapters 7 and 8.

The importance of this feature of social movements can also be developed by looking at the relation between instrumental and expressive dimensions of movement activism. Drawing from the work of Cohen and Arato (1992) I argue that social movements typically have 'dual faces' which dynamically combine instrumental and expressive forms of activism in both the institutional and everyday worlds. The use of this distinction is common in social movement studies (see also Melucci 1989; Scott 1990). Its particular relevance here is that it allows us to engage with, and then transcend, important debates around interests, identities and recognition. This has particular importance for understanding human rights because it opens up crucial possibilities for exploring the significance of non-institutional and pre-institutional aspects of human rights, then allowing us to consider how these relate to institutionalised social action around human rights, including human rights as law. This is discussed in detail in Chapter 6.

Creative Social Praxis

The above discussion lays the groundwork for understanding the potential for the creative praxis of social movements. Earlier on, when discussing the role of actors in the 'agency–structure' debate, I noted both that most accounts of actors' agency tended to be both individualistic and understood in terms of elite agency. I also noted that little space is left for any broader understanding of a creative social praxis within which ordinary people contribute anything at all to the process of historical transformation. Yet we now have an analytic framework through which we can see how social movements can potentially generate connections between the everyday worlds and the institutional world within which elite actors operate. Indeed, some scholars have already identified social movements as important agents of social transformation and as sites of innovation, creativity and knowledge production. For example, Cohen and Arato argue, '[i]t is our thesis that social movements constitute the dynamic element in processes that might realise the positive potentials of modern civil societies' (Cohen and Arato 1992:492). Alberto Melucci (1989, 1996) has depicted recent social movements as laboratories wherein dominant under-standings of the world are resisted and creative and innovative experimentation with ideas and practices takes place. Eyerman and Jamison (1991) argue that what they term 'cognitive praxis' is the core activity of social movements:

> The forms of consciousness that are articulated in social movements provide something crucial in the constitution of modern societies: public spaces for thinking new thoughts, activating new actors, generating new ideas, in short constructing new intellectual 'projects'. The cognitive praxis of social movements is an important, and all too neglected, source of social innovation. (Eyerman and Jamison 1991:161)

While Eyerman and Jamison's work is, in my view, overly focused on the production of ideas, they nevertheless stress the importance of creativity and praxis as key aspects of social movement activism.

Thinking about creative social praxis in these sorts of ways brings us round full circle. It enables us to re-examine the nature of the social and the possibilities for change and transformation and it provides ways of thinking about a particular form of agency in processes of historical transformation, that is, the collective agency of social movements. Once grasped in these terms, the relevance of the role of social movements in constructing and reconstructing understandings of human rights starts to become clear. Yet in order to understand the significance of that for our understandings of human rights we have to re-interrogate the history of human rights. The next chapter begins that task by looking at the sociality of natural rights.

Conclusion

In this chapter I have tried to set the stage for the exploration of the nature and meanings of the linkage between social movements and human rights. By drawing from work in the field of social movement studies and social theory I have tried to show how the creative praxis of social movements contributes to social transformation and historical change. In contrast to many 'top-down' or teleological explanations of social and historical change, this approach provides a way of analysing what we could call 'agency from below'. The chapters that follow will explore such 'agency from below', arguing that a key originating moment in the development of ideas and practices around human rights is their creation as an aspect of social movement struggles against extant relations of 'power over'. Largely because of disciplinary and ideological proclivities and pre-dispositions, the specialist scholarly literature on human rights is particularly ill-equipped to either grasp the links between social movements and human rights or explore its significance. So deep is this problem that I have employed the metaphor of a hall of mirrors to illustrate these points. A key task of the next chapter is to show how the historical emergence and sociality of natural rights has been distorted in the hall of mirrors.

2

THE 'SOCIALITY' OF NATURAL RIGHTS

This chapter takes us back to a period of history beginning some 370 years ago because the emergence of claims to natural rights in the seventeenth and eighteenth centuries is often a key starting point for both proponents and critics of contemporary human rights. One straightforward explanation for this is broad agreement that natural rights were, at the very least, an important precursor of human rights.[1] But there is rather more to it than that because, in fact, such accounts from proponents and critics often share a range of important underlying assumptions. Challenging the accuracy of some of these assumptions, this chapter explores what I have called the sociality of natural rights, a sociality that arises as a dimension of social movement praxis in the seventeenth and eighteenth centuries. It argues that ideas and practices of natural rights:

- had economic dimensions that had more to do with protecting subsistence than bourgeois property rights;
- connected understandings of individual and collective identity to constructions of collective rights;
- were an important element of the first successful revolution against slavery in Haiti in 1791;
- were deployed by radical sections of movement activism to challenge various forms of 'arbitrary power and privilege'.

The chapter begins by looking at distortions that arise from my metaphorical mirrors on the subject of natural rights. The following sections then draw from a range of historical accounts to look at the social struggles and revolutions in England, America, France and Haiti. The concluding section summarises issues that arise and identifies key moments of analytic failure in the mainstream literature on human rights.

Natural Rights in the Hall of Mirrors

Instead of focusing on the social praxis of natural rights, much of the specialist human rights literature relies on images that are little more than caricatures. We can see this at work in three sets of relationships, each of which is crucial to contemporary debates on human rights. These are the relationships between:

- civil and political rights on the one hand and economic and social rights on the other;
- individual rights and collective rights; and
- universal and particular dimensions of human rights.

Over the last 60 years many liberal theorists and representatives of powerful western states have argued that only civil and political rights are real human rights, on the grounds – for example – that correlative duties to such rights simply require states not to interfere with individual freedoms (the notion of negative rights). Concomitantly, economic and social rights are said to be unreal rights because correlative duties require state intervention (the notion of positive rights) that may be impractical and likely to interfere with other people's freedoms. (Cranston 1973; Beetham 1995; Steiner and Alston 2000:181–5 and 249–61). Critics then argue that such claims illustrate the deep ideological nature and limits of human rights as western bourgeois notions and that, if human rights are useful at all, economic and social rights should be considered more real because our basic physical material existence relies upon them (Halasz 1966; Pollis and Schwab 1980; Steiner and Alston 2000:237). In a parallel set of arguments, liberal theorists and politicians argue that only individual human rights are 'real' human rights and are suspicious of an authoritarian potential being necessarily embedded in any concept of collective right. Typically, critics respond that such arguments demonstrate the possessive, egoistic nature of individual rights and that, outside of some understanding of some collectivity/community, the very notion of the individual is meaningless (Freeman 1995:25–40; Robinson 2002). Finally, some proponents have made strong, sweeping claims regarding the universality of particular categories of human rights, arguing that the task of human rights advocates should now be to ensure that such rights are implemented and enforced globally. Critics respond that these are claims to a false universalism which simply confirm human rights as a dangerous form of western imperialism. Much of the history of this debate has been couched in terms of 'abstract universalism' versus 'cultural relativism', with the latter encompassing claims to Islamic, Asian or other value systems.

All of these debates are closely connected to what has happened to human rights globally since 1948 and cannot be easily separated from the shifts in geopolitical realities and structures of power in the contemporary period. For example, the recent renewed interest in the secular universalism of human rights correlates with the rise of Islamic and other religious fundamentalisms whereas, up until the late 1980s, debates often refracted the geopolitics of the Cold War. Yet, as noted in Chapter 1, such arguments are often projected backwards in time and claimed to apply to the entire history of human rights. In particular, the history of natural rights is assumed to be a 'liberal history' by both proponents and critics.[2] This chapter denies the veracity and utility of such claims, proposing an alternative historical account which casts a very different light on the nature of natural rights. However, before engaging with historical detail, let us look in a bit more detail at these distortions of the mirrors and how these are deployed by some contemporary critics of human rights.

Common Distortions and Reflections

Natural rights are seen as quintessentially civil and political rights by many proponents and critics. Underlying this there is typically a shared, though different, conceptual separation of the economic from the political, with the cultural largely being ignored altogether. For proponents, the economic and political are separated into the private and public spheres respectively, with natural rights marking the beginning of developments which led to the establishment of liberal states, wherein state power is constrained by the constitutional setup and a range of rights belonging to individual citizens are institutionalised. From this perspective, while the emphasis appears to be on the political and the public sphere, in fact the economic sphere is privileged as the key aspect of the private sphere. The mirror image, especially from structuralist critics, is that civil and political rights were indeed the political and legal frameworks that arose to consolidate and legitimise new patterns of capitalist economic relations and/or the modern nation state. While the economic and political are connected here, this connection ultimately relies on a conceptual separation which again allows the economic to be privileged over the political.

Interestingly, it is in this historical period that the link between social movement struggles and rights claims is most frequently acknowledged in the human rights literature. For some proponents, movement struggles for natural rights were struggles for the establishment of constitutional liberal states. Other proponents share the position of critics in arguing that ideas of natural rights were deployed by an emerging bourgeois class in the struggles that led to the transformation from feudalism to capitalism. An excellent illustration of the popular distillation of this sort of characterisation can be found in the 2004 edition of *Encarta* under the entry for 'bourgeoisie':

> As the feudal society was transformed into the early capitalist society of Europe, the bourgeoisie were the spearhead of progress in industry and science and of social change. By the seventeenth century, this middle class was supporting principles of natural rights and constitutional government against the theories of divine right and privilege of the sovereign and the nobility. Thus, members of the bourgeoisie led the English revolution of the 17th century and the American and French revolutions of the late 18th century. These revolutions helped to establish political rights and

personal liberty for all free citizens. (Microsoft Corporation, 2004 'Encarta Premium Suite 2004')

The above characterisations of natural rights are underpinned by specific methods of social analysis which are also shared. Particularly relevant here is the orientation towards the analysis of canonical texts used to set the framework for further discussion. John Locke's *Two Treatises of Government* (Laslett 1967) are assumed to be the crucial texts for understanding natural rights and considered foundational for the development of liberal thought. As Jack Donnelly puts it, 'Locke is the seminal figure in the strand of liberalism that grounds the commitment to equal liberty on natural, or what we today call human, rights' (Donnelly 2003:47). Volume after volume from proponents and critics have focused their analysis on this text, as if the whole story of natural rights is to be found within its pages. From the point of view of the critics, of equal importance is Karl Marx's *On the Jewish Question* where he denounced the 'so-called rights of man' (McLellan 1977:52, 54). This was later developed in another crucial text, *The Political Theory of Possessive Individualism*, where MacPherson (1962) sought to demonstrate the origins and development of what we could call the psycho-social personality type that is 'capitalist man'. Of course, this sort of textual analysis is highly selective. So, for example, Tom Paine's various writings on natural rights are much less likely to be regarded as seminal than those of John Locke, despite his role in the formation and dissemination of understandings of natural rights in America, France and England. While *The Rights of Man* (Paine [1791] [1792] 1995) is sometimes included in the canon of western political thought, other works by Paine, such as *African Slavery in America* (Paine [1775] 2008), *Common Sense* (Paine [1776] 1995) and *Agrarian Justice* (Paine [1797] 1995) are rarely mentioned.

Another important shared tendency is the tendency to work from binary oppositions, most importantly here between the individual and collective and between the universal and particular. Proponents and critics are often unable to see complex interaction between what they hold to be incompatible polarities. While there are undoubtedly deep and contentious issues here, my point is that such polarised thinking has fundamentally shaped the terms of the debate about natural rights. This can be illustrated if we look briefly at three examples of how contemporary critics understand and critique natural rights.

Contemporary Critics

Fiona Robinson is a feminist scholar of International Relations who works on the 'ethics of care'. In 'Human Rights Discourse and Global Civil Society: Contesting Globalisation?' (2002), she argues that human rights as currently understood '…can provide neither a practical goal nor a discursive basis for anti-globalization movements because they represent not universal values but a particular set of values and political ends which are Western-centric and which reflect western hegemonic masculinity (Robinson 2002:3).

While acknowledging that contemporary understandings of human rights are a product of the immediate aftermath of the Second World War, she nevertheless underpins her analysis with assumptions about the nature and meaning of natural rights as they emerged in the seventeenth and eighteenth centuries. She argues that 'the ethics and language of human rights has not been wrested from the liberal framework from which it originated…' (Robinson 2002:2) and that, therefore, the idea that rights discourses can challenge dominant ideas of 'common sense' and can be counter-hegemonic in respect of power '…misses the point that the concept of "right" cannot escape its liberal meaning – of an individualistic, negative, "skeleton" concept which upholds the individual's right to pursue his own understanding of the good' (Robinson 2002:16). So here, Robinson reproduces a standard critique of liberal accounts of rights without at any point considering whether either that standard critique or, indeed, the liberal account itself, accurately portrays the history and praxis of natural rights in the seventeenth and eighteenth centuries.

In a not dissimilar vein, but coming from a very different position (which they term 'grassroots post-modernism') Gustavo Esteva and Madhu Suri Prakash (1998) are also principally concerned with contemporary discourses and practices of human rights which they depict as a 'trojan horse of recolonisation'. Again, assumptions about natural rights underpin key parts of their argument. Saying that human rights are the successor to natural rights, they claim 'Human rights are but the formal juridical expression of a specific mode of being and living. It is defined by the kind of man, woman and child who has appeared on earth only very recently: *homo oeconomicus*, the possessive individual' (Esteva and Prakash 1998:121, emphasis in original). Curiously, despite their post-modernism, Esteva and Prakash exhibit a strong communitarian outlook and retain a strong binary separation between the individual and collective, privileging the latter over the former.

One of the most interesting recent elaborations of a critical position has been developed by Stephen Hopgood (2000) in 'Reading the Small Print in Global Civil Society: The Inexorable Hegemony of the Liberal Self'. In a wide-ranging article ultimately aimed at critiquing contemporary post-metaphysical liberal attempts to legitimate human rights, he argues that:

> The institution of rights, most importantly *human* rights, embodies the promise inherent in the logic of one conception of 'global civil society', understood as the 'space of uncoerced human association'. We may call this *liberal* global civil society where social life (the public sphere) is modelled on exchange and persons meet in order to arbitrate their pre-existing interests which have been 'self authored' (chosen in the private sphere). This liberal conception has historically formed a powerful alliance with the expansion of capitalism. (Hopgood 2000:1, emphases in original)

He contrasts this with what he calls a republican conception of global civil society within which:

> ...the 'public sphere' provides a legitimate forum for the collective negotiation of what are to count as 'acceptable' components of personal identity in private life. In liberal global civil society the private pronounces

with authority on the public, whilst in republican global civil society the
opposite is true. (Hopgood 2000:1)

He argues that, because liberal conceptions of human rights
cannot be morally self-sufficient, some conception of the good
life – of republican virtue – is always required to underwrite them.
Thus, liberal understandings of global civil society require a price
of admission: that all members must be 'remade' in a liberal image.
This then is the small print in liberal constructions of global civil
society: a particular liberal republican notion of virtue which turns
out to be none other than the possessive individual in market
society: 'One thus needs to acquire the proper virtues to succeed
in today's world where globalisation makes market exchange the
model for social affairs' (Hopgood 2000:21). Crucially, Hopgood
does not see this state of affairs as any sort of new historical
phenomenon. Indeed, he looks at the treatment of the Native
Americans in the United States to give historical weight to his
argument. Full citizenship rights, he notes, were only granted by
the US federal state in 1924 after a sustained and protracted period
of 're-making' and 'civilising' of surviving Native Americans.

As a critique of liberal accounts of human rights and civil
society, Hopgood's analysis has much to commend it. Yet he
tends to throw the proverbial baby out with the bathwater.
Leaving aside the (nevertheless crucial) questions of whether a
'space of uncoerced human association' is necessarily liberal or
necessarily modelled on exchange relations, the first thing to note
is his essentially philosophical argument, revolving around the
question of whether human rights can be 'morally self-sufficient'
and anchored in the work of other theorists. Note, also, how he
maintains binary oppositions between 'liberal' and 'republican' on
the one hand and 'public' and 'private' on the other. From there he
then simply assumes that human rights were always – and could
only ever be – an ideological aspect of a liberal project, a project
closely associated with the rise of capitalism. There is simply no
space in his argument for admitting the possibility of a non-liberal
praxis of human rights. Significantly, his account of the treatment
of Native Americans is focused on the late nineteenth century,

long after a liberal interpretation of natural rights had indeed been institutionalised within the United States. As his opening sentence makes clear, his concern is very much with human rights as they have been institutionalised. Whilst that is clearly a very important part of the history of human rights it is not the entirety of that history. The next section explores other aspects of that history.

Social Movement Praxis in the Seventeenth and Eighteenth Centuries

Even a cursory examination of the historical emergence of natural rights suggests that the basic assumptions of the above accounts are nowhere near as watertight as their advocates seem to think. Indeed, much historical research indicates that throughout this whole period economic, political and cultural dimensions of social struggles were imbricated and intertwined in ways that suggest most accounts of the emergence and development of natural rights are narrow, reductive and deeply inaccurate.

To begin, we need to recognise the extent to which different facets of power were fused or claimed to be so within European absolutism. In other words, traditional forms of power were assumed to be undifferentiated and were legitimised in terms of an absolute monarch acting as a direct servant of God via the doctrine of the Divine Right of Kings (Mann 1986:475–83; Burns 1990). The importance of this point is that a challenge to monarchical power was not just a challenge to existing political power but rather to a constellation of power within which political, economic and cultural facets were interconnected. The implication of this is that both the liberal focus on political relations and the Marxist focus on economic relations are likely to result in a misrecognition of that constellation of power and, consequently, the 'shape' of challenges to it.

This can be illustrated by looking at the key example of property rights in articulations of natural rights, firstly in terms of the control of economic resources. When natural rights are only understood as civil and political rights, the place of property rights does appear anomalous and this apparent anomaly can then be used to point to the pivotal role of private property rights in understandings of natural rights in the way both liberal and Marxist theorists have argued. However, once it is recognised that claims to natural rights sought to challenge economic as well as political power, the anomalous position of property rights as demands for the control of economic resources disappears and it is, rather, the accuracy of the category of civil and political rights that is brought into question. The particular assertions of Divine Right and attempts by landlords to rescind existing customary rights (for example, grazing rights) through enclosure were dangerous threats to economic subsistence. In this sense, demands for private property can then also be understood as defensive economic and social demands seeking to protect basic subsistence (D. Thompson 2001:287–315; Wood 2002:108–09; Grear 2003).

But property rights have also been understood as 'property in oneself' and, from this perspective, it is perhaps quite rightly seen as a key civil and political right. Clearly there is a strong connection here to the extensive debates over the development of possessive individualism. But what was it that claims to have 'property in oneself' sought to challenge? In this historical period, human bodies were often deeply abused and alienated: tortured, controlled or possessed by some 'other': the king, the slave-owner, the religious hierarchy, or the feudal lord.[3] Put this way, the demand for 'property in oneself' can be understood as a social demand for the recognition of the necessity of bodily integrity and the legitimacy of the 'self'. In other words, this could be seen more as a demand for liberation from oppression than implying the construction of 'capitalist man'. Whilst 'property in oneself' does not fully capture the social nature of the self, the strong emphasis on the individual person makes sense both in the context of seeking to protect bodily integrity and as the sort of strong claim necessary to challenge the legitimacy of Divine Right.

In the context of wide-ranging surveys discussing the nature of liberalism and movements associated with it, Anthony Arblaster and James Richardson have both identified important forms of social movement praxis that they say cannot be reduced to a defence of bourgeois property relations (Arblaster 1984; Richardson 1997). Discussing England in the middle decades of the seventeenth century, Arblaster unsurprisingly identifies the gradual formation of an essentially bourgeois social philosophy that was to become the middle-class orthodoxy of the eighteenth century. But, he argues, '...these ideas were challenged by a more democratic and popular standpoint by the short lived popular movements of the period' (Arblaster 1984:147). Richardson's point is a wider one. He identifies what he calls 'contending liberalisms' that he claims can be traced back to the seventeenth century. Pointing out that 'liberalism' only emerges in the nineteenth century to cover a wide range of movements and ideas, he argues that one historical strand of liberalism is a liberalism of privilege, private property and power. The other strand, he argues, is much more radical, seeking to universalise ideas of liberty, equality and fraternity (Richardson 1997:7, 10).[4] Within this formulation, far from defending bourgeois property relations, Richardson argues that the radical, rights-based strand of liberalism has always challenged power, property and privilege.

If we now turn our attention to the specific social transformations that took place in England, the United States, France and Haiti we find interesting patterns of historical evidence that support the above arguments. In each case, there is evidence that the advocates of natural rights did not represent bourgeois property interests at all. Indeed, claims to natural rights were consistently attacked and denounced by both the old and the emerging propertied classes. Furthermore, some historians argue that claims to natural rights first emerge from multi-ethnic groups and movements (comprising women as well as men) who constructed an everyday praxis of resistance to oppressive power throughout the Atlantic world (Blackburn 1988; Linebaugh and Rideker 2000) At the same time, and as is now well known, many human beings – the poor and propertyless, women, slaves, indigenous peoples – were often not recognised as enjoying supposedly universal rights. Indeed, indigenous peoples and slaves were instead subjected to systematic and genocidal regimes of terror in the cause of European expansion. These exclusions will not be discussed here because my later argument is that such exclusions only became sedimented at points of institutionalisation. They are therefore discussed in Chapter 4.

England

At the very least, the historical transformation in England covered a 50-year period from 1640 to 1689 and needs to be understood in the context of the protestant reformation, what Wood calls agrarian capitalism, and the beginnings of the consolidation of the modern nation state (Hill 1972; Wood 2002). It was a transformation which had an early revolutionary moment at the time of the English Civil War but was also a more drawn out affair. Following the restoration of the monarchy in 1660, the fused issues of monarchical absolutism and Catholicism returned in the crisis of the late 1680s leading to the so-called Glorious Revolution of 1688 and the English Bill of Rights in 1689.

Movement activism persisted throughout this period, well before the earliest beginnings of what we would recognise as political parties. The role of movements such as the Levellers and the Diggers during the English Civil War has been particularly well documented (for example, MacPherson 1962; Arblaster 1984; Wootton 1991, 1992). In his highly influential work *The World Turned Upside Down*, Christopher Hill (1972) provided a hugely rich account of a wide range of activism in this period, a period he depicts as a 'puritan revolution' – emphasising the cultural, religious, dimensions of power rather than the purely economic and political. In other – related – studies, Manning argues that 'popular movements played a part, perhaps the decisive part, in the revolution' (Manning 1996:5) and, more provocatively perhaps, C.H. George describes the revolutionary radicals of the time as 'the rank-and-file who originated the democratic and socialist history of our civilisation' (in Eley and Hunt 1988:25).

With respect to the Levellers there are many differing assessments, ranging from asserting that they were an essentially liberal/ bourgeois movement to claims that their struggles incorporated demands for the abolition of all forms of slavery and control of the 'commons' (Linebaugh and Rideker 2000:Chs 3 & 4). Perhaps most importantly from the point of view of this work, Wootton argues that the Levellers' document the 'Agreement of the People, 1647' was 'the first proposal in history for a written constitution based on inalienable natural rights' (Wootton 1991:412). What Wootton does not mention is that, in this document, we can also see the first suggestion of some notion of collective right because the people who are said to have these natural rights are 'the people of England' (Levellers, 1647).

Given the emphasis on the concept of possessive individualism discussed above, one of the most relevant studies of the Levellers is that by MacPherson (1962) in *The Political Theory of Possessive Individualism*. He argues that 'possessive assumptions' can be found in the theories of the Levellers and examines these via a discussion of the nature of the franchise they advocated. However, importantly, MacPherson concludes '[we] must not, however overrate the proprietorial quality of the Levellers' individualism'. They did not, he says, '...accept the full postulates of possessive individualism.' Further, the Levellers were plainly opposed to the implications of the unlimited acquisition of property, MacPherson noting that they saw '...riches and power as concomitant, and they denounced both' (MacPherson 1962:154). Nor, he says, was their vision of the ultimate good grounded in the self-preservation of the individual. He notes that a '... vision of human society as the ultimate good, and of the ultimate value of living together, is scattered through the Leveller writings' (MacPherson 1962:156). Despite these various points, MacPherson nevertheless argues that the Levellers 'ought to be remembered as much for their assertion of a natural right to property in goods and estate as for anything else' (MacPherson 1962:158). He claims they paved the way for Locke to confuse the equal right to property with the right to unlimited property.

Curiously, MacPherson could not quite see, or else bring himself to admit, what his own researches demonstrated: that the Levellers had some sense of the sociality of the individual – a notion of a social self. They did not work within the binary polarity between the individual and collective that MacPherson puts at the heart of his theoretical framework. It is almost with a sense of puzzlement that MacPherson ponders that '...the Levellers' sense of community may appear to go oddly with their possessive individual rights. Yet they saw no incongruity' (MacPherson 1962:157). As we shall see, far from being an oddity, the Levellers' attempt to link individual and collective in notions of natural and human rights is in fact quite typical in terms of social movement praxis.

The Diggers (or True Levellers as they described themselves) are typically seen as more socialistic in their orientation to property, described by some as agrarian communists. It is not clear whether they used any developed notion of natural rights. According to Linebaugh and Rideker (2000:101) a Diggers' pamphlet of 1648, 'A Light Shining in Buckinghamshire' called for equal rights, free elections, a commonwealth and a just portion for every person. Interestingly, it was subtitled 'A Discovery of The Main Grounds and Original Causes of all the Slavery in the World, but chiefly in England', linking universal and particular and indicating perhaps some idea of 'old wrongs' (see Chapter 5). Certainly, like the Levellers, they sought to defend 'customary rights' against enclosures and restrictions by landowners and argued for the levelling of property. They also had a sense both of ancient liberties of 'the poor oppressed people of England' (Ishay 2004:93) being destroyed by the 'Norman Yoke', property rights being seen as nothing more than the spoils of war and conquest. In MacPherson's view, '[t]he only natural rights of the individual that Winstanley recognised was the natural right of men to labour together and live together, governing themselves according to a natural law of social preservation' (MacPherson 1962:157). While he acknowledges that the Levellers came close to this at times 'in their glimpses of the ultimate value of living together', he argues that the Levellers did not share Winstanley's utopian insight that freedom lay in free common access to the land (MacPherson 1962:157). In short, it seems that Macpherson saw the Levellers pursuing individual rights in contrast to the Diggers pursuing common or collective rights. Arguably, it was more complicated than this claimed binary separation suggests.

Ellen Wood, a contemporary Marxist analyst, has written extensively on the origins and development of capitalism, emphasising the specificity of the origins of capitalism in England. Most standard histories of capitalism, she argues, only serve to obscure such specificity and she points out:

> ...it is a measure of how deeply rooted the old question-begging explanations of capitalism are that they are still present in the most current scholarship – not only in anti-Eurocentric critiques but also in today's conceptions of modernity and postmodernity – and in our conventional everyday language, which still identifies *capitalist* with *bourgeois*, and both with modernity. (Wood 2002:70, italics in original)

John Locke, she says, '...becomes perhaps the first thinker to construct a systematic theory of property based on something like... capitalist principles', acknowledging that his notion of improvement could easily be mobilised to justify colonial expansion and expropriation of indigenous peoples. But she then denies that the English Revolution can be meaningfully described as bourgeois, arguing that '[c]alling this revolution "bourgeois" requires a definition so vague and general as to be vacuous' (Wood 2000:118). Furthermore, she notes, if we contrast the standard accounts of the English and French revolutions, we would be forced to conclude that revolutions can be bourgeois without being capitalist and capitalist without being bourgeois (Wood 2000:119).

Wood also warns against treating popular radical forces as agents of capitalist progress. In the context of the English Revolution she argues:

> It is surely misleading to treat popular struggles as the major force in advancing the development of capitalism, emphasising them at the expense of more subversive and democratic popular struggles that challenged property forms conducive to capitalist development. These popular forces may have lost the battle against capitalist landlords, but they left a tremendous legacy of radical ideas quite distinct from the 'progressive' impulses of capitalism, a legacy that is still alive today in various democratic and anticapitalist movements. (Wood 2000:120)

Evidence presented in this section suggests that it was such radical and proto-democratic movements that initially developed and deployed notions of natural rights in England and I would argue that natural rights cannot be properly understood without grasping this. Without denying the importance of John Locke as a foundational thinker for liberalism, it is crucial to recognise that his particular account of natural rights is not representative of that history. Certainly, exploring the emergence and development of natural rights should not be reduced to an assessment of his texts.

The United States

Of the four transformations considered in this chapter, it is the American case that – at first sight – looks the most conservative. Indeed some characterisations of the American Revolution say that, internally, nothing very much changed: a European propertied elite led the revolution; won the revolution; and sustained their power subsequently. In his overview of the historical literature, Greene (1979) notes that much of the post-war strand of historical research articulates this position:

> The prevailing view thus came to believe that the revolution was predominantly a conservative, Whiggish movement undertaken in defence of American liberty of property, preoccupied throughout with constitutional and political problems, carried on with a minimum of violence – the least when seen in the perspective of other revolutions – and with little changed either in the distribution of political power or in the structure and operation of basic social institutions, and reaching its logical combination with the federal constitution. (Greene 1979:54)

But Greene also details what he calls a 'progressive conception' of the revolution. This literature, he says, identifies a fundamental conflict between an upper-class elite who advocated property rights and the political predominance of special interests and '...the little men... who stood for human rights and democracy' (Greene 1979:8). Such accounts see the revolutionary period as a struggle for democracy on the part of disenfranchised and underprivileged groups. Furthermore, some of these accounts argue that, by the time of the Declaration of Independence and the revolutionary war, it was the radicals not the elites who had won. Indeed, this might explain why there is a right of revolution but no mention of private property rights in the American Declaration of Independence.[5] On the other hand, this victory was apparently short-lived, 'progressive accounts' then arguing that the constitution-building of the late 1780s delivered a decisive victory for the propertied elites. Referring to Beard's study of the economic interests of the members of the Constitutional Convention of 1787, Greene notes:

> Implicit in Beard's conclusions was the idea that the constitution instead of being the logical culmination of the revolution was actually a repudiation of it, the counterrevolutionary instrument conceived by Conservatives to curb the democratic excesses of the war and confederation periods. (Greene 1979:12)

Greene himself is unconvinced by these accounts. He argues that other research undermines such explanations (Greene 1979:27–31) and that, in his view, a central concern 'of the man of the American Revolution' was the search for the means (citing Morgan) 'to check the inevitable operation of depravity in men who wielded power' (Greene 1979:73).

Despite Greene's overall assessment, important radical dimensions of the American transformation have been identified in similar terms. On the basis of a detailed analysis of a range of pamphlets and other writings of the time in the *The Ideological Origins of the American Revolution*, Bailyn (1967) also detects the distinctive influence of 'the peculiar strain of anti-authoritarianism bred in the upheavals of the English Civil War' (Bailyn 1967: viii). This was transmitted to the colonists, he suggests, by a group of early eighteenth-century radical publicists and opposition politicians in England and that – at its core – was indeed a critique of arbitrary power. Furthermore, '...the preservation of liberty rested on the ability of the people to maintain effective checks on the wielders of power, and hence in the last analysis rested on the vigilance and moral stamina of the people' (Bailyn 1967:65).

In his biography of Tom Paine, John Keane (1996) supports Bailyn's central argument about the need for an active struggle against power:

> At the time of Paine's arrival in the colonies, songs, poems, newspapers, political pamphlets, doggerel and books were pouring from the presses of American printing shops. Much of this literature supposed a theory of politics that is strikingly relevant....The colonists worked from the idea that the driving force behind every political development, the key determinant of every political controversy, is power. Power was understood as the exercise of dominion by some men over the lives of others, and it was seen as a permanent temptation in human affairs....The key problem in human affairs, therefore, was how to preserve liberty by inventing effective checks on the wielders of power, apportioning and monitoring it, ensuring its responsible exercise. (Keane 1996:90)

Perhaps the fantastic reception amongst the colonists for Paine's *Common Sense* in the early months of 1776 can be explained in terms of its resonance with this outlook.

While political power was clearly a central concern during the revolutionary period, it was not the only aspect of power that was challenged. Robin Blackburn notes that both the Vermont constitution of 1777 and the Pennsylvania Assembly of 1780 moved towards slave emancipation and that some of the white revolutionaries believed that universal rights should indeed be extended to all (Blackburn 1988:111, 117). Furthermore, not all the social actors were white. Blackburn notes that black slaves sometimes petitioned state assemblies for their freedom and that, although rarely successful, '...the wording of the petitions from blacks typically drew attention to the logic of the revolutionary natural rights doctrine' (Blackburn 1988:116).

Linebaugh and Rideker offer an altogether more dramatic account which, even if only partly accurate, would seriously undermine many accounts of natural rights in the American Revolution. They discuss the role of what they call a 'motley crew' in the American Revolution, by which they mean sailors, slaves and commoners who made up a multi-ethnic, urban and revolutionary 'crowd' in the 1770s. Suggesting direct links back to the struggles of the Levellers and Diggers, they argue that these were 'the real citizens of the world' who 'instructed' the middle and upper class revolutionaries like Paine and Jefferson on natural rights (Linebaugh and Rideker 2000:Ch.7).

France

In England it was some 50 years after the Civil War before natural rights were institutionalised in the constitutional settlement of 1688/89. In the United States it took just over a decade. In France the 'Declaration of the Rights of Man and Citizen' of 1789 was, at least in part, about legitimising and institutionalising a new form of political power (Gauchet 1989; Baker 1990:261–7; Fontana 1992; Van Kley 1994:6). Furthermore, there was a strong and very particular concept of collective right – the sovereignty of the French people represented through the French state – embedded in the French Declaration. So the tension and inter-relation between individual and collective notions of rights was present at the outset. Both the emphasis on institutionalisation and the state-centric formulation of collective right suggest that, in some ways at least, this approach to natural rights was already enmeshed in elements of what I call the 'paradox of institutionalisation' examined in Chapter 4.

These and other tensions are reflected and refracted in many of the historical accounts. The French Revolution has been seen as the starting point of 'modern politics', but it has also been depicted as the first 'popular revolution' and is said to mark 'the unexpected invention of revolutionary politics' (Hobsbawm 1962:1–4; Hunt 1986:3; Doyle 1999). Interestingly, in terms of the development of natural rights, there is little work which sees natural rights in the French revolution as the *culmination* of 150 years of social struggles. Whilst there is some discussion of the specific relation between the texts of the American and French declarations, broader connections are typically projected forward towards the revolutionary upsurges of the nineteenth and twentieth centuries rather than linked back to struggles in the English Civil War or the wider Atlantic world of the seventeenth century.

In his *Origins of the French Revolution*, Doyle (1999) examines the traditions of historical scholarship since 1939. He identifies three broad schools of work which he labels 'classic', 'revisionist' and 'post-revisionist'. The 'classic' account, epitomised he says by the work of George Lefebvre, explained the revolution in terms of the coming to power of a bourgeois class bringing political relations into symmetry with economic realities. Given my argument that liberal and Marxist accounts often 'mirror' each other, interestingly Doyle argues that there was broad agreement on the accuracy of this 'classic' account by the middle of the twentieth century. Yet this consensus broke and a 'revisionist' interpretation of the French revolution emerged after the end of the Second World War. According to Doyle, for example, Cobban's account argued that the revolution '...was not the work of the rising bourgeoisie at all but rather of a declining one. The revolutionaries of 1789 were neither hostile to "feudalism", which the peasants, not they, destroyed; nor were they the standard bearers of capitalism' (Doyle 1999:10–11). Up until the late 1980s, divisions between 'classic' and 'revisionist' accounts often reflected splits on both ideological (between liberals and radicals) and national-cultural grounds (between Francophone and Anglophone historical scholarship). But according to Williams, by the late 1980s, the classic account of the revolution had even collapsed in France, ironically perhaps, under the weight of evidence built upon the previous major advances achieved by Marxist historical scholarship (Williams 1989:ix). Doyle argues that 'post-revisionist' accounts began to emerge at that time. In contrast to 'revisionist' accounts, 'post-revisionism' reinstates a concern with identifying structural tendencies shaping the revolutionary process. But, in contrast to the structural economic processes identified in the 'classic' accounts, emphasis was now placed on cultural factors. Indeed Doyle argues that, by 1989, a new post-revisionist consensus was emerging.

I have dwelt on Doyle's overview because it illustrates two important points. Firstly, it shows how changes in intellectual fashion within historical scholarship closely shadow changes in the intellectual climate in the humanities and social sciences more generally. Secondly, and more importantly for this study, Doyle's characterisation of 'classic', 'revisionist' and 'post-revisionist' reflects different understandings of the importance of the economic, the political and the cultural. In Doyle's account, political explanation supplants economic explanation and then cultural approaches supplant political explanation. Yet each approach seems to share the search for a primary 'driver' of social relations and social change. As I argued in Chapter 1, the approach here seeks to avoid this reductionism seeing the political, cultural and economic as interactive and interconnected realms of 'the social'.

A range of historical accounts look at the role of social movements in the revolution and explore the adoption of the 1789 Declaration. Hunt's (1986) influential work *Politics, Culture and Class in the French Revolution* criticises those accounts which, by focusing on origins and outcomes, ignore the processes of the revolutionary period and the intention of revolutionary actors. She argues that:

> Because the identity of the revolutionaries fits into neither the Marxist nor the revisionist account... both end up denying the importance of who the revolutionaries were or what they thought they were doing. In the Marxist interpretation the revolutionaries facilitated the triumph of capitalism, even while expressing hostility to capital, and in the revisionist interpretation revolutionaries mistakenly dragged the process off its course of liberal, notable rule. What the revolutionaries intended is not what came out of the revolution, hence what the revolutionaries intended matters little. Thus, the focus on origins and outcomes has made the revolutionary experience itself seem irrelevant. (Hunt 1986:10)

Focusing on the processes and practices of the revolutionary period, Hunt argues in contrast that '[t]hrough their language, images, and daily political activities, revolutionaries worked to reconstitute society and social relations. They consciously sought to break with the French past and to establish the basis for a new national community' (Hunt 1986:12).

At the heart of Hunt's analysis is the identification of what she calls a republican political class which both challenged the arbitrary power and privilege of the old order and believed that participation through elections and office-holding should be open to a broadly based citizenry. However, at the same time she notes that while the revolutionaries 'challenged the patriarchal model of power... even the radicals were eager to maintain some kind of legitimate (and, in their eyes, masculine) authority' (Hunt 1986:214). Nevertheless, it is clear that significant contestation took place around the extent to which women, slaves, free blacks, religious minorities and the poor were entitled to citizenship. Hunt argues that the '...question of citizenship helped drive the Revolution into increasingly radical directions after 1789 as one excluded group after another began to assert its claims' (Hunt 1996:16).

Fontana shares Hunt's doubts about liberal and Marxist explanations of the revolution. She points to an enormous volume of research in the last decades of the twentieth century that seriously undermined such accounts, showing that a 'whole series of historical stereotypes... have proved unreliable or confused' (Fontana 1992:110). While this necessarily results in a more blurred and tangled picture of the revolution, she argues:

> It is a real advance to see the advent of democracy in France during the revolution not as the predetermined outcome of socio-economic forces, but as a set of genuinely creative collective practices, in which the energies of different groups of people coagulated around immediate political issues. (Fontana 1992:111)

She goes on to say that it was in the context of the impossibility of sustaining permanent mobilisation that the constitution of 1795 marked a hasty retreat towards a restricted, property-based franchise (Fontana 1992:112).

In contrast to textual analyses of declarations of rights in terms of their philosophical coherence or ideological trajectory, some scholars have instead emphasised the importance of tactics and strategy. For example, Baker notes that members of the revolutionary National Assembly saw issues around the declaration of rights in largely strategic terms. It was, he says, a '...discussion over the very nature of the revolution itself'

(Baker 1990:264). Similarly, Fontana points out that the very term 'declaration' was used tactically and deliberately to echo the same formula of royal pronouncements. The first purpose of the declaration was, she argues '...to confer on popular sovereignty the sacredness which had always accompanied the acts of the monarchy by appealing to universal principles and the authority of God' (Fontana 1992:115).

But there were dangers in this. Having made the point that the National Assembly intended the declaration of 1789 to serve as a foundation for a new government, Van Kley cites the work of Marcel Gauchet who, he says:

> ...has persuasively argued that before it was a text the Declaration was an act, an act justifying the seizure of royal power rather than self-defence against it, with the consequences that the revolutionaries ensnared themselves in 'the trap of power' from the very outset. Unlike the American declarations, concerned above all to make individual rights and civil society immune to power, the French Declaration's main purpose was to use abstract individuals and their rights as the constituent elements of a new and unlimited power. The result for Gauchet as for Furet, was the construction of a sovereignty so collective so as to effect an identification of citizenry with their government archaically reminiscent of the virtual identity of the Old Regime nation with its King. (Van Kley 1994:9)

Despite considerable differences of interpretation, it is clear that collective right appears in a considerably stronger form in the French revolution than was the case in England or the United States. Clause Three of the 1789 declaration states 'the source of all sovereignty resides essentially in the nation; no group, no individual may exercise authority not emanating expressly therefrom' and Clause Six begins 'law is the expression of the general will' (Ishay 1997:138). The more specific claim that collective right was made superior to individual right in the French Declaration is contentious. Marx, for example, argued the opposite case in *On the Jewish Question* (in McLellan, 1977:39–62). But from the point of view of this study, the most important point is simply to recognise that constructions of collective identity and collective right were significant elements of natural rights in the

English, American and French revolutions. So, natural rights were never just individualist. Nor, it is now clear, should it be assumed that they were only of European origin.

Haiti

One looks in vain for any reference at all to the Haitian Revolution in the mainstream literature on the development of human rights. Yet, in 1791, black slaves in the French colony of Saint Domingue launched a rebellion which eventually led to the independent republic of Haiti being established in January 1804. As only the second republic to be established in the western hemisphere, the very existence of Haiti '...clearly had an electrifying effect' (Geggus 2002:37). Mimi Sheller argues that the revolutionary founding of the republic of Haiti '...initiated a long-running debate throughout the Atlantic world over how to react to the existence of a 'black republic' at the core of the system of slavery. Haiti's independence set the terms of debate for nearly a century of anti-slavery struggle' (Sheller 2000:71).

While the Haitian revolution did not produce a text that directly parallels the American and French Declarations, Dubois argues that the Haitian revolution was '...the most concrete expression of the idea that the rights proclaimed in France's 1789 Declaration... were indeed universal' (Dubois 2004:3) and Fischer argues that the early constitutions '...function more like declarations of independence than legal codes; they are expressions of aspirations and desires...' (Fischer 2004:229). Certainly, there can be no doubt that understandings of natural rights were an important dimension of social struggles in Haiti from the 1780s until at least the middle of the nineteenth century.

The absence of the Haitian revolution in mainstream accounts of the development of human rights is highly significant. In this anti-slavery and anti-colonial struggle, natural rights combined demands for freedom and emancipation for slaves, political and civil rights for black and other non-white people, and challenged the economic logic that underpinned the plantation economies of the Caribbean and the Atlantic slave trade generally. Such understandings of natural rights simply cannot be fitted into either liberal accounts of natural rights, or those of their Marxist and post-structuralist critics. Nor can they easily be fitted within the disciplinary proclivities and Eurocentric assumptions found in much academic scholarship (for example, see Buck-Morss 2000).

One obvious area requiring consideration is the connections and relationships between the social struggles in Haiti and France. It has sometimes been assumed that 'liberty, equality and fraternity' were simply exported from revolutionary France to Saint Domingue. For example, Genovese depicts the slave revolution as a first instance of 'bourgeois-democratic' slave revolts; '...true revolutions that, under the influence of the French Revolution, aimed for the first time to eradicate slavery. Slave resistance was thus incorporated into a programmatic history of world revolution' (cited in Geggus 2002:65). Yet such an analysis is too simplistic and retains the Eurocentric assumption of transmission from 'the west to the rest'. On the other hand, arguments that the Haitian revolution was an entirely indigenous affair (see Geggus 2002:40) seem equally misplaced. In his now classic account, *The Black Jacobins,* James (1963) emphasises the creative political agency of black slaves and non-white freemen, as well as acknowledging the importance of events in France. He also recognises the impact of the slave revolution on developments and ideas of natural rights in France itself. In particular, he recounts how three deputies from Saint Domingue were catalysts to the decree of the French National Convention abolishing slavery in all its colonies in February 1794 (James 1963:139–42). In more recent work comparing black publics and peasant radicalism in Haiti and Jamaica, Mimi Sheller focuses on the creative social agency in struggles from below. The central thesis of her study is that:

...those who struggled out of slavery in Haiti and Jamaica also developed a shared radical vision of democracy based on the post slavery ideology of freedom. In addition to the clear demand for political participation and equal citizenship, it was an ideology that included an explicit critique of white racial domination and of the unbridled market capitalism that built a world system of slavery. (Sheller 2000:5)

Rejecting top-down, Eurocentric models, she argues that we need to re-centre our thinking about *where* the impetus for democratisation arose and reconsider *how* subaltern groups engage in politics. Rather than metropolitan governments bringing democracy to the Caribbean, she says it was Caribbean freed slaves who pushed hardest for full democratisation (Sheller 2000:8). In an argument which chimes with the approach taken here, Sheller calls for far reaching changes in how we think about and study emancipation and the abolition of the slave trade:

Emancipation was a multisided, dispersed and constantly interrupted struggle for local expansion in the breadth and depth of democratic rights wherever and whenever progress could be made, accompanied by breathtaking assault on those same rights in countervailing retreat and retrenchment....Emancipation, then, was not the triumphal march of humanitarian progress depicted in early celebratory accounts of the abolition of slavery, yet neither can it be grimly reduced to the grinding imperatives of one-way capitalist exploitation and hegemonic adjustment, as pessimistically depicted in recent neo-gramscian accounts. Understanding the interaction of structural constraints with human agency requires an account that allows room for both the possibilities and impossibilities of social change, and for multiple causation. (Sheller 2000:30)

For Sheller, there is no doubt that the social actors understood themselves as being engaged in struggles for natural rights. Indeed, her specific Haitian case study is of a movement called 'the army of sufferers' who, in the mid-nineteenth century, had to call once again for the establishment of black civil and political rights in the context of an elite-driven and faltering 'liberal revolution'. Yet, that said, it is also important to recognise that rights discourses and struggles for rights were not the totality of the Haitian revolution. In particular, Geggus is sceptical of the importance of ideas of natural rights, arguing that 'the slaves of Saint Domingue rose in the name of king and church rather than the rights of man, although they incorporated both into their rhetoric' (Geggus 2002:66).

Given so much contemporary radical scepticism towards human rights, it is interesting that radical voices feel more comfortable invoking the notion of universal human rights within the context of the Haitian revolution. In an article in *Radical Philosophy* on the bicentenary of Haiti's independence, Peter Hallward noted:

> Of the three great revolutions that began in the final decades of the 18th century – American, French and Haitian – only the third forced the unconditional application of the principle that inspired each one: affirmation of the natural, inalienable rights of all human beings. Only in Haiti was the declaration of human freedom universally consistent. Only in Haiti was this declaration sustained at all costs, in direct opposition to the social order and economic logic of the day. (Hallward 2004)

He also argues that of these three revolutions, it is Haiti's that has most to teach us today. While that may be true, what it has to teach us it may not be what Hallward thinks it is. His contention of sustained consistency is not supported by the historical evidence.

In particular, if we go back to Sheller's study, a very different picture emerges. At the heart of Sheller's analysis is what she calls processes of de-democratisation, crucial to the transition out of slavery (Sheller 2000:6). Explaining this in terms of the structure of ties between state and civil actors (particularly the key role of the military in relations between publics and the state) she argues that the post-independence political development of Haiti forms part of the wider pattern of anti-democratic reaction to slave emancipation. Referring again to the struggles of the mid-nineteenth century, she argues:

> The original anti-slavery, anti-colonial and egalitarian premises of the Haitian revolution did not simply die out but were crushed. Yet, peasant democratic republicanism lived on in a popular vision of liberty, fraternity and equality... It was precisely the threat of this powerful discourse – and the collective action it elicited – that led the liberal faction of the elite to retreat back into their pact with the agrarian-military planters.... In spite

of their democratic rhetoric, liberals were not prepared for real democracy, especially if accompanied by radical calls for land redistribution and political enfranchisement. (Sheller 2000:111)

So, just as in England, the United States and France, the institutionalisation of previously radical rights-based struggles proved highly ambiguous. But that is a different part of the story to be examined in Chapter 4. The complete absence of the Haitian revolution in the standard histories of human rights also points directly towards the general theme of the next chapter. In the hall of mirrors absences are just as significant as the reflected and distorted images.

Conclusion

The evidence presented above has focused on the construction and use of natural rights in social movement challenges to arbitrary power and privilege. Within this, what I have called the sociality of natural rights has been illustrated. This account therefore casts serious doubts on the veracity and utility of those depictions of natural rights as a set of ideas which were: worked out largely philosophically; were individualistic in tone and trajectory; and – wittingly or otherwise – legitimised the interests of a rising bourgeois class in Europe and the United States. Furthermore, the use and reconstruction of natural rights in the Haitian revolution disrupts the accusation that natural rights were a product of exclusively European provenance.

A key question posed by the account presented here is why the mainstream human rights literature has not been able to acknowledge the analytical significance of the sociality of natural rights. Four factors can, I think, be identified. The first is the tendency to substitute the reading of texts for the analysis of historical praxis, discussed above and in Chapter 1. The second factor, also discussed previously, is the propensity for 'reading history backwards', that is, analytically confusing outcomes with processes. In other words, what – with the benefit of hindsight – can be seen and understood as an historical pattern is often taken by analysts and reflected back into explanations of historical processes so as to (re)generate history according to that pattern. History 'is' what history 'became'. In its most extreme form this results in the assertion of an immutable historical law: history couldn't have turned out any differently. The most specific and important issue here is the relationship between natural rights, the history of the development of capitalism and the rise of a bourgeois class. As we have seen, both liberals and their severest critics have often shared the view that the transformations in England, the United States and France can be depicted as bourgeois revolutions and that the emergence and development of natural rights were nothing other than a key ideological legitimation of such bourgeois revolutions. Yet, as soon as we step outside the specialist human rights literature, it is clear that such historical accounts have been vigorously contested and seen as reductive and overly-simplistic. Marxist and other critical scholars have often led the attack on such crude reductionism.

The third factor relates to the applicability of the notion of 'the liberal self'. Critics can hardly be blamed for identifying the problem of the atomised, egoistic possessive individual – 'the liberal self' – precisely because such a conception of human beings has indeed been a crucial element of liberal thought. Yet does this really have very much to do with the emergence of natural rights? Well, yes, in so far as liberal theorists have vigorously sought to shape understandings of natural rights in their own image. It is curious, though, that critics have then been so trusting of such claims, often appearing to accept them uncritically as historical fact. What this chapter has shown is that the emergence and nature of natural rights emphasises not the atomised, egoistic possessive individual but, rather, social beings: social selves, constructing and using rights claims to challenge existing relations and structures of power.

The fourth and final point which intertwines with the above is the persistent Eurocentrism that pervades so many accounts of human rights from both proponents and critics. The almost complete absence of the Haitian revolution in accounts of the historical emergence of natural rights cannot be adequately explained without reference to the range of Eurocentric assumptions that are often the foundation of many accounts of human rights. Perhaps these also explain why the stories of Linebaugh and Rideker's 'motley crew' remain largely untold. But such absences are also part of a wider picture. The next chapter argues that a whole century disappears in many histories of human rights.

3

THE LOST NINETEENTH CENTURY

The nineteenth century all but disappears in many accounts of human rights. When some historical development is acknowledged, it is usually passed over in a sentence or two with little suggestion that any such developments are analytically significant for understanding human rights. While a few authors have recognised the possibility of such significance, in recent years only Micheline Ishay (2004) has elaborated on what that might be. A simple explanation could of course be that human rights played no significant part in nineteenth-century movement struggles, yet such an argument is unsustainable. Readily available historical evidence points towards a strong praxis of human rights within a range of social movements, including important historical continuities and reconstructions in the understandings and use of natural rights. Further, it is clear that the nineteenth century was a critical period of major social transformations on a global scale which remain of world historical importance.

Eric Hobsbawm's 'long nineteenth century' begins with the French Revolution and runs until 1914 (Hobsbawm 1962, 1975, 1987). The beginnings of the industrial revolution in England and the political revolution in France – Hobsbawm's 'dual revolution' – heralded major structural shifts in the nature and quality of social relations, most evidently in terms of new class formation in the emerging industrial societies, the consolidation of the modern nation state, the expansion of European imperialism and the emergence of modern political parties.

The 'social question' and the 'national question' became the dominant arenas of political struggle and movement praxis in nineteenth century Europe. Here, the term 'social question' refers to the vast range of social problems and inequities associated with the reconfiguration of economic power and the rise of industrial capitalism. The special relevance of the 'national question' for this study is in the important continuities between understandings of a people's right to self-determination in the American and French Revolutions (and in a more rudimentary form in the English Civil War) and in their twentieth-century counterpart. In South America, Africa and Asia, self-determination was also sometimes couched in 'national' terms but more typically it signified that people were engaged in desperate struggles for survival against the onslaught of elite and/or imperial power. Sometimes such people used the language of natural or human rights. Often their struggles were lost.

In terms of the historical development of human rights, Hobsbawm's periodisation and framework is unsatisfactory. As mentioned previously, natural rights in the French Revolution need to be understood, at least in part, as a culmination of historical processes which can be traced back to the English Civil War. Thus, Hobsbawm's account separates that which requires connection, obscuring the extent of continuity between human rights claims developed and articulated in the nineteenth century and earlier constructions of natural rights. Also, we should note a degree of Eurocentrism in Hobsbawm's account of historical change (Hobsbawm 1962:ix; 1975:xi–xii, Ch.7; 1987:8–11; Blaut 1999). The relevance of this here is that it allows little space for recognising the impact of anti-slavery and anti-colonial struggles on developments in human rights.

It will be argued below that, in a wide variety of ways, social movement praxis in the nineteenth century has major implications for our understandings of human rights. This chapter therefore explores the human rights dimensions of the 'social question' and the 'national question', the latter in terms of the idea of self-determination. But it is necessary to begin by trying to explain the absence of the nineteenth century in my metaphorical mirrors that shape the specialist academic literature on human rights. I should stress that the choice of topics in this chapter is purposively selective so as to enable me to identify specific weaknesses in that specialist literature. Many other struggles around the world could have been explored, the rise of 'first wave' feminism being an obvious example. But while selectivity is an inevitable by-product of focus, my point here is that we must always guard against such selectivity solidifying into a regime of absence.

Understanding and Explaining Absence

A tendency to assume human rights 'began' in 1948 was noted in Chapter 1. This tendency is especially strong among practising lawyers, scholars of law and international relations and those activists who work in and around the international human rights system. Their respective foci make it easy to ignore what went before 1948 and can lead to the assumption that whatever did happen amounts to nothing more than a primitive pre-history of human rights. For example, when Steiner and Alston characterise the origins of economic and social rights, their entire reference to nineteenth-century history amounts to noting '…the political programmes of the nineteenth-century Fabian socialists in Britain [and] Chancellor Bismarck in Germany (who introduced social insurance schemes in the 1880s)' (Steiner and Alston 2000:242). Their account moves swiftly on to the work of the International Labour Organisation which they claim is the most appropriate starting point from which to look at the evolution of economic and social rights in international human rights law. In his account of *Rights,* Peter Jones (1994) makes no mention of the nineteenth century at all, allowing him to ponder more easily whether economic and social rights should best be understood as institutionalised welfare rights, that is, citizens' rights rather than human rights. In marked contrast, David Beetham (1995) has emphasised both the significance of struggles for human rights and the importance of economic and social rights as human rights. Yet even he, when he considers the future of economic and social rights, sees no need to examine early struggles for economic and social rights. His focus remains, illustratively, on the interplay between philosophy and law since 1948.

Steiner and Alston adopt a similar stance with respect to the origin of a peoples' right to national self-determination. While they recognise that '...nationalism had a profound influence in political discourse and on the cartography of Europe during the nineteenth and early twentieth centuries' (Steiner and Alston 2000:1251–4), they locate significant precursors as the Treaty of Versailles and President Wilson's 14 points speech. What they call the deep historical significance of a people's right to self-determination only starts with decolonisation after the end of the Second World War (Steiner and Alston 2000:1248).

As indicated above, not everyone sees the nineteenth century as irrelevant to the development of human rights. But even when that relevance is acknowledged it is often dealt with in short measure. For example, Jack Donnelly (2003) clearly recognises continuity in struggles for (western) human rights from the seventeenth century to the present day. But the nineteenth century gets just a couple of phrases. Firstly, Donnelly notes that the dichotomy between civil and political rights and economic, social and cultural rights was born of political controversy '... first in working class political struggles in the nineteenth and early twentieth centuries and then in the Cold War ideological rivalry' (Donnelly 2003:28). Then, in summing up the history of economic and social rights, he says:

> ...economic and social rights began to make substantial headway only with the nineteenth century rise of the working class as an effective political force. The resulting political struggles led to new understandings of the meaning of and conditions necessary for a life of dignity, rooted in significant measure in the experience of the social and economic devastation of early industrialisation. (Donnelly 2003:58)

So the struggles are there, in history, but their only apparent significance is that they gave rise to 'new understandings' which, presumably for Donnelly, led on to the institutionalisation of welfare rights in the west. On a people's right to self-determination, Donnelly notes '...we can see a right to self-determination as an appropriate response to imperialism, which usually denied its victims the full range of human rights' (Donnelly 2003:222). But his implication here – like Steiner and Alston's – is that a people's right to self-determination is a consequence of struggles in the twentieth, not nineteenth, century. Concerned as he is to limit human rights to the rights of individuals and not groups, he avoids any discussion of struggles for national self-determination or workers' struggles for collective rights in the nineteenth century (Donnelly 2003:221–4).

Michael Freeman (2005) also acknowledges the relevance of movement struggles in the nineteenth century. For example, in an entry in *The Essentials of Human Rights*, he notes:

> ...several developments that were important for the future of human rights took place in the nineteenth century: the anti-slavery movement... the campaign for the social and political rights of women; workers and socialist movements, trade unions and political parties; the development of the humanitarian laws of war; concern for religious and ethnic minorities; and protests against racial discrimination and colonialism. (Freeman 2005:153)

These developments were important, he says, because of their emphasis on economic and social rights and their internationalism. Yet even he fails to develop these points analytically. He doesn't tell us, for example, what this could mean for understanding or reconstructing human rights, despite his call for interdisciplinary approaches to the study of human rights (Freeman 2002).

The above examples are all illustrative of the general tendencies in human rights literature. Many more could be offered but the point is clear enough. Yet how should this absence be explained? We need to come back to my metaphorical mirrors. In disciplinary terms, it is the supposed lack of significant theoretical developments that ensure that the nineteenth century is ignored by philosophers, political theorists and scholars of the history of ideas. Indeed, philosophically speaking, ideas of natural rights are usually depicted as being in sharp decline or having been discredited during the nineteenth century. This is explained both theoretically (utilitarianism supplanting rights-based theorising plus a turn to more positivist forms of social analysis) but also in terms of many thinkers rejecting the violence of the French revolution (see Douzinas 2000:109–14; Freeman 2002). Yet, with respect to this latter point – as we shall see below – what it could also demonstrate is not just a rejection of the specific violence of the French terror but rather a rejection of the broader subversive potential of natural rights. In other words, natural rights could still be used as a challenge to power. Many nineteenth-century theorists found this possibility deeply unpalatable and thus natural rights were effectively excised from the liberal lexicon at the very moment they took on a new lease of life in movement struggles.

Ideologically, there is an eerie confluence of interest between liberals and their critics to keep the nineteenth century out of debates about human rights. For classical liberals, movement claims to collective rights or to economic, social and cultural rights are already ruled out by *a priori* definition or suppressed so as to avoid questioning their narrow definition of human rights. Similarly, for those critics who understand human rights as bourgeois rights, there is a manifest difficulty in accounting for human rights claims that challenge the legitimacy of capitalist economic power, state repression and imperialism. Between classical liberals and their Marxist and poststructuralist critics are various strands of social liberal and social democratic thinking which, broadly speaking, accept the idea of economic and social rights and are sometimes amenable to the idea of collective rights. Yet proponents of a social democratic approach to human rights, whilst acknowledging the importance of nineteenth-century struggles to both the development of their own political tradition and to the development of economic and social rights, nevertheless tend to leave that history behind. Human rights as struggle concepts disappear and we are magically left with 'already institutionalised welfare rights'. In my view this shift needs to be explained in terms of modern social democracy having become almost exclusively committed to sustaining institutionalised forms of elite and technocratic governance (Stammers 1995; 2001a).

Beyond this, and in summary, my overall argument is that there are good reasons stemming from disciplinary proclivities and ideological commitments as to why social movement praxis around human rights in the nineteenth century has been largely ignored.

One recent study does, however, break through some of these proclivities. In *The History of Human Rights,* Micheline Ishay (2004) gives nineteenth-century developments their own chapter. Describing the struggles of workers, liberal nationalists, suffragettes, surfs and slaves as 'a chain reaction of popular unrest', Ishay argues that '...the human rights vision currently depicted as liberal was in fact indelibly molded by the socialist ideals that grew out of nineteenth-century industrialization' (Ishay 2004:5). In other words, it was nineteenth-century socialism which reshaped and significantly broadened the human rights agenda, not only in terms of the development of economic and social rights but also in terms of recognising other forms of oppression and subordination affecting slaves, women, homosexuals, children, national minorities and colonised peoples. This 'socialist human rights vision' was destroyed, she says, by the rise of nationalism and the descent into the First World War. Aspects of Ishay's account certainly chime with what follows. But it is contextualised through a very broad reading of mostly European and American history and she sustains an argument that – even in its socialist manifestation – human rights are best seen as a gift from the west to the rest (Ishay 2004:7). I questioned the accuracy and implications of such a stance in the previous chapter and will do so again below. For the moment, though, let us follow through on Ishay's point that nineteenth-century socialism made an important contribution to the development of human rights.

The Rise of Workers' and Socialist Movements

The struggles of workers and the rise of socialist movements in the industrialising economies were certainly precursors to modern configurations of economic and social rights. But we must not assume that contemporary categorisations of rights can be simply applied to this historical period, or that nineteenth-century rights claims determined the shape of economic and social rights in the twentieth century. In particular, nineteenth-century claims for civil and political rights often had economic dimensions or were intended to pave the way for economic reform. Moreover, many struggles – especially those for collective labour rights – demanded the application, extension and expansion of civil and political rights. The nature of these concerns and people's understandings of rights varied enormously, both within and between movements. Some activists assumed the primacy of the political, arguing political transformation would enable economic reform. Others assumed the primacy of the economic, believing political reform to be a blind alley. Perhaps the majority did not see these as polarities at all but rather two sides of the same coin. Indeed, as we shall see, political, economic and cultural dimensions of these struggles were almost always interlinked.

The Continuing Significance of Natural Rights

As suggested above, one key explanation for the apparently sharp decline in discussion of natural rights in nineteenth-century political thought was, ironically, that many nineteenth-century struggles were precisely premised on the extension and consolidation of natural rights. In other words, liberals joined with conservative thinkers (epitomised by Bentham and Burke) in rejecting the legitimacy of natural rights because of their subversive potential and their connection to the threat of mass insurrection, as had been demonstrated by the French Revolution (Douzinas 2000:109–14; Freeman 2002:Ch.2).

In movement praxis, 'natural', 'historical' and 'constitutional' justifications of rights were often combined in specific, strategic reformulations of the universal and the particular (see Prothero 1997:29–31) and there was a strong continuity with earlier struggles in the way rights were understood as challenges to arbitrary power and privilege. One clear link is via the ideas and activism of Thomas Paine. A significant actor in both the American and French revolutions, Paine wrote *The Rights of Man* as a riposte to Burke's attack on the French Revolution. Yet Paine was also highly influential in the development of workers activism, at least in England, in the period up to 1830. E.P. Thompson (1980:99) describes *The Rights Of Man* as a foundation text of the English working class movement and Hobsbawm (1967:2) has argued that Paine's *The Age of Reason* has remained the classic statement of working class rationalism ever since. Also, in his short history of Chartism, Royle (1996:7) remarks that Paine's work is one of the most important elements linking Chartism all the way back to the Leveller tradition.

In fact, it was easy for radicals and early socialist activists to work with the natural rights tradition as a critique of arbitrary power and privilege. For example, in his study of *Radical Artisans in England and France, 1830 to 1870*, Prothero notes that:

> The privilege that radicals assailed was often seen in terms of groups or interests that pursued their selfish concerns at the expense of those of the general population, and these interests were often defined in economic terms. The chief element in the ranks of privilege was the great landowners, the traditional enemies who tended to hold the top posts in the state, a corrupt and selfish aristocracy. But 'aristocracy' was an epithet not reserved for nobles and landowners, and embraced a wider ruling class that could include ...all men who wielded local or national power and promoted policies in their own selfish interest... (Prothero 1997:23)

In the context of the industrial revolution and the formation of a wage labouring class, the notion of a right to private property was re-articulated as a claim that workers were entitled to the full fruits of their labour. Prothero notes that the idea:

> ...that labour was the working man's property, and that labour legitimated property, were old ones that could lead in our period to very radical conclusions, in that any property that was *not* the product of one's own labour was illegitimate; this was the basis of Proudhon's attack on property as theft. (Prothero 1997:139)

This basic idea was, he says, common to many nineteenth-century movement struggles. Indeed, a key aspect of Marx's theory of alienation rests precisely on the argument that workers are alienated from the full product of their labour (Avineri 1968:105).[1]

The Real Rights of Man?

Many of the above points are brought together in a collection entitled *The Real Rights of Man: Political Economies for the*

Working Class 1775–1850 by Noel Thompson (1998). The author draws his title from a pamphlet written by Thomas Spence, published in 1793, and he does so in order to argue '[f]or Spence, Paine had failed to grasp that the real rights of man must be grounded in the possession of economic power. Without that, mere political rights were devoid of significance, and demands for liberty, equality and fraternity so much empty rhetoric' (Thompson 1998:vii). Yet, despite Thompson's privileging of the economic, the case studies which make up his book demonstrate that activists saw reality as being much more complex than can be captured by this claim. Indeed, Thompson himself notes that Spence was imprisoned for selling the second part of Paine's *The Rights of Man*, so Spence could not always have been quite so dismissive of Paine's position as Thompson maintains (Thompson 1998:14). Beyond this, it is clear that, far from being 'devoid of significance', political and legal demands were an essential aspect of nineteenth-century struggles and not just for 'reformists,' as Thompson (1998:Ch.9) makes clear in his discussion of Chartism and 'red republicanism'. Despite its limitations, this volume demonstrates how natural rights were an important element of the activism in nineteenth-century England. Spence saw the right to equal property in land as a natural right (Thompson 1998:7) and he echoed the American Declaration of Independence in arguing that 'when the government violates the rights of the people, insurrection becomes to the people... the most sacred and most indispensable of duties' (Thompson 1998:10). Thompson notes that Spence's understandings and arguments were very influential, remaining '... part of the fabric of radical and socialist thinking throughout the whole of the nineteenth century' (Thompson 1998:14).

While some combined Spence's emphasis on land rights with a right to property derived from labour, others formulated natural rights as arising solely through the efforts of labour. Noel Thompson looks at the work of Thomas Hodgskin who, in 1832, published *The Natural and Artificial Rights of Property Contrasted*. Hodgskin, like Marx, argued that labour alone was productive of value and, as the title of his work suggests, drew a contrast between what he saw as the natural rights of the labourer and the artificial property rights of the capitalists (Thompson 1998:49–58).

Interlinking Political and Economic Demands

Understandings of privilege, power and property were ubiquitous in the emergent workers' and socialist movements and could inform the framework for reformist, transformative or revolutionary programmes. Many demands for workers' rights were intended either to protect wage labourers or to provide them with the legal framework through which they could protect themselves. That this should be so is less surprising once it is understood that, in a whole range of ways, workers' movements were struggling against the imposition of new, repressive legislation designed to construct a free market for the new industrial capitalist economy. E.P. Thompson (1980:65) notes, for example, that no less than 63 new offences against property carrying the death penalty were created in England between 1760 and 1810. Summarising regressive legislative changes in England and France, Prothero notes that claims for rights which would vary the terms and conditions of employment or protect workers' abilities to organise and take collective action need to be understood as an attempt to reverse and directly challenge legislation that had systematically worsened the position of the working class. Prothero argues that '[laissez-faire] political economy was rejected, explicitly or implicitly through a stress on rights and a concept of justice which refused to see labour as a commodity' (Prothero 1997:135).

It is also important to recognise both the centrality of the demands for broader political reform and the extension of civil and political rights, and the fact that activism around such demands were not simply 'reformist'. Indeed, such demands and strategies were seen as deeply radical and threatening and provoked violent responses from employers and the state. According to Prothero (1997:42–3), for example, early mass mobilisations and threats of violence on the part of the Chartists only gave way to a more quiescent, gradualist approach to political reform in the face of sustained repression and state violence.

Collective Rights

Another important point to stress here is the extent to which rights claims were formulated as collective rights. Whereas many proponents of human rights see collective rights as being of dubious provenance, if not entirely anomalous, examination of workers' struggles in the western industrialising countries demonstrate how understandings of collective rights have been a persistent and fundamental way in which human rights claims have been formulated and developed. As Cole put it:

> Trade Unions, in every country in which they have grown up, have been compelled to fight a hard battle for the right even to exist, and have won reasonable recognition at law only by stages and at the cost of severe struggles that have called for high courage. Trade Unionism developed in the countries which first went through the Industrial Revolution, at a period when the doctrine of economic individualism was very strong in the rising capitalist classes, and when the older governing classes, terrified by the French Revolution and the assertion of the 'Rights of Man', were disposed to look on every working class combination as a conspiracy against the aristocratic order. Thus, the old governing class of aristocrats and the new rising class of capitalist entrepreneurs, though engaged in a struggle for power, were apt to join forces to repress working-class combinations, which appeared to threaten both alike. (Cole 1953:163)

Combinations and trade unions were seen as conspiracies and attempts to restrain trade and were thus doubly criminalised. Even when combinations were made lawful in England after 1824, the very same Act of Parliament that had legalised them made it almost impossible to conduct a lawful strike (Cole 1953:166).

Demands for collective rights were perhaps, above all, designed to legitimate a wide range of collective and co-operative associations that workers needed as a matter of fundamental material necessity. The main thrust of Prothero's work is precisely to look at that range of benefit, trade, co-operative, credit, insurance, educational and convivial clubs of varying degrees of formality comprising mostly people connected to manufacturing industry. He argues that the obstacles to setting up and continuing these organisations were severe and legion because forms of association and organisations were of such pivotal importance in the nineteenth century. So struggles for collective rights were also fundamental to the legitimation of these very basic forms of mutual support and association (Prothero 1997:5).

Expressive Dimensions of Activism

In the light of the discussion developed in Chapter 6 below, it is useful to stress here that understandings of rights importantly shaped the identities, value systems and moral orientations of ordinary working people during this period. They could validate their own selves and communities through understandings of rights whilst simultaneously critiquing the social order and demanding its reorientation and reconstruction along different lines. As challenges to arbitrary power and privilege, natural rights gave meaning to understandings of what it meant to be free as a person, not in the sense of the egoistic possessive individual posited by MacPherson, but as potentially free from subservience and oppression. In England, understandings of natural rights could be linked to the historical legacies and myths of the so-called 'freeborn Englishman' (E.P. Thompson 1980:Ch.2). In the preface to his celebrated study of the making of the English working class, Thompson rejects economic reductionist accounts of history, emphasising that '[t]he working class did not rise like the sun at an appointed time. It was present at its own making' (E.P. Thompson 1980:8). At many points in his account he stresses that the issues which often provoked the most intensity of feeling among the working class were ones concerning traditional customs, justice, independence and security. Even the Luddites, he says, were seen to be defending 'ancient right' in their destruction of new machinery. (E.P. Thompson 1980:579).

The early 1830s in England were aflame with agitation. But after a period of repression, activists withdrew into their local communities. Thompson implies that it was largely as a consequence of this repression that the focus of dissatisfaction became local and predominantly economic and industrial in character. Nevertheless, he says, while the Jacobins and Painites may have disappeared '...the demand for human rights became defused more widely than ever before. Repression did not destroy the dream of the egalitarian English republic' (E.P. Thompson 1980:545). It was, he says, a combination of repression and collective identity formation that dissolved the remaining ties of loyalty between working people and their masters in such a way that dissatisfaction spread in a manner which the authorities simply could not penetrate (E.P. Thompson 1980:546). Here, Thompson places understandings of human rights at the heart of the construction of a working class culture of resistance.

This brings us back to the relationship between collectivities, communities and rights. As we saw above, many of the rights claims made in the nineteenth century were claims for collective rights and the establishment of friendly societies and other forms of mutual aid. While such demands clearly had vital material and instrumental dimensions, they also had crucial and connected expressive dimensions. Noel Thompson brings out this connection clearly:

> ...the appeal of communitarian socialism must be seen in terms of pre-existing traditions of working class mutuality. The guilds, burial clubs, trade societies, friendly societies, trade unions of the eighteenth and early nineteenth centuries represented collective attempts to provide a measure of material security for those who, individually were unlikely to survive the chill blast of the competitive economic wind... it was also the case that these early institutional expressions of working class mutuality themselves generated a language of harmony, union and community which supplied the rhetorical building blocks of the socialist idiom. (N. Thompson 1998:76–7)

Hobsbawm makes the point somewhat differently but, again, the connection is clear. The Labour movement, he says, 'was an organisation of self-defence, of protest, of revolution. But for the labouring poor it was more than a tool of struggle: it was also a way of life' (Hobsbawm 1962:214). Prothero too stresses the importance of understanding both material and non-material aspects of struggles (1997:4). Specifically on rights, he argues '[t]he language of rights, especially "natural rights", can be a very effective and exhilarating instrument which...can facilitate a change in people's self image and be a liberating and even revolutionary rhetoric' (Prothero 1997:29). He notes that the terminology of freedom, tyranny and slavery suffused trade societies, disputes and strikes and stresses that trade disputes were not simply oriented towards instrumental demands. The '...defence of liberty and rejection of tyranny was an act of self-respect; men deserved respectful treatment from employers...' (Prothero 1997:101).

It needs to be recognised that this expressive dimension of activism around rights remained largely patriarchal. The 'rights of men' were often seen as just that: for men. Prothero notes that manliness was an important aspect of the language of artisan struggle and that, in championing 'the rights of labour and sons of toil', emphasis was often placed on masculinity and manliness which, in turn, was associated with patriotism (Prothero 1997:102–103). In *The Struggle for the Breeches: Gender and the Making of the British Working Class*, Anna Clark (1995) takes up this link between rights and masculinity. She argues that, during the 1830s and 1840s, working class consciousness often focused on the political rights of skilled men, only occasionally mobilising women and the unskilled as part of larger communities. But, she says, the discourses chosen by the radicals were shaped by the extant realities of power. Put another way, radicals made strategic use of rights discourses but this usage was shaped by a recognition of '...their own lack of political clout and working men's desire to retain control over women at home and at work' (Clark 1995:8–9).

Yet Clark does not see human rights as necessarily and inevitably liberal and masculinist in the way, for example, Fiona Robinson has argued (Robinson 2002 and see Chapter 1 above). Rather, she sees understandings of rights and gender as being combined by activists in specific and strategic constellations. While she concludes that '[t]he fatal flaws of misogyny and patriarchy ultimately muted the radicalism of the British working class' (Clark 1995:271), she also argues that Paine's formulation of the *Rights of Man* had a universalising and egalitarian trajectory which could be opened up and radicalised by women. She notes that, as the nineteenth century progressed, the issue of gender and other forms of oppression came to be understood as being both linked and extending beyond national borders (Clark 1995:145, 157).

Universal Rights and Socialist Internationalism

Over the nineteenth century an increasing emphasis was often placed on the particularity of rights claims, the achievement and instantiation of specific rights within national polities and legal jurisdictions. But the universal dimensions of rights claims never disappear. For example, E.P. Thompson cites from 'Instructions of the London Corresponding Society to its travelling delegates' of 1796 to open Part One of *The Making of the English Working Class*, '[y]ou are wrestling with the Enemies of the Human Race, not for yourself merely, for you may not see the full Day of Liberty, but for the child hanging at the breast' (E.P. Thompson 1980:17).

The importance of Paine's work and the emphasis on natural rights in the nineteenth century also strongly indicates the continuing significance of the universal dimension of human rights. However, as Ishay (2004) argues, an important new emphasis was provided by the internationalism within socialist movements in the latter part of the nineteenth century. The way universal and particular dimensions of rights could be combined in this context is well illustrated by the Erfurt Programme of the German Social Democratic Party, drafted by Kautsky and Bernstein and adopted in 1891. While this programme was criticised by Engels (for failing to stress the dictatorship of the proletariat) and its authors later denounced by the Bolsheviks, Donald Sassoon argues it '...became one of the most widely read texts of socialist activists throughout Europe.... [and that] Kautsky's commentary [upon it], *The Class Struggle*, was translated into sixteen languages before

1914 and became the accepted popular summa of Marxism' (Sassoon 1997:11).

The programme comprises a statement of principles followed by a detailed list of demands. The statement of principles is worth considering in some detail. Having called for the transformation of capitalist private ownership into social property and socialist production 'by and for' society, the statement continues:

> This social transformation amounts to the emancipation not only of the proletariat, but of the entire human race, which is suffering from current conditions....The struggle of the working class against capitalist exploitation is necessarily a political struggle. Without political rights, the working class cannot carry on its economic struggles and develop its economic organization. It cannot bring about the transfer of the means of production into the possession of the community without first having obtained political power....The interests of the working class are the same in all countries with a capitalist mode of production. With the expansion of global commerce, and of production for the world market, the position of the worker in every country becomes increasingly dependent on the position of workers in other countries. The emancipation of the working class is thus a task in which the workers of all civilized countries are equally involved. The German Social Democratic Party therefore does not fight for new class privileges and class rights, but for the abolition of class rule and of classes themselves, for equal rights and equal obligations for all, without distinction of sex or birth. Starting from these views, it fights not only the exploitation and oppression of wage earners in society today, but every manner of exploitation and oppression, whether directed against a class, party, sex, or race. (German Social Democratic Party 1891)

There are a number of very interesting aspects to this statement. The internationalist aspirations for the working class are clearly set out in terms of what, today, would be understood as economic globalisation. Then there is the degree of emphasis placed on the necessity of political struggles and the achievement of political rights, illustrating again the interlinking of political and economic demands. Perhaps most fascinating is the emphasis placed on ending every kind of exploitation and oppression including those based on sex and race. Taken together, these elements suggest an underlying analysis of power as complex and multidimensional. In this sense, the Erfurt programme not only connects back to earlier critiques of arbitrary power and privilege but also prefigures the orientations of the so-called new social movements in the latter half of the twentieth century.

The specific demands of the programme incorporate a wide range of civil, political, economic, social and cultural rights, including: 'universal, equal, and direct suffrage'; 'abolition of every limitation of political rights'; 'abolition of all laws which limit or suppress the right of meeting or coalition'; 'abolition of all laws that discriminate against women'; 'the secularisation of the public sphere including schools'; 'free education'; 'free administration of justice and free legal assistance' and 'free medical care, including midwifery and medicines. Free burial.' The programme also calls for the settlement of all international disputes by arbitration and for effective national and international legislation for an eight hour working day, the prohibition of the employment of children under the age of 14 and a general prohibition of night work where practicable. It is clear that these demands range across all realms of social relations, including the cultural sphere. Of particular interest are the demands for secularisation and the challenge to the legitimacy of church control of information and knowledge in education. Then there is the emphasis on international legislation around economic rights which, even today, are often understood primarily as a national concern. In short, the Erfurt programme combined economic, political and cultural dimensions with a positive orientation towards rights, both universal and particular.

All of the above discussion demonstrates the extent to which, albeit varying, understandings of human rights were central to the praxis of the rising working class and socialist movements in the nineteenth century. Moreover, at the century's end, economic and social rights were already being acknowledged as signalling a major shift in social relations. In *The Age of Capital*, Hobsbawm notes that demands from below had become so vocal and so politically effective that, by 1870, the historian Jacob Burckhardt considered that 'the modern version of the Rights of Man...includes the right to work and subsistence' (Hobsbawm 1975:305–306).

So, on one level, struggles for workers' rights could be said to have been a significant success. Yet the specific construction of these rights in terms of legal protection and state duties left open the question of their effectiveness. Unfortunately, answers to this question then came to be shaped by broader debates around the dichotomy between revolution and reform, between revolutionary Marxism and anarchism on the one hand and gradualist and reformist programmes of social democracy on the other. In some ways these debates continue today and link directly to the arguments of the uncritical proponents and uncritical critics discussed in Chapter 1. The line of argument to be developed in Chapter 4 is that proponents and critics of human rights coming out of these ideological traditions have failed to engage properly with what I call the paradox of institutionalisation. But before moving on to that issue, we need to look at another key dimension of nineteenth-century movement praxis, struggles around self-determination.

At the Heart of the Nineteenth Century: Struggles for Self-Determination

Even a quite thorough examination of the human rights literature would suggest to a student fresh to the subject that a people's right to self-determination was a twentieth-century invention, a 'third generation' right which made its first appearance at the end of the First World War and which came of age in the anti-colonial struggles after the end of the Second World War. Yet understandings of individual and collective self-determination were central to movement struggles all around the world in the nineteenth century. The historical evidence suggests a missing link between the earlier constructions of collective identity and collective rights examined in the last chapter and those understandings of a people's right to self-determination as that developed in the twentieth century. The implications of this are significant because reconnecting these histories makes it clear that collective identity and collective right (whether or not the latter is understood as a group right or as an aggregation of individual rights) has been a persistent continuing element of the unfolding of understandings of human rights. As Michael Freeman neatly puts it '[t]he concepts of individual rights and collective rights have a similar history and a similar general theoretical rationale. Individuals and collectivities have been oppressed throughout history and in the modern period protection has been sought in the form of institutionalized rights' (Freeman 1995:28).

The 'National Question' in Nineteenth-Century Europe

The absence of discussion of self-determination prior to the twentieth century in the specialist human rights literature is more than curious because, beyond that literature, the strong historical connections are clearly and explicitly acknowledged in a range of studies across the disciplines. For example, in *The Quest for Self-Determination*, Ronen (1979) begins his preface by citing the American Declaration of Independence, claiming '[t]his very same quest for self-determination that gave birth to the United States of America re-emerged in a new geographical and political setting in the French Revolution' (Ronen 1979:ix). The French Declaration of the Rights of Man and the Citizen proclaimed, he says, both popular sovereignty and the right to resist oppression. It:

> ...embodied forcefully the ideas and aspirations of former revolutions, and its impact on institutions and political thought was lasting. By proclaiming the principle of popular sovereignty, the revolution altered the then prevailing conception of the state; the divine right of kings was not only discredited, as it had been in England since the beginning of the 18th-century, but was also replaced by the divine right of the people. (Ronen 1979:2)

It was these ideas, Ronen says, that subsequently 'fired nineteenth-century Western Europe with nationalist fervour' (Ronen 1979:2).

In *Nations and Nationalism Since 1780*, Eric Hobsbawm (1992) also makes a direct connection between the American and French revolutions and subsequent understanding of the relationship between the concepts of 'nation', 'state' and 'people'. In excavating the meaning of the term 'nation' in the nineteenth century, the most frequent usage – he claims – was political. 'It equated "the people" and the state in the manner of the American and French revolutions…[t]he "nation" so considered, was the body of citizens whose collective sovereignty constituted them as a state which was their political expression' (Hobsbawm 1992:18–19). Citing the French Declaration of Rights of 1795, he argues that the equation nation = state = people not only linked nation to territory but also implied a '…multiplicity of nation states so constituted, and this was indeed a necessary consequence of popular self-determination' (Hobsbawm 1992:19). Hobsbawm suggests two levels of interrelation between the universal and the particular here in terms of rights. Inside the nation state, individuals had rights in relation to one another within a collectively defined community, a 'we the people'. Outside particular nation states, different collectivities – different 'peoples' – had rights as col-lectivities *vis-à-vis* other 'peoples'.[2]

But how then was the notion of 'a people' understood? While detailed interrogation of this question is beyond the scope of this work, a couple of points need to be made. Firstly, both Hobsbawm and Ronen argue that the 'national question' and the 'social question' were intimately connected and intertwined for much of the nineteenth century. As Ronen (1979:2) put it, the fight was on two fronts, 'the national fight for political freedom and the social struggle for economic reform'. Hobsbawm says that, during the first part of the nineteenth century, what constituted 'a people' did not necessarily involve a connection with a particular territorial state or with ethnic or linguistic bases of group membership. Indeed, he argues:

> If 'the nation' had anything in common from the popular revolutionary point of view, it was not in any fundamental sense, ethnicity, language and the like, though these could be indications of collective belonging… what characterised the nation-people as seen from below was precisely that it represented the common interest against particular interests, the common good against privilege. (Hobsbawm 1992:20)

Hobsbawm's language here is strongly resonant of the language of earlier articulations of natural rights, especially those of Paine. Understandings and practices around 'a people's right to self-determination' were an integral aspect of struggles against arbitrary power and privilege.

But there was another crucial dimension of nationalism that first emerged in the nineteenth century and which has subsequently become the dominant understanding of the term. Hobsbawm distinguishes between what he calls the 'revolutionary democratic' and the 'nationalist' understandings of the nation. While the equation of state = nation = people applied to both, he argues that:

> For nationalists the creation of the political entities which would contain the nation derived from the prior existence of some community distinguishing itself from foreigners, while from the revolutionary democratic point of view the central concept was the sovereign citizen-people = state which, in relation to the remainder of the human race, constituted a 'nation'. (Hobsbawm 1992:22)

This distinction is important in so far as it points to the problem that has often been noted with respect to contemporary implications of a people's right to self-determination – that it carries significant exclusionary potential. Both Hobsbawm and Anderson suggest related processes already at work in the middle of the nineteenth century. Hobsbawm talks of the 'principle of nationality' changing its guise in the most dramatic way during the period from 1830 to 1880 and Anderson argues that 'official nationalisms' developed inside Europe as a response by powerful groups threatened with exclusion or marginalisation from popular imagined communities. 'Such official nationalisms were conservative, not to say reactionary *policies*, adapted from the model of the largely spontaneous popular nationalisms that preceded them' (Anderson 1991:109–110, emphasis in original).

Having been 'imagined', these models of nationalism could then be exported or pirated and Anderson claims this official nationalism was picked up by ruling groups around the world. So was it this process that led to the hegemony of states in the global order and the assumption that only states (usually one's own state) have correlative duties in respect of human rights? Hegemony, of course, is never complete. Even in the context of this conception and construction of European nationalism, Anderson sounds an appropriate note of warning. In the preface to the second edition of *Imagined Communities*, he says that part of his original plan had been to stress the New World origins of nationalism, so to disrupt the assumptions of European scholars 'accustomed to the conceit that everything important in the modern world originated in Europe....'. Yet Anderson was startled to discover that in many reviews of the first edition '... this Eurocentric provincialism remained quite undisturbed, and that the crucial chapter on the originating Americas was largely ignored' (Anderson 1991:xiii). The same pattern can be seen with respect to self-determination.

Self-determination in Struggles against Imperial Oppression

Europe was not the only part of the world in which struggles for self-determination were of crucial importance in the nineteenth century. Such struggles were worldwide and some consideration here is instructive for a number of reasons. Firstly, the relationship between a people, a nation and a state comes to the fore again. Secondly, so too does the question of the relationship between forms of struggle that use understandings of human rights and other struggles that do not, even though the forms of oppression and domination challenged may be the same. Thirdly, the relationships between individual and collective notions of self-determination suggest another way in which individual and collective understandings of rights have been linked historically.

Struggles for Independence in Latin America

The first quarter of the nineteenth century saw the collapse of Spanish and Portuguese colonial power in Latin America as a consequence of revolutionary armed struggles across the region.

What is more, it is clear that understandings of natural rights both inspired many of these independence struggles and that, when the construction of nation states began at the end of that period, various commitments to natural rights were included in many of the Latin American constitutional documents and declarations. Yet, once again, we look in vain for any substantial analysis of this history in the dominant literatures on human rights. In a paper dedicated to 'retrieving a Latin American tradition of the idea of human rights', Carozza complains that 'Latin America has long been regarded as the *object* of human rights concerns more than a *contributor* to human rights thinking' (emphasis in original) and that human rights in Latin America have been seen as '...tarnished and inferior copies of grand, rich European ideas'. Even among critics, he says, the history of human rights in Latin America has been lumped into a monolithic understanding of 'western human rights' (Carozza 2003:283). On one level there appear to be good reasons for this. Historians generally agree that these revolutions were driven by Creole* elites who were familiar with the intellectual and political developments of the European Enlightenment and the importance of natural rights in the North American and French revolutions as portrayed by writers such as Rousseau, Locke and Paine. Carozza, for example, argues that Simón Bolívar was deeply influenced by the works of European thinkers, especially Rousseau (Carozza 2003:300–302).

Although Carozza rejects the argument that natural rights in Latin America were simply derivative, he does not stray too far from mainstream orthodoxies. No indigenous peoples, black people or slaves appear as social actors in his account of the human rights tradition in Latin America. Neither is any mention made of the impact of the Haitian revolution. Yet, on the latter point, it is clear that Bolivar travelled to Haiti and received significant military and logistical support from Haiti in return for a pledge that the liberation of slaves would become part of the Bolivarian revolution (Langley 1996:194).

---

* Creole here refers to people of Spanish or Portuguese descent who were born and lived in Latin America.

In *The Americas in the Age of Revolution*, Langley agrees that the independence struggles in Latin America were led by, and resulted in the subsequent domination of, Creole elites. Yet, he also makes many references to the activism, rebellions and armed insurgency of indigenous groups, slaves and free blacks across the region, arguing that they had a significant impact on subsequent developments. Indeed, he argues that the 'outbursts and insurgencies' by the mass of Indians, mestizos, mulattoes and blacks 'antedated and in many ways anticipated the rebellion the Creoles had proclaimed' (Langley 1996:185). Langley also suggests that it was Bolivar's encounter with, and defeat by, a largely 'pardo'* royalist army led by commander, José Tomás Boves, that changed Bolivar's thinking on slavery and prompted his journey to Jamaica and Haiti. From then on, according to Langley, for Bolivar '…the revolution had a singular purpose – to liberate the continent – and to that cause Bolivar vowed to enlist Creole, pardo, and slave' (Langley 1996:194).

This raises two interesting points. Firstly, as well as depicting the Latin American revolutions as liberal, many historians have also depicted them as nationalist. Yet, these independence struggles also had a pan-Spanish American dimension and, in fact, consolidation into nation states was a post-revolutionary development. Thus, struggles for self-determination in Latin America, while certainly struggles against Spanish rule, should not be simply seen as struggles for *national* self-determination. The second point is much broader and poses the question 'self-determination for whom?' Langley argues that Bolivar knew that slaves would demand freedom as the price of their service and that 'pardo' and slave would demand a stake in the post-revolutionary order. Yet Bolivar apparently despaired at post-revolutionary developments. While, 'the French Declaration uniformly did serve as the principal source for individual rights and guarantees in virtually every early Latin American constitution' (Carozza 2003:299), Creole elites attempted to sustain their hegemony, were reluctant to abolish slavery and maintained strict ethnic

---

* 'Pardo' is a nineteenth-century Spanish term for people of black and white mixed ancestry.

social hierarchies. To what extent any of these various struggles 'from below' used understandings of natural or human rights is unclear, but given the influence of the Haitian revolution – particularly on the slave populations – it would be surprising if they did not.

The Ending of the Slave Trade and Imperial Expansions

The economic and political elites in the United States and Europe gave little thought to any rights of self-determination that might be held by indigenous peoples or slaves. As the Atlantic slave trade ended, the so-called 'scramble for Africa' began and the United States began its own form of imperialism. The 1830s witnessed a period of aggressive expansionism by the United States, acquiring new territories by purchase, conquest and pushing 'the frontier' westwards (Carroll and Noble 1988:Ch.4). This latter strategy involved abrogating treaties previously signed with Native American peoples recognising their autonomy and guaranteeing their land rights. Moreover, by the nineteenth century at least, Native Americans were familiar with concepts of equal rights and self-determination. For example, whilst trying to construct an economic and military alliance among different tribes to oppose the expropriation of Indian lands, Shawnee Chief Tecumseh is cited as arguing:

> The white people have no right to take the land from the Indians, because they had it first; it is theirs. They may sell, but all must join. Any sale not made by all is not valid. The late sale is bad. It was made by a part only. Part do not know how to sell. It requires all to make a bargain for all. All red men have equal rights to the unoccupied land. The right of occupancy is as good in one place as in another. There can not be two occupations in the same place. The first excludes all others. It is not so in hunting or traveling; for there the same ground will serve many, as they may follow each other all day; but the camp is stationary, and that is occupancy. It belongs to the first who sits down on his blanket or skins which he has thrown upon the ground; and till he leaves it no other has a right. (Chief Tecumseh 1810)

Prior to their forced removal from their traditional lands, the Cherokee nation had adopted a constitution in 1827 that, while following the textual traditions of white constitutions (including the exclusion of people of African descent) nevertheless spelt out in detail individual and collective rights of self-determination and the boundaries of the nations' land (Cherokee Constitution 1827).[3]

Langley notes that an 'exclusionary doctrine applied as emphatically and systematically to black Americans as well' (Langley 1996:228). While further examination of the gradual abolition of slavery in United States is not discussed here, we saw in the previous chapter that slaves and free blacks used understandings of natural rights during the American Revolution and this continued throughout the nineteenth century (see Blackburn 1988; 2007). One expression of increased white racism was the 'American Colonisation Society' whose members believed that blacks should be resettled in Africa. What we now know as Liberia was founded by this society in the early 1820s when a small number of former slaves were 'repatriated'. It is no small irony that the establishment of the first, ostensibly democratic, sovereign state with a constitution including a declaration of rights on the African continent was created by emancipated slaves who saw themselves as more American than African. Liberia declared itself a free and independent sovereign state in July 1847. Independence arose from detailed negotiations. Nevertheless, the preamble to the constitution describes Liberia as 'an asylum from the most grinding oppression' and the Declaration of Rights both explicitly prohibits slavery in its assertion of 'natural, inherent and inalienable rights' and limits citizenship to 'Negroes or persons of Negro descent' (Constitution of Liberia 1847).

The European imperial conquest of Africa only accelerated in the last quarter of the nineteenth century. Before the 1880s, only 10 per cent of the African landmass was under European control but, by 1900, only 10 per cent was not. The Berlin Conference of 1884/85 sought to regulate and formalise European colonisation and trade in Africa. The European powers drew lines across the map of Africa that have blighted the possibilities for the self-determination of African peoples ever since. In *Rethinking Resistance: Revolt and Violence in African History*, Abbink, de Bruijn and van Walraven (2003:1) begin by stressing that 'throughout African history, distant as well as recent, Africans have resisted forces of domination'. While that may seem obvious enough, we must not forget the dominant Eurocentric rationalisations of the time for 'civilising the natives' and accepting 'the white man's burden'. The systematic denial of individual and collective self-determination is perfectly summed up by two verses of Labouchère's (1899) retort to Kipling, 'The Brown Man's Burden':

> *Pile on the brown man's burden,*
> *And through the world proclaim*
> *That ye are Freedom's agent –*
> *There's no more paying game!*
> *And, should your own past history*
> *Straight in your teeth be thrown,*
> *Retort that independence*
> *Is good for whites alone.*

> *Pile on the brown man's burden,*
> *With equity have done;*
> *Weak, antiquated scruples*
> *Their squeamish course have run,*
> *And, though 'tis freedom's banner*
> *You're waving in the van,*
> *Reserve for home consumption*
> *The sacred "rights of man"!*

Whether pre-colonial African cultures utilised any understandings of human rights has been a subject of more general debate (Shivji 1989:12–13). Unfortunately, much of this has got caught up in the distortions of my metaphorical mirrors, with critics often assuming that human rights are necessarily individualistic and bourgeois and thus assumed alien to the claimed communalism of pre-colonial African societies. A similar problem recurs in trying to look at understandings of rights and self-determination in India.

'Rightful Dissent' and 'Dharmic Protest'

In India, the first war of independence of 1857/58 was preceded by ten years of direct annexation of lands. According to Wolpert, supposedly independent princes '...were stripped one by one of their privileged domains under the spurious legal doctrines of "lapse" and "paramountcy". [The British] could always find something "debauched" or "depraved" about the Indian princes... that would justify tearing up treaties and stealing their states' (Wolpert 1993:226–7).[4] Wolpert argues that the emergence of national consciousness among Indians during the nineteenth century was primarily the product of responses, both negative and positive, to the consolidation of British power (Wolpert 1993:250). One indicator of this, he says, was that all major leaders of the first nationalist movement had received some English education. This fact alone makes it clear that, from the outset, this was an elite-led movement.

The Indian National Congress was established in 1885 and early leaders feared that, without modernisation, political freedom would mean a return to religious and regional wars, the continuation of the caste system and the continuing subjection of women to men. Yet, at the same time, 'it soon became painfully clear to more and more middle-class Indians... that... the system they served was fundamentally unresponsive and hostile to many basic Indian needs, aspirations, and desires' (Wolpert 1993:256). Talking of what he calls 'the illusions of the first liberals', Ranjit Guha cites Rabindranath Tagore, 'We had just graduated and undertaken to translate such foreign phrases as equality, liberty, fraternity, etc. into Bangla. We thought that Europe, with all its physical prowess, acknowledged the weak as its equal in terms of human right' (cited in Guha 1997:68). But, as Guha puts it, '...such sentiments proved wrong. The British were quick to demonstrate that they would not treat Indians as equals after all' (Guha 1997:68–9). The secular, liberal reformist, approach of key Congress leaders came to be challenged by an emerging Hindu nationalist resistance. In particular, Bal Gangadhar Tilak adopted the demand for *swaraj* (self-rule or self-governance) as his personal mantra and, in the early part of the twentieth century, became a key leader of the *Swadeshi* movement, a movement built around the boycotting of British cotton goods and the use of home spun cotton. Gandhi subsequently described *swadeshi* as the soul of *swaraj*.

In *Dominance without Hegemony: History and Power in Colonial India* Ranajit Guha (1997) has sought to analyse resistance during the colonial period. He argues that, at that time, there were two idioms of resistance at work, one British and one Indian. The British idiom, which he describes as 'rightful dissent', owes – he says – nothing to any Indian tradition. He claims it derives directly from English liberalism of the eighteenth and nineteenth centuries which, in turn, is grounded in the example of the glorious revolution of 1688 and on natural rights based on an originating social contract as propounded by Locke. In contrast, 'the purely Indian idiom' was, Guha argues, informed by Dharma. Thus, he calls it Dharmic protest and points to a range of peasant uprisings, mass desertions, sit-down protests, suspension of public activities, withdrawal of labour and measures designed to destroy the offenders caste. He claims that what distinguishes Dharmic protest from 'rightful dissent' is that it is derived from a pre-colonial tradition and has no notion of rights at all. Interestingly, he does talk about attempts on the part of what he calls the liberal elite to marry together the two idioms. He argues that Bankim Chandra Chattopadhyay sought to link the western concept of right to the Hindu idea of a spiritually legitimised dissent and that Gandhi tried to graft notions of liberty and citizenship onto the Hindu ideology of Dharma in his theory of *satyagraha* (Guha 1997:59–60).

Guha is concerned with recovering the agency of the subaltern in histories of India which, he argues, has been systematically expunged by both neo-colonialist and nationalist historiographies through a shared commitment to reducing the analysis of power to a contest between colonial and nationalist elites and designed to keep resistance out of history (Guha 1997:ix–xii, 91). Yet Guha's own framework assumes 'rights' are necessarily 'liberal' and that 'liberal' (whether in its colonial or nationalist guise) means 'bourgeois'. In other words, he relies on a binary separation between an elite-driven liberal discourse of 'rights' contrasted to a subaltern discourse of Dharmic protest. But this separation appears to be derived more from the underlying assumptions of his framework than from concrete historical analysis. This is particularly unfortunate because the concept of *swaraj* implies important connections between individual and collective understandings of self-rule and self-determination.[5] Furthermore, self-determination in *swaraj* does not necessarily imply a commitment either to nationalism or to the construction of a nation state, though it did evolve to mean this within Indian nationalism. Interestingly, in *The Illegitimacy of Nationalism*, Ashis Nandy (1994) argues that by the 1920s there was ambivalence within the anti-colonial movement towards nationalism and the construction of a nation state, some activists at least regarding nationalism as a by-product of the western state system fostering an unhealthy homogenous universalism.

This section has indicated the worldwide importance of ideas of self-determination in the nineteenth century but also shows that much more detailed historical research is required on understandings of human rights. What is clear from even this brief discussion is that human rights cannot simply be assumed to be, or reduced to, a 'western discourse'.

Conclusion

The failure to integrate the rights dimensions of nineteenth-century struggles into the human rights literature has had a decisive impact upon contemporary understandings of human rights. In particular, it has allowed the historical separation between natural rights and human rights which has enabled proponents and critics to keep understandings of both in a box marked 'liberal'. Yet it is clear that, throughout the nineteenth century in the industrialising countries, the rising workers and socialist movements placed particular emphasis on both collective rights and economic, social and cultural rights. Furthermore, a range of movements developed ideas and practices rooted both in a critique of arbitrary power and privilege and recognition that power was complex and multi-dimensional. In this respect, some nineteenth-century movement praxis prefigured challenges to power more usually associated with movement struggles of the latter half of the twentieth century.

Across the colonised world, North America and Europe, the nineteenth century witnessed enormous struggles organised around understandings of self-determination. Many commentators agree that, in Europe, 'the social question' and 'the national question' were two sides of the same coin. Some have argued that the equation of state = nation = people was understood in deeply contrasting ways, suggesting that demands for self-determination in Europe did not necessarily imply the model of the nation state that has become hegemonic in the contemporary world. We can identify similar tendencies in struggles for self-determination by colonised peoples in other parts of the world. It is particularly unfortunate that human rights scholars have paid no attention at all to the concept of *swaraj* developed in the struggles against British imperialism in India because it potentially offers quite different ways of thinking both about the relations between individual and collective dimensions of self-determination and the relation of self-determination to what has emerged as the modern nation state.

4

THE PARADOX OF
INSTITUTIONALISATION

While continuing to explore the history of human rights this chapter examines what, in my view, should be a key issue in the analysis of human rights. It is less concerned with the relationship between social movements and human rights, exploring instead what happens when human rights are institutionalised. To focus specifically on institutionalisation is to focus on social processes in a way rarely seen in the specialist literature on human rights. Certainly, there are discussions of institutionalisation in that literature but they are usually subsumed within, or derivative of, a focus elsewhere. On the other hand, there can be no doubt that a focus on institutionalisation raises issues crucial to a proper assessment of the potentials and limits of human rights. For anyone actively working in the human rights field today, engagement with issues thrown up by institutionalisation cannot be avoided. The focus on institutionalisation also throws interesting light on questions relating to the universality and particularity of human rights and the extent to which they should be understood as abstract or concrete. These are issues which lie at the very heart of many academic debates around human rights.

The first section below looks in more detail at the way institutionalisation is dealt with in the specialist human rights literature and situates my paradox in the broader context of the literature on institutions and institutionalisation. The next section looks at the way human rights have been institutionalised historically, focusing on their 'liberalisation' and 'nationalisation', framing these in terms of what I call the institutionalisation of particularity. The previous chronology of the history of human rights is then brought back into the picture by looking at the international institutionalisation of human rights in the United Nations (UN) system from 1948, with complexities of the paradox of institutionalisation being illustrated through a brief discussion of self-determination after 1948. This section is framed in terms of what I call the institutionalisation of universality. The final section of the chapter shifts perspective to look at human rights activism and how the paradox of institutionalisation can impact on such activism.

Institutions and Institutionalisation

Underpinning my concern with institutionalisation is the relationship between 'power to' and 'power over' (see Chapter 1) and how power is embedded within, and works through, institutions and organisations. This is hardly a novel concern. Indeed, it is the stuff of much sociological analysis and social theory. All the more curious, one might think, that so few attempts have been made to make institutionalisation a specific focus in the literature on human rights.

Institutionalisation in the Human Rights Literature

Again, my metaphor of the hall of mirrors works well here. The disciplinary and ideological orientations of the human rights literature can help to explain this absence. In this case, both proponents and critics tend to share the key assumption that the study of human rights is, or should be, the study of human rights *that are already institutionalised*. For uncritical proponents, the institutionalisation of human rights is seen as largely unproblematic and the nature of the relation between institutions and power left well alone. In contrast, uncritical critics usually assume that institutionalised human rights (and human rights activism that engages with the institutional world) cannot have any meaningful emancipatory dimension because institutions can only ever reflect existing relations and structures of 'power over'. Once again, proponents and critics typically establish their positions as a binary polarity: a polarity which relies on grossly simplified understandings of human rights struggles, the nature of institutions and relations between the institutional and everyday worlds. In contrast, I argue that in their institutionalised form, human rights stand in a complex and ambiguous relation to power.

Institutionalised human rights certainly retain the capacity to challenge and constrain various forms of power. This can be evidenced directly through innumerable court cases – some celebrated, most forgotten – around the world, and in many aspects of the work of the UN human rights bodies and large (I)NGOs such as Amnesty International and Human Rights Watch. But is this continuing capacity to challenge power the whole story of what institutionalised human rights are all about? Consider for a moment the domain of law. Stressing what he calls 'the virtues of legalization', Jack Donnelly argues that law ought to be central to the struggle for human rights because it is 'a domain of social values and practices with a distinctive character and normative force' (Donnelly 2006:69). While Donnelly is undoubtedly right, we might ponder why other domains of the social – where values and practices are also generated – are left out in the cold. Donnelly makes no attempt at a comparative justification of the domain of law. We can also ask whether this distinctive character and normative force is always and necessarily beneficent and benign. In my view, critics are right to argue that when human rights are institutionalised they necessarily become embedded in relations and structures of power. There is abundant evidence that institutionalised human rights have been structured to support power or sustain exclusivity and used quite explicitly by powerful actors in pursuit of their own interests. Even Donnelly recognises these points. He has acknowledged that '[l]aw, both domestic and international, does tend to reflect the interests of the powerful', although he claimed this to be much less of a problem than the fact that '[h]uman rights are daily abused by raw national power operating in defiance of international human rights law' (Donnelly 2006:70–71). Donnelly has also argued that '...we must overcome the dangerous illusion...that the state can be a neutral instrument of technocratic management and an impartial arbiter of politically neutral rules of social order' (Donnelly 2003:33).

But then, if this is so, don't we need to interrogate this supposedly distinctive character of law much more critically? Annelise Riles, for example, has identified what she calls 'the iron cage of legal instrumentalism' which, she argues, shapes and constrains praxis around the international human rights system and international human rights law, even among critical legal scholars (Riles 2006:52, 59–62).

Recognising law as being necessarily embedded in wider institutional frameworks, Philip Allott – defending a specifically idealist view of human rights – offers this trenchant commentary:

> ...the installation of human rights in the international constitution after 1945 has been paradoxical. The idea of human rights quickly became perverted by the self-misconceiving of international society. Human rights were quickly appropriated by governments, embodied in treaties, made part of the stuff of primitive international relations, swept up into the maw of an international bureaucracy. From being a source of ultimate anxiety for usurping holders of public social power, they were turned into bureaucratic small change. Human rights, a reservoir of unlimited power in all the self-creating of society, became a plaything of government and lawyers. The game of human rights has been played in international statal organizations by diplomats and bureaucrats, and their appointees, in the setting and ethos of traditional international relations. (Allott 2001:287–8)

In his own way, Allot makes it clear that analysis of human rights solely through the lens of law is seriously inadequate. A broader focus on institutions, institutionalisation and power is needed. Critics of human rights might claim that they have already offered such a focus. Yet, despite the power of many of their arguments, such critics often rely on an overly static view of both power and the institutional world. While there is undoubtedly a strong capacity for power to reproduce itself through institutions, it is also the case that institutional processes and structures can be subjected to challenge, contestation and transformation. As we have seen in the previous two chapters, human rights claims and human rights activism have been key ingredients of such contestation and struggle.

The paradox here is found in the complex issues at the heart of this chapter – in the necessity of institutions to social life and human civilisation combining with the apparently intractable problem of institutional 'power to' so easily morphing into forms of 'power over' – and it captures what look like contradictions when viewed from the stances of the uncritical proponents and uncritical critics of human rights. For proponents, the idea that human rights might serve power cannot be entertained whilst, for many critics, the idea that human rights can do anything other than serve existing relations and structures of power is equally unthinkable. I reject the underlying premises of their positions, instead recognising the complexity of 'the social' (see Chapter 1). The term paradox also points to specific dimensions of social processes imbricated in this chapter's subject matter. Social movement struggles are typically rooted in the everyday world but have persistently constructed human rights claims in ways that demand their institutional instantiation. In other words, non-institutional activism has historically demanded the institutionalisation of human rights. Furthermore, a clear trajectory can often be identified in the historical development of social movements themselves which I characterise below as a tendency towards the institutionalisation of activism. While ordinarily familiar to those studying social movements, this is rarely examined in the human rights literature and often ignored by human rights activists themselves. So key strategic questions identified by this paradox are whether the emancipatory thrust of human rights and human rights struggles can be sustained through processes of institutionalisation and, if so, to what extent and how?

The Paradox in Context

Like so many terms in the social sciences, the concept of an institution is wide ranging and contested. Indeed, some definitions of what institutions comprise are so wide that they appear to encompass nearly all forms of social relations.[1] In contrast, the concept of institution is used here to mean formally organised structures of social relations: political, economic and cultural. It should be stressed that this emphasis on formally organised structures is not meant to imply that cognitive, normative or discursive aspects of institutions are unimportant, nor does it imply that institutions are hermetically sealed, unchangeable entities. Rather, conceptualising institutions in this way coheres with the distinction drawn in Chapter 1 between 'the institutional world' and 'the everyday world'. Social movements typically arise and develop in the everyday world but are then often oriented towards the institutionalised world and can come to straddle the institutional world and the everyday world through their organisations, that is 'their' (I)NGOs (see Chapter 1, Figure 1.3).

Understood in this way, the importance of institutions and the institutional world can hardly be underestimated. Using a slightly wider understanding of institutions than employed here, but with formally organised structures firmly in mind, Campbell – for example – argues:

> Institutions are the foundation of social life. They consist of formal and informal rules, monitoring and enforcement mechanisms, and systems of meaning that define the context within which individuals, corporations, labor unions, nation states, and other organizations operate and interact with each other. Institutions are settlements born from struggle and bargaining. They reflect the resources and power of those who made them and, in turn, affect the distribution of resources and power in society. Once created, institutions are powerful external forces that help determine how people make sense of their world and act in it. They channel and regulate conflict and thus ensure stability in society. (Campbell 2004:i)

Campbell assesses institutions as being crucial to – and a positive force in – social life, arguing that '...[w]ithout stable institutions, life becomes chaotic and arduous...' (Campbell 2004:i).

Yet, in a range of other important work influential across the whole of the humanities and social sciences, much of what Campbell sees as positive about institutions has been dramatically questioned. Institutions are at the heart of that aspect of Weberian sociology that emphases tendencies towards the rationalisation and bureaucratisation of modern life. The key roles of regulation, discipline and normalisation of social relations is developed in many studies inspired by the work of Michel Foucault. Particularly important for the analysis of activism is the work on the development of oligarchy (the rule of the few) within even supposedly democratic associations. Initially identified by Roberto Michels (1962 [1915]) as an 'iron law', strong tendencies towards oligarchy have been subsequently identified and confirmed in studies of both social movements and organisations. Indeed, in a recent volume examining commonalities and differences between the fields of organisational studies and studies of social movements, Davis et.al. begin by noting 'Michel's "iron law of oligarchy" may have been overstated, but it nicely captured the transformation of what had been participatory and less bureaucratic organizations into formal organizations with hierarchic and self-reproducing authority structures' (Davis et al. 2005:xiii). Other approaches have explored specific aspects of institutional power in ways compatible with their own orientations. Much Marxist scholarship has focused on how political institutions serve to protect capitalist economic relations and scholars from the Frankfurt School have also subjected cultural institutions to critical scrutiny. In *Civil Society and Political Theory*, Jean Cohen and Andrew Arato capture the general point well:

> Societal rationalisation has been dominated... by the imperatives of the subsystems; that is the requirements of capitalist growth and administrative steering have predominated over lifeworld concerns. The 'selective institutionalisation' of the potentials of modernity has thus produced overcomplexity and new forms of power on the system side and the impoverishment and underdevelopment of the institutional promise of the lifeworld. The 'colonization of the lifeworld' related to capitalist development and the technocratic projects of administrative elites has blocked and continues to block these potentials. (Cohen and Arato 1992:525)

Even from the brief discussion so far it is clear that, for good or ill, institutions and processes of institutionalisation are of enormous import. Yet, because proponents and critics assume that human rights are essentially institutional phenomena,[2] there is little reference in the human rights literature to the detail of the social processes connecting pre-institutional forms of human rights claims with any subsequent institutional instantiations of them. Similarly, very little attention has been directed towards non-institutionalised forms of human rights, their place and dynamics in the everyday world, or how they connect to institutionalised forms of human rights. So, in the manner of a self-fulfilling prophecy, a narrowed and impoverished understanding of human rights then allows proponents and critics to diverge to their respective binary poles. My suggestion is that, by analysing non-institutional and pre-institutional forms of human rights, the necessity of examining what happens to human rights when they are institutionalised would come sharply into focus.

It is here that the paradox of institutionalisation comes into its own as an analytic tool. The emphasis on complexity, on the continuities and discontinuities between the institutional and the everyday worlds, the rejection of naive advocacy and naive critique, the fact that these sorts of issues have been largely ignored by the dominant political ideologies of the last 150 years – all these suggest the potential richness and texture of analysis of human rights that takes the question of the paradox of institutionalisation seriously. On the other hand, it also makes it clear that we are not going to get any simple, easy answers. No political ideology or political programme, perhaps with the exception of the most utopian strands of anarchism, has ever proposed that humans can or should attempt to live without formally organised structures of social relations, that is, to live without institutions at all. So, accepting that institutions are indeed a social necessity, it looks as if we must learn to understand and live with the paradox of institutionalisation. If this is the case then the apparently paradoxical impulse of extra-institutional activism demanding human rights be institutionalised begins to look like a quite ordinary, almost routine, aspect of social and historical change. If this, in turn, is right then close study of the social processes involved would surely advance our understanding of human rights.

The Institutionalisation of Particularity

To look at the institutionalisation of human rights as a set of contested historical social processes means leaving behind many basic assumptions in the human rights literature but it also means returning to elements of the historical accounts examined in the previous two chapters.

The 'Liberalisation' of Natural Rights

To specify the 'liberalisation' of natural rights requires us to look at a range of issues that already appear in the human rights literature, but from a different angle. It is to consider the extent to which rights became effective exclusionary devices at the point of their institutionalisation and also how they evolved so as to be understood as the rights of possessive individuals with all that follows from such an understanding.

Exclusions

In the transformations discussed in Chapters 2 and 3 it was at the point when understandings of natural rights were institutionalised in constitutional provision and law that explicit exclusions were formalised and fixed. Having asserted particular notions of collective identity and collective right, usually in the form of a 'we the people' during the struggles for social transformation, it was at the point of institutionalisation that definitions were made and decisions taken as to who was 'in' and who was 'out' of any particular collective 'we'. Today, we are broadly familiar with the results of those processes. Whole categories of human beings living within the geographical areas of these political and juridical communities were excluded. Full citizenship was variously denied to women, indigenous peoples, slaves, the propertyless or poor and a range of minorities. Even in Haiti, there was an explicit post-revolutionary struggle around entitlement to full citizenship. But there is a further, crucial, dimension here too. The institutionalisation of rights within particular political and juridical communities also excluded all those physically outside of those communities. In other words, natural rights institutionalised as citizenship rights left the non-citizen without rights. Amongst other things, this left the conceptual and ideological space for rationalisations of imperial conquest. Liberal attempts to explain these exclusions might claim they were unwitting errors or that they simply arose from the extant cultural *zeitgeist*. In other words, the historical struggles which challenged absolutist monarchical and early imperial power somehow missed these other dimensions of 'power over' or else did not understand them as a problem of power at all. But such arguments are untenable. The historical evidence shows that these exclusions were debated and disputed, often hotly so.

From the time of the Spanish conquest there had been arguments, especially among theologians, regarding the status of indigenous peoples (Carozza 2003). During the American Revolution, at least some revolutionaries expressed a good deal of sympathy with the plight of both slaves and the Native Americans (Blackburn 1988; Ishay 2004:113–14). In France, Condorcet denounced slavery as a crime in 1781 because it deprived slaves of their natural rights (Hunt 1996:10, 55–7) and the revolutionary period was marked by explicit debates about the entitlement of free blacks, slaves and women to rights and citizenship and also the extent to which rights should be granted to Jews and homosexuals (Hunt 1996; Ishay 2004:110–16). What is more, at least some of those excluded used understandings of natural rights to challenge their continuing oppression. The Haitian revolution itself is perhaps the most compelling case but a range of other examples were discussed in the previous two chapters. In respect of women, de Gouge's *Declaration of the Rights of Women* in 1790 and Wollstonecraft's *Vindication of the Rights of Women* in 1792 are famous examples of direct responses by women to their exclusion from full citizenship (see Ishay 1997:140–57).

The ideological world views justifying such exclusions certainly did not somehow suddenly appear at the moment of institution-alisation, but institutionalisation required a degree of closure in so far as political and juridical status had to be formally set out and defined. Put another way, these decisions and definitions were shaped by the prevailing balance of social forces at the point of institutionalisation. But it does not then follow that they were either necessary or inevitable. That is why I reject the arguments of many critics that these exclusions were somehow an essential and necessary ingredient of natural rights. That said, if contemporary liberals want to claim heritage and lineage back to these revolutions, then they should acknowledge these points of exclusion as analytically significant. All the more so because similar problems have been persistently identified in both liberal theory and in the practices of supposedly liberal states ever since.

As noted above, as well as excluding categories of people *inside* the geographical territory, the institutionalisation of natural rights within a particular political and juridical entity also excludes those physically *outside* of that community. In the context of Europe in the eighteenth and nineteenth centuries, this led to the establishment of different national citizenships and contributed to the catastrophic consequences suffered by populations around the world as a result of imperial conquest. Again, those who seek to defend a liberal conception of natural rights should interrogate the analytical significance of such linkage, but this rarely happens. More often, history is conveniently re-written. For example, while Ishay recognises key exclusions from citizenship, her apparent lack of any understanding of the mass and systematic violations of human rights resulting from imperial conquest leads her to make a remarkable claim. Talking about the 'rise of the west' and the 'honing' of universal rights in the English, American and French Revolutions, she argues '[t]he emerging commercial nation-state was then entrusted to diffuse these ideals worldwide in the spirit of peace and cooperation' (Ishay 2004:69). At later points, she does acknowledge the impact of imperialism but that impact is not related in any way to her conceptualisation of human rights.

'Embourgeoisment'

In the previous two chapters I sought to demonstrate that, in contrast to the usual arguments of critics, natural rights were neither necessarily individualistic nor 'bourgeois'. Rather, they were typically deployed by the most radical sections of movement activism to challenge both old and new forms of property relations and that emerging propertied elites saw rights talk as dangerous and revolutionary and were highly suspicious of the subversive potential of rights claims. Again, the moment of institutionalisation is important. England in 1688 was quite different from England in 1640 and in the United States it appears that the balance of forces shifted decisively between the revolutionary period leading up to 1776 and the moment of constitution-making in 1787. In Haiti, the original anti-slavery, anti-colonial and egalitarian premises of the Haitian revolution were crushed as political developments in Haiti became part of a wider anti-democratic reaction to slave emancipation. So, in each of these cases, rights discourses were significantly reconfigured as the powers of new elites were institutionalised, politically, economically and culturally. France appears to be the exceptional case, in so far as the processes of challenging and overthrowing one form of power were directly linked to the processes of institutionalising new forms of power. But, here again, a key shift in the balance of social forces towards propertied elites by 1794 has been noted by many historians. Even Ishay, who links the emergence of natural rights to the rise of a bourgeois class, identifies a pattern of more radical social forces being defeated in and through the processes of institutionalisation. As she puts with respect to France, '...the progressive forces of the Enlightenment era were in retreat, challenged by the interests of a greedy commercial class' (Ishay 2004:109).

Yet, whereas the exclusions discussed above were sedimented at the moment of institutionalisation, the embourgoisment of natural rights was much more a process that developed and deepened over time as bourgeois relations and structures of power were consolidated and embedded throughout social relations. Partly, of course, this involved seeking to privilege property rights above other forms of rights as well as arguing that property rights were the quintessential natural rights. Yet, at the same time, this process also involved the intellectual denigration of arguments for universal natural rights, precisely – as we have seen – because of their subversive potential.

The Nationalisation of Workers Rights and Struggles against Imperialism

As we saw in Chapter 3, despite liberal re-interpretations and reconfigurations, the language of natural rights was extensively used and reconstructed by socialist, anti-colonial and workers' movements. But as also noted there, while understandings of natural rights retained an important universal dimension, rights claims became increasingly directed towards that specific particularity that became the modern nation state. Claims for rights became increasingly directed *at* one's own nation state in the case of struggles for workers rights, or articulated as the demand *for* one's own nation state in the case of struggles against imperialism. The importance of this increasing focus on the nation state in the history of human rights can hardly be overestimated since it sets the framework within which duties correlative to rights claims were effectively 'nationalised'. In part this followed from the extent to which these movements themselves and the rising social democratic parties in Europe became largely statist in their orientation. A key consequence was the way in which claims to economic and social rights gradually became translated into the welfare rights of citizens. Alan Hunt (1990) has made the perceptive point that the shift from human rights to welfare rights turns rights holders into welfare supplicants and Cohen and Arato (1992:445) point to the same issue. They suggest that the structure of benefit entitlements associated with welfare rights encourages bureaucratic implementation, is more attuned to 'clients' not 'citizens' and strengthens the administrative state and not civil society. This is all a very long way from understandings of economic and social rights challenging the inequities of economic power, locally and globally.

In early struggles for self-determination, we find parallel processes of 'nationalisation'. While notions of collective identity and collective right had been expressed in the English and American revolutions, it was in the French revolution that the sovereignty of a people was more directly linked to the sovereignty of a state. This link was sustained in the Haitian revolutions and was also eventually manifested in the struggles for self-determination in Latin America. As we also saw in Chapter 3, the French revolution is widely credited with being the catalyst for the nationalist fervour that gripped Europe from the middle of the nineteenth century.

Institutionalisation and the State

So human rights were historically institutionalised in a very particular sort of way. The processes I have called the 'liber-alisation' and 'nationalisation' established a crucially strong relationship between human rights and the state – a relationship so strong that, to this day, many authoritative commentators cannot imagine human rights existing in any meaningful way outside of the institutions of the nation state. Taking an admittedly enormously broad historical sweep, we can nevertheless say that what started out as challenges to economic, cultural and political power fused within monarchical absolutism, then unevenly morphs and transforms into something intimately connected to the particular forms of political power found in the modern nation state. In terms of the capacity of human rights to challenge power once institutionalised within a state form, there are twin dangers. Firstly, threats of 'power over' emanating from outside a nation state cannot easily be constrained at source. At best, such power can be constrained at the state borders or made the subject of inter-state diplomacy. Secondly, the possibilities of human rights being effectively used to challenge the power of the state within which they have been institutionalised are inevitably constrained through their very imbrication in those structures of power. In part, this arises because of the reliance on the state to 'deliver' human rights. Thus, overall, the institutionalisation of human rights within modern nation states has resulted in understandings, approaches and policies with respect to human rights which are often deeply ambiguous in relation to power.

The Institutionalisation of Universality

1948: An Historical Anomaly?

As we have seen, when many people talk about human rights their reference point is the international system that began with the United Nations Charter and the 1948 Universal Declaration of Human Rights (UNDHR). Yet from the point of view of this study, the origin of this system is historically anomalous. In contrast to human rights arising out of social movement struggles and then being institutionalised, the construction of the international human rights system was an institutionalised process from the outset. That said, at the same time this process was the first attempt in history to begin to concretise the universal aspects of human rights for the whole of humankind. So, whatever its limitations, it clearly demands serious exploration and analysis. Unsurprisingly, all the ambiguity and ambivalence of the paradox of institution-alisation can be found here in stark and intricate forms. At one end of the complex continuum, we can see international human rights being manipulated by the world's most powerful states and economic actors to their own ends while, at the other end, we find social movements using the international system of human rights in attempts to open up new challenges to power in all sorts of different ways, all over the world. Between these lie a range of practices which are complex, multifaceted and ambiguous.

The standard histories of human rights contextualise the origins of the UN and the international human rights system in terms of an acknowledgement of the horrors of the Second World War and, in particular, the genocide of the Holocaust. Within this account, 'politicians of goodwill' sought to forge a set of international arrangements so that such horrors would never be repeated. These standard accounts make it clear that the origins of the UN system of human rights was, from the very outset, an institutionalised process between elite actors at the level of the inter-state system. While this overall assessment may be accurate, even around this easily researchable and relatively straightforward topic, there has often been significant narrowing of perspective and distortion in the accounts of both proponents and critics. Perhaps of most importance is the claim from critics that the UNDHR contained an inbuilt western bias, serving the interests of capitalism and powerful western states (Evans 1998). Yet such a claim seems hard to reconcile with at least some of the evidence in detailed historical accounts (see especially Morsink 2000; Glendon 2001). Ishay argues that the initial orientation and commitment of the UN to human rights was significantly shaped by a range of non-western states, by notable critics of the west such as Gandhi, Nkrumah, Ho Chi Minh and a small number of American NGOs. She claims that all of these condemned the absence of a commitment to human rights in an early draft of the UN Charter and it was only under considerable pressure that the United States, the USSR, Britain and France finally agreed to such a commitment (Ishay 2004:214–15). Carozza stresses the contribution of Latin American states to the UNDHR, arguing that their delegates became the guardians of the social and economic provisions of the draft declaration and that their 'understanding of rights consistently emphasised the social dimensions of the human person' (Carozza 2003:287).

Focusing specifically on the role of NGOs, Korey claims that they played a major role in ensuring that the UN Charter made reference to human rights and were also influential in the drafting of the UNDHR. He notes that Charles Malik credited NGOs with acting as '...unofficial advisers to the various delegations, supplying them with streams of ideas and suggestions' (Korey 1998:46). John Humphrey, responsible for an early draft of the UNHDR, has made a similar point arguing that 'some of the most ardent and innovative contributions to the process of constructing the UNDHR came from individual delegates and non-government organisations' (cited in Waltz 1999). That said, it should be stressed that these various NGO contributions came from influential elite actors already well embedded in the institutional world (see Korey 1998:Ch.1). So this does not challenge my general depiction of the process being institutionalised from the outset and conducted by elite actors at the level of the inter-state system.

What the various points above suggest is that the process that led to the UNHDR and establishment of the UN human rights system was not one that was simply in the pocket of the dominant western powers. Interestingly, in the subsequent 60 years of sustained contestation around the content and meaning of human rights and the functioning of the UN system, successive governments of the United States have been regularly and explicitly hostile towards developments in international human rights and the UN human rights system. Mertus, for example, notes the long track record of the US government in opposing economic rights and mentions how a United States representative sneeringly denounced the right to development (Mertus 2005:13–14).

The Problem of Inter-national Institutionalisation

The basic state-centrism of the international political institutions since 1945 has simply been assumed to be the permanent and natural state of affairs by many commentators. Yet the institutionalisation of human rights within this inter-state system clearly sets strict constraints and limits both on how human rights may be defined and incorporated into international law and also on the activities of the international human rights institutions, most obviously the office of the High Commissioner and the UN Human Rights Commission. Certain sorts of issues cannot get on to the institutional agenda and some specific policy developments are nigh on impossible within the current inter-state set up. Two contrasting examples are the extent to which gay and lesbian rights on the one hand, and the duties of transnational corporations on the other, struggle to make headway. In the former case, opposition comes especially from states influenced by religious ideologies, especially in the United States and a range of nonwestern states (Donnelly 2003:229–37). In the latter case, the simple fact that international human rights law largely comprises treaties and other instruments agreed by 'states parties' means that transnational corporations have no formal duties under these arrangements. That is not to say that movements, NGOs and the international human rights institutions cannot try to hold transnational corporations to account. The UN Norms on the responsibilities of transnational corporations adopted in 2003 may be able to generate some normative constraints but, by themselves, their impact is likely to remain very limited (OHCHR 2003; Sorrell 2006).

Some proponents of human rights accept that the existing inter-state system seriously disrupts and distorts the potential of international human rights (for example, see Donnelly 2003:168–71). Indeed, the use and abuse of human rights by the most powerful western states to serve their own foreign policy interests have clearly devalued and de-legitimised both human rights and the UN human rights system to the point that critics and those on the receiving end of western foreign policy simply assume that human rights can be nothing other than a form of western imperialism. But does that mean positive developments are impossible within the international institutional set up? Not necessarily. Indeed, arguably, some considerable progress has been made as links between social movement struggles and human rights have been reinvigorated. For example, several commentators have argued that the political framework for participation and involvement in the preparation and advocacy of the draft treaty on the rights of indigenous peoples was a highly open and participatory process (for example, Steiner and Alston 2000:1301) which could serve as a model for future democratisation of UN structures. Many have also commented on the apparent (I)NGO successes achieved at the Vienna Conference in 1993 (for example, Korey 1998:Ch.12). However, in order to illustrate the complexity and ambivalence associated with the existence of an international human rights system in more detail let me return to the question of a people's right to self-determination.

An Illustration of Complexity: Self-determination after 1948

With respect to relations between states there was no reference to a people's right of self-determination in the UNDHR. However, Article 21 referred to a people's right to self-determination in stipulating that 'the will of the people shall be the basis of the authority of government'. This has usually been understood as specifying internal democracy: the relationship between government and the governed inside a nation state. The UNDHR was understood as being silent on the problem of power imposed from the outside: the issue of colonial domination (see Walker 1993; Steiner and Alston 2000:Ch.15). Despite this, the UNDHR did help to focus and legitimate the struggles against the colonial powers and it is widely acknowledged that it was the impact of the anti-colonial struggles and the subsequent emergence of newly independent states within the inter-state system that led to the incorporation of a people's right to self-determination as a central clause in both of the international human rights covenants agreed in 1966 (Steiner and Alston 2000:Ch.15).

While such developments might be regarded as positive, at another level these processes of focusing and legitimation were themselves shaped by the embedded structural framework of international human rights. In other words, the tendency already strongly present in the late nineteenth and early twentieth centuries was now strongly reinforced. A people's right to self-determination came to be understood as a right of *national* self-determination and the struggles of the anti-colonial movements came to focus largely on the achievement of independent statehood (Rajagopal 2003:186–94). The achievement of independent statehood was equated with the achievement of freedom. But, as is now clear, this was often a very limited notion of freedom, in terms of both 'outside' and 'inside'. In terms of the 'outside', political independence may have been a step forward but, as Baxi puts it:

> The practices of the right to self-determination became incarcerated in the 'superpower' hegemony and domination [of the Cold War]. The 'self' proclaimed to be entitled to 'determination' thus stood constituted by the play of hegemonic powers... In this sense, neocolonialism is born just when the practices of the right to self-determination seem to succeed. (Baxi 2002:35–6)

In terms of the 'inside', what typically became legitimised was not a people's right to self-determination as proposed in Article 21 but rather the right of the state itself and, thus, the power of the ruling elites in those societies. Indeed, Rajagopal makes the point that – contrary to much popular wisdom – Third World states embraced the notion of human rights because it enabled the expansion of the state and sphere of governance (Rajagopal 2003:192–3). Mamdani goes further, arguing that the state centrism of a people's right to self-determination has a very 'European flavour' because the construction of collective right that grew out of nineteenth-century struggles in Europe was essentially statist (in Mohanty, Mukherji and Törnquist 1998:94).

There are a range of further substantive issues that arise from the way in which a people's right to self-determination has been institutionalised. Firstly, its inclusion has meant that other groups and movements have been able to locate and orient their own challenges in terms of the international recognition of self-determination. Richard Falk has argued that the right of self-determination provides '...a powerful mobilising instrument with which to resist involuntary governance' (Falk 2000:97). Neatly combining 'inside' and 'outside', he argues that the very idea of self-determination recognises that the legitimacy of *any* political arrangements must depend on the will of the people subjected to its authority (Falk, 2000:124, emphasis in original). On the face of it that does, indeed, provide a yardstick for assessing the legitimacy of political power.

But, secondly, despite the fact that indigenous peoples and internal minorities might regard the existence of the right as a spur to their further activism, in international law the remit of the right is severely circumscribed. It excludes both indigenous peoples and internal minorities (Steiner and Alston 2000:Ch.15). As Falk puts it, the right '...only seems to sanction the repudiation of alien rule at the level of the state' (Falk 2000:102).

Even in the context of anti-colonial struggles, the inherent statism of the right clearly limits its applicability. Baxi, for example, argues:

> The 'new' nations of Asia and Africa somewhat understandably insisted that the right to self-determination extended only to situations of 'classic' colonialism, available to their 'peoples' only once in history: to determine their collective status as sovereign states within the meaning of international law. That right once exercised was extinguished for all

times; this presumed that the 'logic' of colonialism, which made all sorts of different peoples, cultures, and territories vessels of imperial unity, should continue in the post-colony. (Baxi 2002:36)

Underlying this indefensible process – whereby lines drawn on a map by the colonial powers in the nineteenth century can determine what constitutes 'a people' with supposed self-determination in the twenty-first century – is the statist logic of the inter-state system within which human rights have been institutionalised. Here we are back to the point made earlier that when rights are institutionally fixed they necessarily become embedded within the relations and structures of power pertaining at that point in history. Thus the paradox plays itself out both in the contestation of meanings of rights within an existing institutionalised framework and then in struggles to transform that institutional framework.

International Human Rights: A Particular Universal?

Prior to 1948, the universal aspect of human rights had only ever been expressed in particular ways, including through those exclusions sedimented by such instantiations. Put another way, we could say there was no 'concrete universal' to match either the 'abstract universal' in understandings of human rights or the 'concrete particulars' of human rights as (differently) institutionalised in various societies. But the establishment of the UN human rights system and the adoption of the UNDHR established the beginnings of some sort of 'concrete universal' of human rights. For all its serious limitations, this then opened up the possibility of challenge, development and transformation of that concrete universal. This has happened regularly and in a variety of ways since 1948. Rajagopal notes that, from the 1960s, developing countries used human rights both to oppose the apartheid regime in South Africa and also in attempts to achieve equitable and just economic conditions in the global political economy. He argues further that it was this impetus that led the UN General Assembly to affirm in 1977, for the first time, that all human rights were equal, indivisible and interdependent – challenging the often claimed hierarchy of human rights (Rajagopal 2003:217). Mohanty develops a similar theme, noting a process of evolution from an initial 'liberal humanist formulation' at the time of the Universal Declaration to a more subtle and complex understanding of human rights by the time of the UN summit in Vienna in 1993. In line with one of the key themes of this work, Mohanty goes on to argue that this demonstrates the limits and inadequacies of both traditional liberal advocacy and traditional radical critique of human rights (in Mohanty, Mukherji and Törnquist 1998:22–3).

Baxi's work is particularly salient on this point and on the paradox of institutionalisation more generally. He contrasts what he calls the 'contemporary' paradigm of human rights characterised by a logic of inclusion, with what he calls a 'modern' paradigm characterised by a logic of exclusion (Baxi 2002). Although he does not spell it out, it appears that – for Baxi – the contemporary paradigm only emerges after the end of the Second World War. In a schematic which parallels the analysis here, what Baxi calls the politics *of* human rights deploys symbolic or cultural capital in order to manage the distribution of power in national and global arenas. In other words, it is used as a disciplinary device and serves power. In contrast, what he calls the politics *for* human rights seeks an alternative politics, an order of progress which makes the state more ethical, governments more progressively just and power increasingly accountable. While Baxi does not put institutions and processes of institutionalisation at the centre of his analysis, he nevertheless argues that '…the global institutionalisation of human rights signifies the interpenetration of the world of politics *for* human rights with the worlds of power harnessing the politics *of* human rights' (Baxi 2002:40, emphasis in original). Here Baxi grasps the essential complexity and ambivalence of the paradox of institutionalisation but he does not then develop the point. While arguing that social movements and NGOs have been crucial to the construction of his contemporary paradigm, he has no analytical way of assessing the potentials and limits of such activism. More attention paid to institutions and institutionalisation together with a more developed understanding of the relationship between social movements and NGOs would, I suggest, help to shape and flesh out Baxi's argument.

The Paradox and Human Rights Activism

The Organisational Question

Despite widespread acknowledgement of the importance of (I)NGOs to the contemporary international human rights system, there have been relatively few detailed empirical studies of (I)NGO activism in the dominant literatures (although see Keck and Sikkink 1998; Risse, Ropp and Sikkink 1999; Welch 2000). Uncritical proponents tend to assume that (I)NGO and movement activism is generally beneficial and unproblematic, while uncritical critics tend to assume the opposite. Furthermore, almost entirely absent in the specialist human rights literature is any discussion of the distinction between social movements and (I)NGOs and how they might differentially impact on the development of ideas and practices around human rights (Stammers and Eschle 2005).

As made clear earlier, the paradox of institutionalisation connects to a much wider set of issues in social analysis which link a whole range of processes to questions of organisation and power and, through them, to notions of participation, representation and democracy. This general 'organisational question' has rarely been given the attention it deserves since virtually all political ideologies assume the necessity for organisations to be formally structured. This is often coupled with an explicit argument in favour of elite leadership on the basis that such forms of organisation and leadership fundamentally increase the 'power to' of the organisation in question. While those committed to revolutionary change often see contact with the existing institutional world as a 'sell-out', they rather blithely assume – with some important exceptions such as Alexandra Kollantai and Rosa Luxemburg – that revolutionary organisations and post-revolutionary institutions will somehow be immune to, or be able to transcend, the general tendencies towards bureaucratisation and oligarchy discussed earlier in this chapter. Yet not even social movements are immune from these trajectories. There is considerable and persistent evidence that, while social movements begin as spontaneous, participatory, forms of association outside the institutional world and with little or no formal organisation, formal organisations with traditional forms of leadership and hierarchy gradually emerge. These formal organisations then both increasingly engage with the institutional world and become institutions themselves. Brief historical reflection on the history of the workers' movements in the west – how movements turned into political parties and trades union organisations, firstly engaging with and then often entering institutional structures of power – makes the point clear enough. A similar trajectory can also be identified with respect to many of the so-called New Social Movements that began to emerge from the 1960s onwards (see Chapter 5).

The Institutionalisation of Activism

Now, just as the institutionalisation of human rights can be seen as a success, so the institutionalisation of social movements can be seen as a victory, especially when parties and organisations that have emerged from movements accede to government. Yet, the reality is much more complex and ambiguous. Cohen and Arato (1992:555–63) pick up many of these points. In particular, they reject the argument that the institutionalisation of movement activism is an indicator of success. Rather, they argue:

> ... the traceless transformation of movements into bureaucratic political parties or lobbies remains both a negative and an avoidable model...[but that]... the movement form cannot survive the step over the boundaries of the lifeworld. Movements cannot influence structures coordinated through means other than normative or communicative interaction without succumbing to the pressure for self-instrumentalization. (Cohen and Arato 1992:561)

Interestingly, having linked human rights to social movement struggles, Baxi also identifies this trajectory of the institutionalisation of activism but does not problematise it. He argues:

> Much of the history, and future of human rights lies congealed in this enunciatory struggle for the creation of human rights in which human rights *movements* faced undeniable repression, on their way to becoming legitimate and legal *organisations*... this translation from illegitimacy to legality of social movements is an ineluctable aspect of juridical and social flourishing of civil society associations. Human rights movements undoubtedly need to articulate themselves into some sort of juridical form, conferring an order of comparative social and political advantage. Indeed, the histories of trade union movements richly illustrate everywhere the struggle of *movements* to become *organisations*, in ways that testify to the power of social movements to constrain and compel the state to acknowledge the legitimacy and legality of certain forms of associational activity. (Baxi 2002:45, emphases in original)

Baxi is insufficiently critical here. The suggestion that processes of institutionalisation are both unambiguously necessary and positive cannot be sustained. His reference to the histories of trade union movements should have alerted him to some of the ambiguities and complexities involved in processes of institutionalisation

To take this organisational question seriously means taking a much more critical – but not dismissive – approach to analysing the relationships between social movements and (I)NGOs and the relationships of these entities to the institutional world. While I would not accept many of the sweeping condemnations of all forms of activism of the uncritical critics (see Chapter 7) tendencies towards bureaucratisation, oligarchy and the emergence of an (I)NGO elite sector in the human rights field are all clearly present.

As well as internal dynamics, there are strong external 'pulls' towards oligarchy and bureaucratisation from the institutions that (I)NGO activists seek to engage with. Sometimes this is clear and explicit, for example, in the rules laid down for admission to a particular forum (for example, becoming an NGO recognised by Economic and Social Council of the UN) but often it is opaque and Machiavellian, in so far as institutional actors seek to quell opposition and criticism through a strategy of co-option and assimilation which involves drawing activists into dialogue and engagement with a range of institutional fora. There is, of course, nothing new about this. It is routine and recognised. Much literature in political studies and international relations have analysed 'insider' and 'outsider' groups, what groups have to do if they want to get 'inside', and what price they have to pay (for example, see Grant 1985; Page 1999). In *Contesting Global Governance*, O'Brien et al. (2000) examined how 'global social movements' interacted with global economic institutions. In fact, the vast bulk of their work focused rather on the activities of a range of (I)NGOs from three movements: the women's movement, the labour movement and the environmental movement. While the authors identify some positive accomplishments arising from this engagement, at the same time they are clear that the motivations emanating from these institutions were far from innocent. While the different economic institutions (the World Bank, the IMF and the WTO) have different orientations to their engagement with (I)NGOs, in each case the institutions sought to 'draw in' the (I)NGOs both to further and to safeguard the interests of the institution. With respect to the women's movement, the strategy of 'gender mainstreaming' which had been accepted and adopted by many women's (I)NGOs throughout the 1990s, is now being significantly criticised. For example, Ann Marie Goetz cites a speech by the UN special envoy to Africa on AIDS, Stephen Lewis, who she describes as 'an increasingly vocal and, frankly, agonized speaker about the problem of gender mainstreaming'. She reports that he has dismissed gender mainstreaming as 'a pathetic illusion of transformation leaving nothing but a cul-de-sac for women' (Goetz 2006:4–5).

Very occasionally, these sorts of issues do surface in the human rights literature. For example, in the collection edited by Mahmood Mamdani, *Beyond Rights Talk and Culture Talk* (2000), Kimberle Crenshaw reassesses the American debate about civil rights. She claims that the era in which civil rights produce meaningful reformist victories has come to a decided close. Focusing on the juridical realm, Crenshaw argues that court decisions began to reflect competing interpretations of civil rights moving from a pro-victim perspective to a pro-perpetrator perspective, leading civil rights activists then to engage in activism and practices that largely comprise 'rearguard actions meant to protect hard-won concessions against pressures of retrenchment' (in Mamdani 2000:63). She claims that the central observation arising out of her review 'confirms that rights discourses can both facilitate transformative processes and insulate and legitimise power' (in Mamdani, 2000:63). Her analysis is subtle and multifaceted and she maintains that human rights institutions may be crucial to back up the demands of disempowered groups. But we are back precisely to the complexities of the paradox of institutionalisation.

The Problem of Representational Power

At the heart of the paradox of institutionalisation is a fundamental question about how various relevant aspects of social relations might be reconstructed and democratised. Leaving aside for the moment the huge issues of democracy *within* movements and organisations, *between* movements and organisations, and *between* the everyday and institutional world (see Chapters 6 and 8) there is a question which is even more directly linked to the concerns of this chapter. Baxi calls it the 'problematic of representational power' (Baxi 2002). There are clearly circumstances in which relatively powerful organisations, such as Amnesty International or Human Rights Watch, claim to speak on behalf of others. Indeed, it is probably the case that the vast bulk of work around human rights in the institutionalised world – most obviously monitoring for violations – relies very heavily on the work of these large (I)NGOs. They are key players in the transnational advocacy network that focuses on human rights (Keck and Sikkink 1998). There is not necessarily a problem with large (I)NGOs speaking on behalf of the oppressed and those whose rights are being violated or threatened. But clearly those (I)NGOs must ensure that they do properly represent the interests, views and demands of those they claim to represent. One question that then arises is the extent to which there are any democratically constructed channels of communication and representation between the (I)NGO and the peoples they claim to speak on behalf of. Lack of such channels potentially poses serious problems. We have already seen the extreme dangers of this in the context of what I have called the 'nationalisation' of human rights, when states claim to speak on behalf of their citizens on all matters concerning human rights, often leading not to the protection of human rights but to their violation.

As indicated above, this leads towards a much wider discussion about the nature of democracy, the potentials and limits of representation and the potentials and limits of relationships between social movements and (I)NGOs. This all necessarily goes far beyond the specific concerns of this volume but it is clear that critical work in such areas is desperately needed on the part of both analysts and activists. I come back to some of these issues in the final chapter.

Conclusion

Institutionalisation is a social process. As such, it cannot be reduced to philosophy or law. What I have tried to demonstrate in this chapter is that the institutionalisation of human rights and activism around human rights requires a focus on complex issues and questions rarely addressed directly in the literature on human rights. I summed these up by using the notion of a paradox of institutionalisation. At its most basic, my argument is that, once institutionalised, human rights stand in a complex and ambiguous relation to power. Typically constructed in social movement struggles to challenge extant 'power over', institutionalised human rights do maintain a capacity to challenge or constrain power over. Yet they can also be 'switched' or 'turned' so as to serve or sustain power. Activism, whether by social movement or (I)NGOs, often follows similar or parallel trajectories.

The chapter identified two key dimensions and processes of institutionalisation, what I called the institutionalisation of particularity and the institutionalisation of universality. In contrast to many commentaries, I argued that many of the problems that dog the praxis of human rights arise from both their institutionalisation within particular juridical and political communities and their institutionalisation within the existing state-centric international system. Having said that, there are also dynamics and developments which indicate that the international institutionalisation of human rights has opened up possibilities for challenging historically sedimented exclusions from human rights and for providing a framework through which contemporary and emerging relations and structures of power may be challenged. What is certainly the case is that, since 1948, social movements have been able to orient their struggles not just to particular instantiations of human rights but also towards the 'concrete universal' of human rights as institutionalised in the UN system. What is especially interesting about this is that many of the social movements that have come to the fore in the last 40 or 50 years have sought to renew challenges to dimensions of 'power over' which had been obscured or occluded for many years. The next chapter moves on to look at this topic in detail. However, it remains clear that the activism of social movements around human rights needs to be understood in the context of the paradox of institutionalisation.

5

NEW MOVEMENTS? OLD WRONGS?

In historical terms, this chapter looks at the relationship between human rights and the so-called New Social Movements (NSMs) that are usually said to have emerged from the 1960s onwards. Analytically, it sketches out an alternative framework through which the significance of the link between human rights and social movements can be understood and evaluated. The historical and analytical aspects of this chapter merge in an argument that one of the key factors leading to consideration of 'newness' in the NSMs was that, taken together, these movements re-opened the debate on the nature of 'power over' after a closure of that debate for some 70 years or so. This closure had been created through both the limits of academic analysis and the orientations of the workers' and socialist movements in their reformist and revolutionary manifestations. I will argue that, by reopening this debate, these movements made connections back to earlier critiques of arbitrary power and privilege discussed in previous chapters. This leads us to consider the extent to which the so-called NSMs resurrected claims to 'old rights' and whether their critiques of power were in fact identifying old, maybe even universal, wrongs in terms of social and historical practices. I will suggest that, by the end of the twentieth century, historical struggles for human rights had effectively identified five key sites of power through which the perpetuation and persistence of such wrongs may be located and understood.

The chapter begins by looking at the rise of the so-called NSMs and the ways they were conceptualised. It then moves on to consider the extent to which the so-called NSMs re-opened the analysis and critique of power. The following section then broadens this discussion out to argue that movement struggles around human rights have *de facto* identified five trans-historical and trans-cultural sites of 'power over' and a range of 'old wrongs'. The last section considers the extent to which organisations emerging from the NSMs have 'aged' while, in contrast, some more recent movements are challenging 'power over' in ways that are contiguous with specific radical aspects of the so-called NSMs.

Conceptualising 'New Social Movements'

Upendra Baxi has argued that many developments in human rights over the last 30 or 40 years cannot be understood outside of an understanding of the dynamics of the NSMs. These movements, he says, were not just 'human rights reinforcing' but also 'human rights creating' (Baxi 2000:36). Noting that few analysts of human rights have examined the link to social movements, Baxi also points out that NSM theorists have rarely considered the relevance of human rights to the NSMs and that human rights movements have not often been depicted as NSMs. Baxi's observations here relate closely to key themes of this chapter. However, to get to these it is necessary to do some preliminary groundwork. The concept of New Social Movements was initially developed in the early 1980s to refer to a range of movements that first emerged in the west from the 1960s onwards (for overviews see Dalton and Kuechler 1990:Ch.1; Scott 1990; Buechler 2000:45–51). The students' movement, 'second wave' feminism, peace movements, green movements and lesbian and gay movements were considered the archetypal NSMs. The black civil rights movement in the United States is sometimes seen as an NSM but is more usually excluded or seen as a transitional movement between 'old' and 'new' movements (Eyerman and Jamison 1991:145). Indigenous peoples' movements in the west have also sometimes been seen as NSMs. During the 1980s a wide range of movements in Eastern Europe, Asia and Latin America were also identified as NSMs by both activists and scholars (see Escobar and Alvarez 1992:Ch.1; Wignaraja 1993). Towards the late 1990s a wave of studies of transnational and global social movements focused on organisations and activism which had strong connections and affinities with movements previously depicted as NSMs, even though many of the authors rejected the NSM concept (Maiguascha 1994; Smith, Chatfield and Pagnucco 1997; Keck and Sikkink 1998; Cohen and Rai 2000). Finally, there are a few claims that the orientations of the contemporary critical movements such as the Zapatistas and movements associated with the World Social Forum, G8 and WTO protests display NSM-type characteristics (Williams 2005; Bradley 2005).

It is also important to stress that a range of movements active from the 1960s have rarely, if ever, been depicted as NSMs. Neither the anti-apartheid movement nor anti-imperialist movements in the south attracted the appellation and – as Baxi points out – neither, typically, have human rights movements. Below, I suggest that the 'borderline' between 'NSM' and 'not-NSM' is best explained in terms of different understandings of 'power over'. Within the specialist field of social movement studies it became clear that the NSM concept – no matter how configured – was unable to carry the theoretical weight required of it and its usage largely abandoned. But because of claims such as Baxi's and because of its continued use in other fields (even if only as a residual or implied category) some discussion of the NSM concept is required here. At first sight, the literature on NSMs displays a confusing array of analytical distinctions, but closer examination indicates many interconnections. Below, I firstly identify two dominant constellations of ideas/distinctions in theorising the NSMs. Then I point to some particular aspects of that theorisation which can be re-interpreted as attempts at redefining radicalism in ways that transcended the then dominant currents of reformist and revolutionary socialism.

Structural Change, Interests and Identities

The link between social movements and broader structural change and the rise of the NSMs was explained in one of two ways. Some theorists argued that NSMs arose in the west as a consequence of the failures of social democratic corporatism and the welfare states in the 'advanced capitalist countries' (Castells 1983; Offe 1985; Scott 1990:25–6). As they saw it, when the post-war settlement between capital and labour came under pressure from the 1960s onwards, NSMs emerged as an expression of social groups excluded from that settlement and who were, consequently, increasingly marginalised and disenfranchised. This form of explanation precludes the possibility that NSMs could arise in countries where no such settlement had previously occurred. The other, much more dominant, structural explanation for the rise of the NSMs identified some sort of qualitative or epochal structural shift in the nature of social relations. While described in many different ways (for example, from industrial to post-industrial society, or from modernity to post-modernity) NSMs were explained as responses to, or products of, such fundamental structural change. Old movements were then similarly associated with the old epoch. Given that many theorists of NSMs had backgrounds in Marxism it was not perhaps surprising that the term 'old movements' was almost always used as a euphemism for workers' movements and NSMs were believed to be the 'progressive forces' of the new epoch (Touraine 1981; Boggs 1986). Again, it tended to be assumed that these epochal shifts were principally taking place in the west, but such developments in other parts of the world were not precluded. These analyses were first developed in the early 1980s and mostly pre-dated debates about globalisation, although interestingly one or two writers emphasised the 'planetary' dimensions of the NSMs (Melucci 1989; Hegedus 1989). They also pre-dated the resurgence of right-wing, nationalist and religious fundamentalist movements around the world from the late 1980s (for contrast see Castells 1997).

Closely linked to these structural explanations for the rise of NSMs was an assumption of a dichotomy, a binary polarity, between interests and identities. This was mapped on to the old/new distinction so that it was typically argued that old movements (read workers' movements here) were fundamentally concerned with material interests while the NSMs were fundamentally concerned with questions of identity. This made sense in so far as the epochal structural shift in social relations was understood as a shift in the key dynamic of societies from the production of material goods to the control and manipulation of information and knowledge (Touraine 1981: Melucci 1989, 1996). Studies claimed to show 'a silent revolution' with the rise of 'post-materialist values', evident among participants in the so-called NSMs in the west (Inglehart 1977; Dalton and Kuechler 1990:Ch 3).

These various points were taken up by supporters and critics of the NSMs in a wide-ranging intellectual and political knockabout. For those who analysed the world in terms of the conflict of material interests, especially via class analysis, the apparent concern with identity was often taken as pejorative proof of activists' naïveté and immaturity. NSMs could be dismissed as middle class. In contrast, for other intellectuals the apparent focus on identity in the NSMs was celebrated and taken as evidence of the need for the cultural turn in the social sciences. I would suggest that there is a good case to show that the emergence of these movements was, in fact, the catalyst for the cultural turn in the humanities and the social sciences (Darnovsky, Epstein and Flacks 1995) thus challenging the strong tendency amongst academics to assume that the world follows where intellectuals lead (see also Buck-Morss 2000).

Without foreclosing the argument that identity has indeed become a more important aspect of social movement activism as a consequence of broader structural changes in social relations, it is nevertheless clear that the dichotomy between interests and identity was hugely overblown. There is compelling evidence that, generally, social movements – including the archetypal 'old' and 'new' movements – have always contained elements which relate to both interests and identity (D'Anieri, Ernst and Kier 1990; Tucker 1991; Calhoun 1993). Analysts should never have separated interests and identity into a binary opposition because they necessarily co-joined in complex ways. Further, and as I will argue in the next chapter, interests and identity may be better understood within a wider analytic categorisation of instrumental and expressive dimensions of movement activism.

Central Empirical Characteristics

This second constellation of distinctions identifies differences between old and new movements in terms of their claimed central empirical characteristics – loosening, but not abandoning, both the connection to structural change and the concern with interests and identities. For example, Alan Scott set out the differences between old and new movements in terms of their location, aims, organisation and medium of action. Scott's chart (1990:19, Table 1.1) reproduced here explicitly contrasts 'new movements' with the 'workers' movement'.

	Worker's Movement	New Movements
Location	increasingly within the polity	civil society
Aims	political integration/ economic rights	changes in values & lifestyle/ defence of civil society
Organisation	formal/hierarchical	network/grass roots
Medium of Action	political mobilisation	direct action/cultural innovation

Figure 5.1   Contrast between 'new movements' and 'workers' movements' (Scott 1990)

While the dichotomy between interests and identities reappears in a broader form under 'aims', the other three categories of Scott's chart each relate to other instrumental and expressive dimensions of movement activism. Significantly, each of them encompasses important strategic and organisational dimensions. Scott agrees that the distinctions between old and new movements were too firmly drawn and, again, many commentators have pointed out that one can find supposedly old characteristics in new movements and supposedly new characteristics in the old movements (D'Anieri, Ernst and Kier 1990; Tucker 1991; Calhoun 1993: Plotke 1995; Buechler 2000). In other words, these supposedly central empirical characteristics have been reified, the historical and empirical evidence suggesting instead much greater complexity. In particular, when contrasted with formally structured organisations such as NGOs or political parties, one of the key characteristics of social movements as movements is precisely their diversity in terms of ideologies, goals and organisation (Stammers 1999b). Furthermore, these reified characterisations were also historically static, a snapshot of what these movements were supposed to have looked like in the 1970s and 1980s. One need only consider what the supposedly 'old' movements looked like when they first emerged in the nineteenth century to see the problem. Moreover what do the so-called NSMs look like now, in the first decades of the twenty-first century?

Redefining Radicalism?

Though the above two constellations of explanation and characterisations of the NSMs have been dominant, they do not exhaust ways in which the 'newness' of NSMs was understood. Three other points require emphasis. While often weaved into the above forms of explanations, they were neither intrinsic to them nor did they rely on their specific conceptual configurations. They can, in other words, be extracted from them and interpreted differently. The first point is that NSMs were both non-institutional in their form of activism and adopted explicitly anti-institutional and anti-bureaucratic orientations (Dalton and Kuechler 1990:Chs 1, 12; Cohen and Arato 1994:510–23). The historical contrast was again with the workers' movements in the west, which were seen to have become bureaucratised and ossified into trades unions and political parties. Certainly, significant currents in many of the so-called NSMs were acutely aware of what I have termed the paradox of institutionalisation, in particular the dangers of 'the iron law of oligarchy'. Many activists were determined to avoid what has been described as a 'life-cycle process' by which social movements have historically succumbed to such tendencies. The second point is that NSMs were often understood as being 'self-limiting', although this meant different things to different commentators. For some, it meant that the NSMs were 'anti-vanguardist' – rejecting the Leninist insistence on the necessity of a vanguard party – whilst nevertheless seeking revolutionary change. For others, the NSMs sought substantive social transformation but were not revolutionary in terms of the tradition of insurrectionary violence, the lineage which connects Marxist, anarchist and anti-imperialist ideas of revolution back to Europe in the seventeenth and eighteenth centuries. So self-limitation here was often interpreted as a commitment to non-violence taken from the Gandhian model and given a new lease of life in the black civil rights movement in the United States (Ackerman and DuVall 2000). In a much more moderate formulation, self-limitation was explained by Cohen and Arato (1992) in terms of activism that did not seek to transcend the 'steering systems' of state and market. This latter notion of self-limitation was directly drawn from Eastern Europe. Prior to 1989, the dissident movements were especially concerned, as Jacek Kuron put it, 'not to lure the wolves out of the woods', that is, provoke the deployment of Soviet tanks (Kuron 1981). In an interesting and pithy formulation, it was sometimes suggested that the strategy of the Eastern European movements during the late 1970s and 1980s was one of 'reform from below' in contrast to the failures of 'revolution from below' (i.e. Hungary, 1956) and 'reform from above' (i.e. Czechoslovakia, 1968). Yet this apparently self-limiting strategy nevertheless contributed to the social transformations in Eastern Europe and the collapse of the Soviet bloc from 1989.

The above two points have wide implications, especially regarding the key strategic relationship between ends and means. Yet they neither relied on a structural explanation for the emergence of NSMs, nor on any binary polarity between interests and identity. They do still rely on a division between old and new, but old is now understood not just in western terms but more broadly in terms of: the histories of the reformist and revolutionary wings of the transnational workers' and socialist movements; their orientations to social change, and the apparent failures of these orientations. This brings me to the third and final aspect of 'newness' which can now be reinterpreted. While distinctions between old and new were hugely overdrawn, there were undoubtedly vibrant and strong currents within the so-called NSMs which sought to redefine, or perhaps better reconstruct, understandings of what radicalism was (Stammers 1999b). What is more, such reconstructions appear to have strong antecedents in movement challenges to arbitrary power and privilege discussed in previous chapters. In other words, while there was little that was actually historically new about such reconstructions, they could appear new in so far as they challenged dominant understandings of what radicalism was. So let me now interrogate continuity and change, oldness and newness in a somewhat different way by bringing us back to the question of power.

Re-opening the Analysis and Critique of Power

Breaking 70 years of Closure?

My central argument here is that the NSMs appeared new because, together, they re-opened the analysis and critique of 'power over', an issue which had been closed for the previous 70 years or so. But what was this closure and how was it effected? In a way we are looking into another hall of mirrors because this closure has to be understood in terms of how, from the middle of the nineteenth century, the emerging academic disciplines and political worldviews in the west understood the social world. In terms of disciplines, while political philosophy and political economy had already developed and achieved a degree of authority, other strands of the social sciences were still very much in their infancy. Ideologically, the nineteenth century also saw the construction and consolidation of liberalism (Richardson 1997) and the emergence and development of socialist thought.

In the social movements examined in previous chapters we have seen elements of a broad understanding of 'power over', with some activists grasping the importance of cultural dimensions of power and quite explicitly expanding the fields within which they saw 'power over' operating. But even when undeveloped, the way in which movement actors constructed challenges to arbitrary power and privilege left open the possibility of re-interrogating what arbitrary power and privilege comprised across different cultures and in different historical periods. Yet, the strands of the liberal and socialist traditions that became dominant by the beginning of the twentieth century largely closed that possibility of re-interrogation. Whatever else their differences, much liberal and socialist thought came to share important assumptions about the nature of social relations and how the world 'worked'. The first was that economic power was the key locus of social power in general. Consequently, social conflict could be best understood in terms of struggles around material interests. It then followed that 'power over' should be understood in relation to material interests. Thus, from the middle of the nineteenth century, liberals, social democrats and Marxists alike came to the view that the conflict between capital and labour was the central conflict and fault line in western capitalist societies and that it should thus be privileged in all forms of social analysis. Cohen and Arato (1992:452) argue that liberal and socialist 'utopias' shared an attempt to totalise a single model of a rational society. They associate the liberal project with 'an economy-centred instrumental reason' and the socialist project with a 'state-centred functional reason'. While this is neatly put, in my view they are wrong to propose such a strong distinction. These two forms of reasoning were in fact co-joined in much liberal and socialist thought.

From the 1960s onwards a range of social movements began to develop an analysis and critique of power which, in their different ways, significantly broke with these perspectives. This has been recognised by a number of commentators. In the context of Latin America, Escobar and Alvarez argue that the 1980s 'witnessed the appearance of new forms of understanding and discussion of resistance and social change that marked a significant discontinuity with past forms of analysis' (Escobar and Alvarez 1992:2). These new forms of theoretical awareness were fostered, they say, by equally significant changes in historical conditions, specifically changes in popular practices of resistance and collective action. Together, they say, this forced recognition of the '... limited character of the approaches widely accepted until the 1960s and 1970s...' (Escobar and Alvarez 1992:2). Claus Offe also comes close to identifying this trajectory, this time in terms of the impact of institutionalised rationality across the whole field of social relations. Contrasting NSMs with reactionary forms of social protest, he suggested that NSMs:

> ...represent a non reactionary, universalist critique of modernity and modernisation by challenging institutionalised patterns of technical, economic, political and cultural rationality without falling back upon idealised traditional institutions and arrangements such as the family, religious values, property, state authority or the nation. (Offe 1990:233)

In the context of a discussion of women's movements, forest struggles and anti-dam movements in India, Pramod Parajuli emphasises self-limitation and the multifaceted nature of power. He argued that:

> New social movements are distinct from traditional anti-systemic movements such as oppositional parties [sic] in two ways. First, the focus of these movements is not to capture state power through elections or a violent revolution but rather to transform the nature of politics itself. Second, new social movements in India and elsewhere dispel the myth of the vanguard. In these movements, antagonisms are expressed not only through class but through multiple 'sites of power' such as gender, ethnicity, caste and regional identity. (Parajuli 1991:176)

Finally, Darnovsky, Epstein and Flacks note that theorists of the NSMs often emphasised the importance of reconstituting aspects of everyday life stressing that '...social transformation is mediated through culture as well as politics narrowly defined – that the personal and cultural is as politically real as, and are not reducible to, power struggles in the state and the economy' (Darnovsky, Epstein and Flacks 1995:xiv).

There is undoubtedly something curious here because – in contrast to these general assessments – NSMs often appeared quite separate and distinct, so much so that critics often dismissed and derided them as single issue movements. Yet, while the women's movement did focus on women, indigenous peoples' movements on indigenous peoples, lesbian and gay movements on lesbians and gay men and so on, what they shared was a focus on a dimension of oppression that had been largely written out of stories of power and oppression as told by liberals, social democrats and Marxists alike. From here we can explain why certain movements were not considered NSMs. The black civil rights movement in the United States, the anti-apartheid movement in South Africa, anti-imperialist movements in the South and human rights movements could all be understood as challenging 'known' relations and structures of power and could also all be reasonably analysed in terms of the pursuit of material interests. In other words, they were 'old' in the sense that the sites of power being challenged were 'familiar territory'. In longer historical perspective, it is also clear that many of the so-called NSMs had significant antecedents, at least in terms of associational groups or cultural formations, if not necessarily as social movements. So, in terms of rights claims, perhaps Baxi's suggestion that the NSMs were 'rights reinforcing' and 'rights creating' should be extended to suggest that the so-called NSMs were also 'rights resurrecting'.

NSMs and Human Rights: Reinforcing, Creating........Resurrecting?

The suggestion that rights claims made by the so-called NSMs had a much older pedigree is most easily demonstrated in respect of the civil rights movement in the United States, indigenous peoples' movements and second wave feminism. It is much less clear with respect to gay and lesbian rights, environmental rights, a right to peace and other issues often associated with NSM activism.

In the black civil rights movement in the United States and in the struggles of various indigenous peoples' movements around the world we can clearly identify a confluence of contemporary rights claims with much older (albeit often unsuccessful) struggles by those groups subjected to conquest, genocide and slavery on the basis of their ethnicity. The extent to which some of these struggles were couched in the language of natural or human rights was discussed in Chapters 2 and 3. But, regardless of whether anti-slavery struggles and indigenous resistance to European conquest specifically used any notions of rights, it is certainly clear that recent movements have articulated a strong sense of continuity with such forms of historical oppression. For example, in *The Alchemy Of Race And Rights*, Patricia Williams depicts the black civil rights movement as 'making something out of nothing' which, she says, took immense alchemical fire, '...the resurrection of life from ashes 400 years old' (Williams 1993:163). While indigenous peoples' movements around the world have met with mixed success in their particular national jurisdictions, the continuities with the historical dimension of their oppression have always been emphasised. More interesting is the fact that these movements have been able to forge an important global 'unity in diversity' as a consequence of the commonalities of their oppression. From 1985 to 1993, a UN working group prepared a draft declaration on indigenous peoples' rights. For years this draft was stalled largely because of persistent opposition of state representatives to clauses specifying rights of restitution and the return of land taken without consent (Anaya 2004; OHCHR 2007), an amended text only finally being approved by the UN General Assembly in September 2007.

Claims for women's rights from second wave feminists (see Brems 1997; Kiss 1997) had new and creative dimensions, but they also had very old resonances. By the end of the nineteenth century, first wave feminism had become a powerful international movement (Sarah 1983) and demands for women's rights to be understood as natural rights were clearly also articulated in the eighteenth century (Hunt 1996:119–39; Ishay 2004:160–65). More generally, in a global anthology of women's resistance, Delamotte, Meeker and O'Barr (1997) claim to trace women's resistance to oppression to 600 BCE. A similar argument is developed (though with a reminder of the contingency of social construction) in a special issue of *New Internationalist* devoted to women's rights:

> A snapshot of history as far back as 900 BCE shows that women have always struggled for their rights – and that progress is not a straight line. Many societies where women are most repressed today were the most enlightened in the past. History shows us that what has been won can also be taken away (New Internationalist 2004, 373:13)

By 'their rights' I presume the author here means 'what we understand as their rights today'. But, in fact, this journalistic shorthand neatly reminds us of the importance of the intimate connection between struggles against oppression that use under-standings of rights and those that do not.

Charlotte Bunch (1993) has identified four approaches in contemporary feminism to the relationship between women's rights and human rights. Firstly, a liberal current which seeks to ensure that women's needs are properly taken into account within the context of the international covenant on civil and political rights. A second approach, most often taken up by socialist and third world feminists, puts the issue of women's rights as socio-economic rights centre stage. The third approach identified by Bunch seeks to create new legal mechanisms to protect women's rights as a distinct form of human rights. The fourth approach seeks to transform ideas and practices in respect of human rights from a feminist perspective. It is this last approach that Bunch calls the most distinctly feminist '...with its women's centred stance and refusal to wait for permission from some authority to determine what is or is not a human rights issue' (Bunch 1993:976). It is Bunch's fourth approach that explicitly identifies social movement struggle. Yet, at the same time and taken together, her four approaches illustrate both the ideological and strategic diversity typical of social movements and the extent to which the orientation of second wave feminism to human rights was rights 'resurrecting', 'reinforcing' and 'creating'.

In a book published just as this volume was going to press, Brooke Ackerly (2008) has sought to reconstruct a political theory of universal human rights drawing insights from contemporary women's activism around the world. Deploying a range of arguments, some of which chime closely with arguments in this study, she claims that:

> Feminist activists have done the apparently impossible: they've shown us how to think about human rights as local, universal, *and* contested. They have show us that contestation over human rights is not evidence that human rights do not exist. Rather, contestation provides a basis

for understanding their universal meaning. (Ackerly 2008:1, emphasis in original)

Without disagreeing with Ackerly on the importance of contemporary feminist activism to understanding human rights, my argument in this study is much wider: that activists from a wide variety of social movements have been potentially showing us how to think about human rights for a very long time.

If the above examples indicate continuity between historical movement struggles and human rights, there are other instances where rights claims appear to be quite novel. Given the depth of the global ecological crisis, perhaps the most important of these is the green movement which has generated a range of claims to environmental rights and environmental justice. Elements of early green movement agendas have been incorporated into mainstream politics as the evidence of the potential impacts of climate change has mounted. Furthermore, a number of relatively powerful and well resourced (I)NGOs – such as Greenpeace and Friends of the Earth – have emerged out of the movement whilst, at the same time, claiming to retain their movement connections. The broader relevance of such developments will be discussed in the last section of this chapter. Below, I provide one illustrative example of how the reinforcing, creating and resurrecting dynamic can be manifested in green activism.

Following a 2003 conference in Colombia, Friends of the Earth International (FoEI) (2004) produced a substantial report *Our Environment, Our Rights: Standing up for People and the Planet*. The report argues that environmental rights and environmental justice will only be promoted both through a struggle for the recognition of new rights and through the effective protection of existing human rights. Acknowledging that people all over the world are claiming their rights, they suggest that many such claims are based on people's environmental rights defined as 'access to the unspoiled natural resources that enable survival, including land, shelter, food, water and air.' At the same time, they argue that protection of environmental rights necessitates political rights including rights for indigenous peoples and other collectivities, a right to information and participation in decision making, freedom of opinion and expression and the right to resist unwanted development. Arguments in these terms are largely rights reinforcing, in terms of creativity they propose the development of '...the right to claim reparations for violated rights, including rights for climate change refugees and others displaced by environmental destruction, the right to claim ecological debt and the right to environmental justice' (FoEI 2004:5). They argue that marginalised people around the world, including women, people of colour and impoverished people in industrialised countries, suffer from environmental injustice by bearing the brunt of pollution. Moreover, they say that we must recognise:

> ...that the existing enshrined rights are the fruit of the efforts of communities that have historically resisted violations and demanded their rights, and that we can only move further if we join the resistance of those whose rights are being violated today. For this reason, alliances with social movements, both on the ethical and political levels, must form the basis for our campaigns. (FoEI 2004:4)

The bulk of the report then comprises a series of case studies from around the world but organised around the delineation of specific rights. Part One, 'Sustainable Societies', specifies rights to 'a sustainable livelihood', 'a clean and healthy environment', 'water' and 'food safety and security'. Part Two is organised around information, participation and security and specifies 'collective rights', 'the right to know', 'the right to decide' and 'the right to resist'. Part Three is entitled 'Redress' and specifies 'rights for environmental refugees', 'a right to claim ecological debt' and 'a right to environmental justice.'

As well as demonstrating the way in which the reinforcing, creating and resurrecting aspects can be combined as an integrated whole, this document also neatly illustrates the extent to which green activism – supposedly a key archetype of the so-called NSMs – is in fact rooted in a clear set of material (because ecological) concerns that cannot be reduced to questions of identity.

At first sight, the same cannot be said of Lesbian, Gay, Bisexual and Transgender (LGBT) movements and these movements do not appear to have significant historical predecessors in terms of rights struggles. While variety in sexual orientation may have a history as old as human history itself, the first time that a self-proclaimed gay person spoke out publicly for gay rights is often credited to Karl Heinrich Ulrichs in 1867 (Adam 1995:16) and the first organisation committed to ending legal and social intolerance of homosexuals was founded in Germany in 1897 (Adam 1995:1). Rightly or wrongly, many prominent gay activists have argued – in a distinctly Foucaldian register – that the self-identification of people as homosexual only really becomes possible after nineteenth-century classifications of homosexuality. Lesbian and gay movements have apparently had some significant successes in incorporating rights around sexual orientation into the law of their particular jurisdictions, for example in Canada and South Africa (although in Canada the impact is contested, see Herman 1994; Smith 1999). But they have made little progress internationally, despite efforts of the International Lesbian and Gay Association and The International Gay and Lesbian Human Rights Commission. Compared to indigenous peoples' campaigns, lesbian and gay activists have achieved only very limited recognition and accreditation in the UN human rights institutions (HREA 2007). Much of the opposition to lesbian and gay movements is driven by Christian and Islamic religious traditions. Indeed, in parts of the Islamic world and global south, lesbian and gay movements are seen as symptomatic of northern/western decadence, in contrast to the oft-assumed virtue of indigenous peoples' struggles.

While there is a strong identity dimension to LGBT struggles that does not mean material interests are not involved. People face discrimination and often severe persecution in clear and systematic violations of existing civil, political, economic and social rights. So LGBT movement struggles are rights reinforcing in so far as they attempt to ensure that existing human rights protections apply to people of non-heterosexual orientation. While there appears to be no 'resurrecting' dimension to lesbian and gay rights claims, they nevertheless challenge a range of long-entrenched ideological, especially religious, orthodoxies. In this sense, they importantly remind us that a key aspect of the early history of human rights was to challenge power organised around the control of information and knowledge through religious hierarchies.

Five Sites of Power and 'Old Wrongs'

In re-opening the analysis and critique of power, actors in the so-called NSMs rarely denied the extent or salience of economic or political power. Rather, they rejected reductionist arguments which sought to explain all forms of oppression through analysis of one particular form of power, especially economic power. It is in this sense that we can see a connection back to that broader critique of arbitrary power and privilege discussed in Chapters 2 and 3. In particular, these movements variously re-identified three other key sites through which 'power over' has been historically organised and sedimented across all domains of the social – cultural, political and economic. These were sites of power organised around sex and gender, ethnicity and the control of information and knowledge. Second wave feminism and lesbian and gay movements focused on power organised around sex and gender. The black civil rights movement in the United States was clearly a catalyst for other movements (especially indigenous peoples' movements and anti-racist movements) to focus on power organised around ethnicity. Virtually all of the NSMs made some critique of the way in which information and knowledge was controlled and organised as a form of power, especially through the production of academic and scientific knowledge (Seidman 2004:274–6). Feminists identified malestream traits, lesbian and gays identified heterosexist traits and a range of black, indigenous and anti-racist movements identified the depth and persistence of racism. The green movement identified major deficiencies in dominant Enlightenment understandings of the natural world. In other words, these movements identified the intimate link between information, knowledge and power, popularised in intellectual circles through Foucault's work on power/knowledge (Foucault 1980; 1982).

But these movements were not identifying sites of power that were historically new. On the contrary, they were re-identifying sites of power that have histories that extend back over many thousands of years and certainly predate the dominant contemporary forms of organised economic and political power, that is, capitalism, nation states and the inter-state system. So my contention here is that, by the end of the twentieth century, social movements involved in the historical construction and reconstruction of understandings of human rights had effectively identified five sites through which 'power over' has been organised and sedimented. Of course, these sites of power are not necessarily either separable or distinct. Indeed, their actual configurations have been typically deeply interconnected whilst, at the same time, varying significantly across space and time. While this argument is distinct, it can be linked to a number of important strands in academic analysis. Let me point briefly to three of these. In talking about the nature and potential of the NSMs, Alberto Melucci argued that one of their systemic effects was 'rendering power visible' (Melucci 1989:76). Derived from this insight, my argument extends it to social movement activism in general, a feature recognised by many movement commentators (see Diani 2000). In political theory, David Held (1995) has identified seven sites of power in *Democracy and the Global Order*, which he then links to a range of rights. But he does so abstractly through a 'thought experiment' rather than making any link to the history of social movement struggles around human rights. Finally, from historical sociology, Michael Mann identifies four sources of social power in his IEMP model (Ideological, Economic, Military, Political) which, he argues, have trans-historical and trans-cultural purchase and which have been organised and sedimented via institutional networks resulting in the institutionalisation of dominant structures of power in particular geographical and historical conjunctures (Mann 1986:29).

If we can indeed identify trans-historical and trans-cultural sites of power, then this clearly implies that we can also identify trans-historical and trans-cultural forms of 'power over' – forms of oppression – emanating from these sites. The question that then arises is whether the history of social movement struggles around human rights has, at the level of socio-historical practices, identified a corresponding set of 'old wrongs'. This is certainly not an issue that has been interrogated in any depth within the human rights literature but there are some hints in that direction. Interestingly, they come from a range of contrasting, usually highly antagonistic, positions. Micheline Ishay, begins her introduction to *The Human Rights Reader* by stating '[at] every stage of history, voices of protest against oppression have been heard; in every age, visions of human liberation have also been eclipsed' (1997:xiii). In an essay 'Righting Wrongs', leading post-colonial theorist Gayatri Chakravorty Spivak, argues that '... "Human Rights" is not only about having or claiming a right or a set of rights; it is also about righting wrongs...' (Spivak 2004:523). While Spivak argues that human rights are a western product and, in this sense, dispensed from above by the powerful to the powerless, she refuses to complain about the Eurocentrism of human rights, arguing that '[o]ne cannot write off the righting of wrongs. The enablement must be used even as the violation is renegotiated' (Spivak 2004:524).

The above are no more than hints, but Alan Dershowitz (2004) offers what he calls a secular theory of human rights in *Rights from Wrongs*. In a chapter entitled 'What, then, is the source of rights?', he argues that '... rights are those fundamental preferences that experience and history – especially of great injustices – have taught are so essential that the citizenry should be persuaded to entrench them and not make them subject to easy change by shifting majorities' (Dershowitz 2004:81). Thus, he says, his theory of rights is, in fact, a theory of wrongs. As examples of great wrongs he refers to the Crusades, the Inquisition, slavery, the Stalinist starvation and purges, the Holocaust, the Cambodian slaughter and other abuses that reasonable people now recognise to have been wrongs (Dershowitz 2004:81). Without disputing any of his examples, what is curious about Dershowitz's account is that he offers no theoretical or historical explanation of how particular actions, sets of actions or processes become seen as 'wrongs' beyond what 'reasonable people now recognise'. In other words, what counts as wrongs is simply asserted. There is no history, no conflict and no struggle in his account of the wrongs that have generated human rights.

In contrast, and in an account of what he calls three tyrannies in the way we conceive, approach and talk about human rights, Ken Booth (1999) argues that a universalist understanding of human rights '...can be based on the secure but sad fact of universal human wrongs' (Booth 1999:46). Human wrongs, he says, are everywhere and are universal in a way that human rights are not. Rejecting normative relativism, he argues that it is, as a matter of fact, a bad thing to be tortured or starved, humiliated or hurt. He notes approvingly Richard Wilson's comment that '... human misery is relatively uniform, leading to a notion of human frailty as the universal feature of human existence' (cited in Booth 1999:63). But Booth does not stop with vulnerability (see Turner 2006). He adds that a universalist perspective favouring the bottom-up perspective of human wrongs '... has the crucial effect of humanising the powerless' and '...allows the victim to assert and define his or her humanity, with the help of solidarist groups elsewhere' (Booth 1999:63). Thus, Booth argues that universal human rights are derived '...from our animal nature (the need for food and shelter) and from our social character and potentiality. The *is* of wrongs demands the *should* of emancipation' (Booth 1999:63, emphasis in original).

In summary, by drawing together these otherwise disparate hints and threads, we can see that at least some commentators have identified a range of 'old wrongs' – forms of oppression, domination, exclusion and silencing. In my view these can be associated with the five sites of power identified and challenged by a range of historical social movements. Tempting though it may be to adopt Booth's suggestion of 'universal' rather than 'old' wrongs, I will not do so. This is partly because the term 'universal' tends to drag us away from the analysis of social praxis towards philosophical debate but also because the 'timelessness' associated with 'universal' implies that these wrongs will always be with us. While the threat of such wrongs may well be ever present, the point of originating constructions and reconstructions of human rights has been precisely to limit and/or mitigate such threats, the complexities of the paradox of institutionalisation notwithstanding.

'Ageing' and Resurgence

In the previous chapter I argued that, despite the very real problems of institutionalisation, the establishment of a 'concrete universal' of human rights through the UN system opened up possibilities for assessing human rights in particular jurisdictions and also for challenging, developing and transforming the international human rights system itself. In Chapter 4, I used the example of self-determination to illustrate the complexity involved but, clearly, a vast range of movement activism has operated in the same context since 1948, including all of the so-called NSMs. In other words, these various movements could both contextualise and orient their struggles in terms of the international human rights system. The importance of this point should not be under-estimated. For the first time in the history of rights struggles, movements could meaningfully orient human rights activism both locally and globally.

Huge efforts have been made to develop and transform the international human rights system – perhaps most notably by women's movements, indigenous peoples' movements and movements focusing on achieving basic economic, social and cultural rights. Moreover, such efforts have often been led by (I)NGOs that either directly emerged from movements seen as NSMs or were established or grew significantly in the broader political and cultural context of what we might describe as the broader 'NSM milieu' of the 1970s and 1980s. Important and influential western-based (I)NGOs such as Friends of the Earth, Greenpeace, Action Aid, The World Development Movement, The International Lesbian and Gay Association, Amnesty International and Human Rights Watch were established or developed significantly in these decades. Indeed, a wide range of literature has assessed a range of such (I)NGOs through an explicit or implicit assumption of their links to the movements seen as NSMs

(Thiele 1993; Otto 1996; Smith, Chatfield and Pagnucco 1997; Keck and Sikkink 1998; Cohen and Rai 2000). So the last 40 years or so have witnessed the development of a plethora of (I)NGOs with human rights concerns that have attempted to engage with the relations and structures of power of the institutional world in a variety of ways. Sometimes actors within the UN human rights system have played an important role in facilitating (I)NGOs relations with the UN human rights institutions. The degree of this sort of engagement has been explored and analysed by Keck and Sikkink (1998) in their work on transnational advocacy networks. At least some of these organisations seek to straddle the porous boundaries between the institutional and everyday worlds. Indeed, as illustrated above in the Friends of the Earth conference report, some elements of networks are specifically committed to facilitating the further empowerment of social movements.

My discussion of the paradox of institutionalisation in the previous chapter suggests we should expect to find ambiguity and complexity in trying to assess success and failure in these engagements with the institutional world. For example, while the draft declaration on the rights of indigenous peoples stalled for many years, the eventual outcome and the process of getting there could be judged a significant achievement. Likewise, some feminists have seen the declaration at the end of the Vienna Conference in 1993 as a tremendous success in terms of embedding women's rights within the framework of international human rights law (Bunch 2003; Abeysekera 2003). So Baxi's argument – that one cannot understand recent development in human rights outside the context of those movements seen as NSMs – seems well founded. Moreover, given that many of these (I)NGOs developed within the 'NSM milieu' of the 1970s and 1980s, perhaps we should not be surprised to find that many of them have taken on board the necessity of 'redefining radicalism' as explained above. As a consequence of such commitments, some organisations are forging alliances with new forms of critical social movement activism (see below) whilst, at the same time, continuing to pursue institutional engagement. The paradox of institutionalisation defies simplicity.

The 'Ageing' of the NSMs?

In the section above on 'redefining radicalism', I drew attention to the non-institutional forms of activism and the anti-institutional and anti-bureaucratic stance sometimes seen as a defining feature of the so-called NSMs and as a key aspect of their radicalism by movement activists themselves. I also drew attention to the unfortunate tendency to see NSMs ahistorically, through static snapshots of movement activism in the 1970s and 1980s. So, from both of these perspectives, we are drawn to the question of what has happened to the so-called NSMs over the last 40 years or so. Have they 'aged'? Should they now be understood as 'old' in terms of these distinctions and arguments? The picture is both mixed and complex. As made clear above, the so-called NSMs have spawned a vast range of formally organised and hierarchically structured organisations that engage with the institutional world. The extent to which specific organisations retain meaningful connections to broader forms of movement activism is an open and important question, as is the degree of internal democracy within (I)NGOS and also their broader accountability to the 'constituencies' they claim to represent – the issue of 'representational power' discussed at the end of Chapter 4.

In terms of internal dynamics there are important examples of well-resourced and powerful (I)NGOs being structured so as to negate the possibility of large scale membership democracy. One typical way this is achieved is by signing up 'supporters' who – whilst making regular donations to the organisation – cannot become members and have no constitutional voice in the organisation. Greenpeace (2007) and Friends of the Earth (2007) are two prominent examples here. Despite their largely positive reputation (due in no small part to their apparent continuing commitment to the green movement and forms of activism) at the time of writing their websites are entirely opaque on how someone can become a formal member of their organisations. While one can become a member with voting rights in some national sections of Amnesty International (2007) there is not even a link on the Human Rights Watch (2007) website allowing someone to become a 'supporter' although there is a link allowing contributions to be made. In a study of internet use on the part of Amnesty International, Oxfam and The World Development Movement, Anastasia Kavada (2005) concluded that these organisations had – at that stage – only developed those internet functions considered instrumental for the achievement of organisational goals and that their profile on the internet had been limited by their high degree of institutionalisation as established political organisations. She argues that what seemed to be missing was a spirit of trust and solidarity and that these organisations failed to show any deeper commitment towards transparency and cooperation.

All of this chimes with the more general findings in the social movement literature which remains sensitive to the problems of bureaucratisation and oligarchy. Looking at transnational social movement organisations, Dieter Rucht outlines some of the consequences of the paradox of institutionalisation:

> ...a declining performance in relation to organizational resources, and a loss of initiative and emphasis particularly among the rank and file ... [C]hanges in structure tend to be accompanied by changes in ideology .... [whereby] some organizations ... become more interested in their own maintenance and growth than in the original goal for which they were set up. A related aspect of this is the threat of an instrumentalization and commercialization of the movements' aims .... [and the possibility of] co-option and deradicalization. (Rucht in Della Porta and Kriesi 1999:218)

Parallel claims have also been made in respect of movements being 'NGO-ised' and INGOs and movement organisations being professionalised and institutionalised (Meyer and Tarrow 1998:20; Alvarez 1999). Talking about INGOs in general, Donini (1996) argued that an oligopoly of INGOs was emerging and that a handful of 'operational' INGOs had become 'market leaders', dominating interactions with the UN and stifling diversity within the sector as other (I)NGOs were forced to adopt similar practices and management styles in order to survive. These various points are poignantly summed up by Hulme and Edwards (1997) in terms of (I)NGOs being 'too close to the powerful, too far from the powerless' in their conclusion to *NGOs, States and Donors: Too Close for Comfort*.

Alberto Melucci argued that a trajectory towards stable organisation and leadership is essential for a social movement to survive, claiming that the Weber/Michels model of bureaucratisation oversimplifies the complexity of organisational phenomena and the empirical reality of social movements (Melucci 1996:313–15). Melucci is right to stress that bureaucratisation, professionalisation and institutionalisation is not inevitable, but his point again emphasises the importance of exploring the paradox of institutionalisation when trying to analyse social movement activism. All the more so given that many activists in the so-called NSMs were acutely aware of the dangers of institutionalisation and bureaucratisation and yet, despite this, many of their organisations have subsequently succumbed to these tendencies.[1] The subtlety of Melucci's point has been interestingly developed by Paul Nelson (2006) in a study of interactions between development and human rights organisations and between social movements and INGOs around issues of economic, social and cultural rights. Nelson argues that insights from both organisational theory and theories of social movements are essential to account for major changes occurring in the two organisational fields of human rights and international development. In terms of social praxis, Nelson concludes that:

Formal human rights and development NGOs at the international level have been drawn into advocacy work on [economic, social and cultural] rights, and into human rights based approaches to development, largely by the force of rights based social movements in the poorer countries. A prominent set of international NGOs – Oxfam, Action Aid, MSF, Amnesty International, OMCT – are not only associating themselves with social movements in health, trade, land and water, but presenting themselves as international flagship organisations for such movements. (Nelson, 2006: 21–22)

This ties in with the approach specified in the Friends of the Earth International report cited earlier which clearly argues for an alliance with, and support for, a range of social movements struggling for human rights and resisting neo-liberal economic globalisation. So are 'ageing' NSMs providing an 'already institutionalised' platform for the most recent wave of critical social movements?

Contemporary Critical Social Movements: Key Continuities?

The resurgence of 'critical social movements' (Walker 1988) around the world since the late 1990s (variously described as anti-globalisation movements, anti-capitalist movements, a 'movement of movements' or simply 'the movement') raises the question of the extent to which these movements should be seen as some sort of continuation of those movements depicted as NSMs. Certainly some of the (I)NGOs that arose out of the NSMs do participate in processes such as the World Social Forum and in protests against the G8 and WTO. Furthermore, as we have just seen, there is evidence that some important (I)NGOs have embraced links to contemporary critical movements. Yet, at the heart of this new activism is a renewal of the challenge to economic power, which certainly does not fit with those depictions of the NSMs as cultural movements largely concerned with questions of identity and lifestyle. But the problem here lies more in reified descriptions and portrayals of the NSMs than in their actual orientation of those movements to economic power. Regardless of this, it is clear that contemporary movement activism continues and builds upon those orientations discussed above in terms of 'redefining radicalism'. A critique of existing forms of institutional power – not just economic power – is strong throughout the new movements and many significant currents of activism explicitly argued for the necessity of reinventing radicalism, emphasising that such radicalism must be self limiting, sometimes in terms of a commitment to non-violence (Brecher, Costello and Smith 2000; Fisher and Ponniah 2003; Sen et al. 2004; Mertes 2004). These points suggest strong continuities with important aspects of the so-called NSMs.

An anthropological study of contemporary anti-capitalist activism in France (Williams 2005) identifies a clear consciousness on the part of movement actors of seeing a direct and important continuity with NSM-type struggles of the 1970s and 1980s. Importantly, the study also identifies a strong positive orientation towards human rights and an understanding of anti-capitalism as being, above all, a critique of power. Analyses of this contemporary critical movement activism will be looked at further in Chapter 7. To conclude here, it is worth noting that by the end of the 1980s, one or two NSMs theorists (Melucci 1989; Hegedus 1989) had begun to provide some potential conceptual bridges between the NSMs and contemporary movement struggles through early articulations of what came to the fore in the 1990s as a concept of globalisation.

Conclusion

Since the 1960s, social movements have had an enormous impact on local and global social relations. Many of these movements have been engaged in struggles for human rights and some of these were conceptualised as New Social Movements. I have argued that the so-called NSMs crucially reopened the analysis and critique of power and attempted to reconstruct understandings of radicalism, rejecting the binary polarity between reform and revolution. Many of these movements have been rights resurrecting, reinforcing and creating and may be conceptually linked to historical struggles against oppression arising from three sites of power – organised around sex and gender, ethnicity, and the control of information and knowledge – which, in addition to political and economic power, have been organised trans-historically and trans-culturally. In terms of social-historical practices, I have argued that we can see struggles for human rights as struggles against 'old wrongs' emanating from all five of these sites of power.

One thing that this discussion makes clear is that the integration of non-legal and pre-legal dimensions of human rights is critical for achieving an holistic understanding. Unfortunately, very little literature in the human rights field has attempted to address systematically the sorts of arguments developed in this chapter despite some hints and nods in the that direction. In social movement studies and social theory, the rise of the so-called NSMs led to much intellectual energy being turned towards a focus on issues of identity, difference and recognition. The next chapter brings these two points together by looking at what I term the expressive and instrumental dimensions of human rights activism.

6

EXPRESSIVE AND INSTRUMENTAL DIMENSIONS OF MOVEMENT ACTIVISM

This chapter explores the analytical significance of non-legal and pre-legal forms of human rights as movement generated social processes – a sort of combined culture and politics 'from below'. To the extent that non-legal aspects appear at all in the specialist academic literature on human rights, they typically appear in a 'top-down' focus whereby law is assumed to 'lead' culture. So the orientation adopted here requires us to reconsider two basic questions 'where do human rights come from?' and 'how do non-legal forms of human rights relate to human rights as law?' Although this chapter involves something of a pause in my account of the history of human rights, it is only something of a pause because the intellectual debates discussed below have their own very distinct history. They arose as a response to the emergence and rise of the so-called New Social Movements, illustrating the more general point made throughout this study that ideas and intellectual developments around human rights have often arisen from movement praxis.

By the end of this chapter I will be in a position to examine what I call the 'expressive/instrumental dynamic' of social movement activism and how this impacts on the social construction of human rights. But in order to get there I need to take a somewhat circuitous route. Firstly it is necessary to specify what I mean by expressive and instrumental dimensions of movement activism and explain why this terminology is preferable to, and provides more purchase on, the link between human rights and social movements than debates that focus on interests, identities and recognition. Particular emphasis is placed on delineating my usage of the term 'expressive' because it may be unfamiliar to many readers. The term 'instrumental' is clarified through, and in conjunction with, my more detailed discussion of the expressive dimension. These tasks are made especially difficult because of the ways that the terms instrumental and expressive have been used in social theory and because of the range and complexity of recent debates around identity, difference and recognition. It is impossible to do justice to these various debates, so those familiar with them may find my discussion overly superficial. Conversely, those unfamiliar with such debates might suspect that this part of my overall argument is tangential and doubt its relevance. To both concerns, I can only reiterate my conviction that a proper grasp and conceptualisation of these dimensions of movement activism is crucial to understanding not just the link between social movement and human rights, but also the possibilities for how human rights might play a positive part in future transformative social change. In particular, this chapter forces open a range of key questions: the nature of the relationship between formal and substantive rationalities and how these link to expressive and instrumental dimensions of movement activism; the relationship between means and ends; the place of 'strategy' in the history of creative human rights praxis, and the question of the 'fixity' of law. On this last point, I argued in Chapter 4 that the institutionalisation of human rights sedimented particular exclusions. But how 'fixed' is such sedimentation?

Some instances of expressive activism as aspects of struggles for human rights were discussed in previous chapters. This chapter examines the expressive/instrumental dynamic at the analytic level, arguing that this dynamic of movement activism is crucial to our understanding of human rights.

Locating the Expressive Dimension

Because of the dominance of philosophy and law in the human rights literature, it is all to easy for proponents to see the history of human rights as a history of 'great men' coming up with 'great ideas' which were then instantiated as 'great laws', firstly, in those western states that became liberal democracies and then, after 1948, as international law in the UN system. Interestingly, in terms of the role of social actors, critics can tell the same story without disturbing the underlying logic by simply substituting 'capitalist' or 'imperialist' for the term 'great'. In other words, these are 'top-down' stories of elite creativity and elite governance. To the extent that social movements get into that story at all they get inserted between 'ideas' and 'law'. But, even when acknowledged as agents of change, social movements are hardly ever seen as *creative* agents. They are depicted as simply responding to the 'great ideas' of the 'great men' and are quickly supplanted by new or transformed institutions of governance and law.[1] Thus it is no surprise there are so few attempts in the dominant literatures to explore non-legal and pre-legal dimensions of human rights, nor any consideration of the significance of such dimensions and their connections to human rights as law.

Of course, this is hardly a novel story. The view that ideas of morality are (and should be) handed down by priests or philosophers is commonplace, certainly in those societies with a Judeo-Christian tradition. Moreover, assumptions and justifications of the necessity, inevitability and legitimacy of top-down governance are as old as top-down governance itself – most obviously sedimented in the western intellectual tradition in the work of Hobbes and, much later, in a social democratic manifestation, by Schumpeter (1976). But familiar as these sorts of accounts may be, that does not make them accurate. Indeed, from the perspective of the framework adopted here, these familiar accounts are little more than caricatures of the complex processes of socio-historical change. An understanding and integration of expressive and instrumental dimensions of movement activism is one thing that can reduce the distorting effects of these caricatures.

The use of the pairing of 'instrumental' and 'expressive' to describe dimensions of activism is commonplace in the field of social movement studies (Scott 1990; Melucci 1989; Darnovsky, Epstein and Flacks 1995) and I began to use this pairing (Stammers, 1999a/1999b) in an attempt to transcend the narrow and restrictive dichotomous separation between interests and identities in accounts of 'old' and 'new' social movements as discussed in the previous chapter. However, in the social movement literature, the way the term 'expressive' is used can be very narrow. Some scholars have used the term to designate those psychological needs of individuals required to facilitate engagement in collective action. A less individualistic formulation sees expressive activism as a key *internal* dynamic of social movements, one that facilitates the construction of a collective identity within a movement and which thus also helps movement activists to mobilise resources or to take advantage of political opportunities (for an overview see Della Porta and Diani 1999:Chs 3, 4). Without denying the potential salience of these two factors, other social movement scholars have used the term 'expressive' more widely, to denote forms of activism that also proffer alternative norms, values and ways of living and being to the wider society.

Alberto Melucci's work can be used to illustrate the point well. Although at times he too has depicted the expressive dimension as an internal dynamic of movements (Melucci 1996:326), his broader arguments are suggestive. Movements, he says, often prefigure the goals they pursue. Furthermore, public dimensions of movement action usually coincide with the proposed cultural models elaborated and lived in networks submerged in everyday life (Melucci 1989:Ch.3). In a distinctly functionalist tone, Melucci (1989:73) argues that the 'hidden efficacy of social movements' lies in their capacity to provide messages and signs to the wider society of its social ills and dysfunctions. Indeed, without the challenges posed by contemporary movements '...complex societies would be incapable of asking questions about meaning; they would entrap themselves in the apparently neutral logic of institutional procedures' (Melucci 1989:11). For Melucci then, social movements are not only creative, they are crucially so.

The key thesis of Jean Cohen and Andrew Arato's voluminous work, *Civil Society and Political Theory* (1992) is similar. They argue that 'social movements constitute the dynamic element in processes that might realise the positive potentials of modern civil societies' (Cohen and Arato 1992:493) and make the expressive dimension of movement activism central to their argument. Drawing from, but also critiquing, Habermas' dualistic social theory separating 'system' and 'lifeworld', they use feminist theory and the example of the western feminist movement to argue that contemporary social movements have a dual face and a dual organisational logic. As well as making instrumental demands for changes in social policy aimed at political and economic institutions, feminist movements directly contest the norms and structures of male dominance in civil society. They argue:

> The dual logic of feminist politics thus involves a communicative, discursive politics of identity and influence that targets civil and political society and an organised, strategically rational politics of inclusion and reform that is aimed at political and economic institutions. (Cohen and Arato 1992:550)

Moreover, Cohen and Arato insist that the legislative and judicial successes that feminist movements have achieved in some parts of the world would have been impossible or much more limited without the accompanying struggle to reconstruct the norms and practices in society more generally. They explain their dual organisational logic in terms of 'two branches' of second wave feminism. They say, inaccurately in my view, that an 'older' branch of long-standing interest-type groups pursued instrumental strategies whilst 'younger' grassroots groups emphasised expressive activism. But they also argue that activists crossed the organisational divide in both directions. 'Nor has learning on the part of activists entailed a one directional shift from expressive to instrumental rationality...learning has occurred on both sides and in both directions' (Cohen and Arato 1992:558).

My usage of the term 'expressive' is intended to designate the affective and normative dimensions of social movement activism. This dimension is foundational for what social movements are and what they try to do. Indeed, the instrumental dimensions of movement activism are usually derived from this foundation. Expressive activism is oriented towards the construction, reconstruction and/or transformation of norms, values, identities and ways of living and being. It is not just about 'who we are' (the key theme of many of the debates about identity and recognition, see below) but also about 'how we are' in the world, consequently requiring evaluation of 'what we do' and 'how we do it'. Unsurprisingly therefore, the expressive dimension of movement activism is usually directed both inwards and outwards. The inwardly directed element can be thought of as legitimating or valorising the position, values, outlook and identities of the actors involved in social movements. The outwardly directed element is about projecting alternative norms, values, identities and ways of living and being into the wider societal milieu, both in terms of seeking acknowledgement and recognition and in terms of proposing alternative ways of living and being.

Now, both Melucci and Cohen and Arato were particularly concerned with analysing the movements of the 1970s and 1980s and – at various points – claim it is the emphasis on expressive activism that marks these movements as significantly different from previous movements. In other words, it is the significance of expressive activism that distinguished 'old' and 'new' movements. So we are back to some of the arguments discussed in the previous chapter. As mentioned there, without wishing to foreclose the argument that expressive dimensions of activism may have become increasingly prominent and significant over recent decades, what I want to do here instead is emphasise historical continuity in the importance and significance of expressive dimensions of activism. In fact, neither Melucci nor Cohen and Arato would seek to deny this. Cohen and Arato, for example, note that Charles Tilly's work on action repertoires of social movements in the eighteenth and nineteenth centuries admirably describes 'richly symbolic and expressive action...despite his overall stress on ...strategic rationality' (Cohen and Arato 1992:501). Furthermore, in arguing against the view that collective actors only learn 'along the cognitive-instrumental dimension' and that movements combining 'the politics of identity and strategy' cannot succeed, Cohen and Arato argue that the empirical evidence is much more ambiguous. They give the example of the achievements and continuity of working class movements which they suggest was due, in part at least, to their ability to combine cultural and political concerns.

Cohen and Arato's linking of identity to culture and strategy to politics brings us to another important point. There is also a strong tendency across the social sciences to see expressive activism as purely cultural and instrumental activism as purely political and/ or economic. My usage of instrumental and expressive does not make or imply such a linkage.

By instrumental activism I mean activism directly oriented towards achieving specific goals. While such activism is often oriented politically and/or economically, it can be directed towards the cultural realm, for example when feminist activists demand an immediate end to male violence. Here the aspect of the instrumental that is being emphasised is the concrete demand for behavioural change on the part of men. Expressive activism can similarly be oriented towards the political and economic realms. Indeed, the typical historical trajectory of human rights is precisely an account of the way in which expressive activism oriented towards the social construction of human rights addresses itself to the political and economic realms. In other words, social movement demands for the institutional instantiation of human rights are attempts to reconstruct the norms, values and assumptions that pervade the institutional world. This is, in other words, a key element of human rights as a challenge to power.

While a useful analytical distinction, the instrumental and expressive dimensions of activism are rarely separable and should certainly never be set up as a binary polarity. Rather, 'instrumental' and 'expressive' need to be understood as usually being in a dynamic and complex relation. The importance of this point can be illustrated by reference to Max Weber's conceptualisations of social action and rationality. Weber's typology of social action moves along a continuum from rational to irrational action. His most rational form of social action is 'instrumental action' dominated by means-ends calculations. Social actors consider alternative means to achieve given ends and attempt to weigh up and calculate the consequences of particular courses of action. Weber's next category is 'value rational action' and this involves conscious consideration and formulation of values and ends. Social action is then oriented towards these values or ends with less emphasis on calculation of consequences. 'Affectual action' is Weber's third category and here action is dominated by the actor's emotions or passions. Finally, Weber identifies 'traditional action' as the most irrational form of social action. It is largely unreflexive and dominated by custom and tradition,

While there is considerable debate over Weber's usage of the concept of rationality (Elliott 1998:4) his distinction between formal and substantive rationality is quite clear. Formal rationality 'denotes the pursuit of the most efficient and technically correct means' of achieving a given end, displaying 'an inherent tendency towards maximum ability, escalating impersonality and general indifference to all substantive considerations' (Elliot 1998:8). In contrast, substantive rationality denotes action oriented to means considered appropriate or correct for a chosen end or value (Elliott 1998:8). In other words, substantive rationality is largely ends driven, formal rationality, means driven. Weber saw his categories as 'ideal types' and recognised social reality as much more complex. But his categories are helpful here. My distinction between 'instrumental' and 'expressive' only partly correlates with the means-ends distinction in Weber's typology of social action and his distinction between formal and substantive rationality. Instrumental movement activism typically displays degrees of strategic thinking and calculation but that rarely becomes divorced from ends. Thus, while close to Weber's notion of instrumental action in terms of rationalities, instrumental movement activism does not depend solely on formal rationality as does Weber's. On the other hand, expressive activism straddles Weber's categories of value rational and affective action and exhibits strong orientations to ends and values akin to Weber's understanding of substantive rationality. Moreover, as we shall see, expressive movement activism can encompass strategic elements intended to facilitate shifts in norms, values and ways of living and being across the whole of the social field.

Social movement activism is not generally oriented towards, nor does it require, the formal rationality exhibited in formally structured organisations – including (I)NGOs and political parties – and which is an essential feature of those large organisations:

corporations, state bodies and international institutions that are key elements of the institutional world. However, when formally structured organisations emerge from social movements, they are very likely to begin to adopt methods and practices of formal rationality. For Weber, formal rationality is both the necessity and the problem of the modern world. It is, in other words, a key aspect of the paradox of institutionalisation. These points are summed up diagrammatically in Figure 6.1.

1. Social Movements	→	challenge to power	→	Institutional transformation
2. Instrumental/ Expressive Activism	→	institutionalisation	→	Activism becomes subjected to formal rationality
3. Human rights as movement activism	→	institutionalisation	→	Human rights subjected to formal rationality, especially as law and constitutional provision

Figure 6.1   Formal rationality and the paradox of institutionalisation

In point two of Figure 6.1 we can now see the institutionalisation of instrumental and expressive dimensions of movement activism as a key part of the paradox of institutionalisation in so far as they become, or are subjected to, the formal rationality that pervades large organisations in the institutional world. Elliott puts it like this:

> The internal logic of formal rationality produces escalating indifference and outright hostility to all substantive considerations. This results, Weber argued, in a system where the cultivation and pursuit of efficient means is elevated to a position functionally equivalent to substantive value, increasingly exposing the system to accusations of substantive *irrationality*. (Elliott 1998:9 emphasis in original)

While Weber's famous metaphor of the iron cage may be too strong, my argument here is that there is indeed a clear problem in that both instrumental and expressive dimensions of movement activism can be subverted through processes of institutionalisation.

In an interesting recent study of these phenomena, Annelise Riles (2006) examines what she calls the 'hegemony of legal instrumentalism'[2] among experts in the human rights field. Her study is based on her own ethnographic work among 'critical human rights lawyers' who share 'scepticism about various aspects of the human rights regime – its theoretical claims, its institutional practices and its archetypal subjectivities' (Riles 2006:55). While, she says, these critics often present complex and apparently compelling support for their arguments, including 'sophisticated critiques of the technocratic instrumentalism of legal knowledge' (Riles 2006:59), at the same time they remain trapped within that legal instrumentalism as the condition of their own daily work as elite actors working in the field of law. What Riles captures so well in her study is the fact that the 'critical human rights lawyers' are necessarily embedded in wider social processes. The same is true of political theorists and philosophers. Too often they seem unable to recognise social processes, either in relation to their own positions as academics or in terms of the orientations of their disciplines (though see Ackerly 2008). So since expressive and instrumental dimensions of movement activism are, above all, social processes it is perhaps no wonder that they have been largely ignored. We could expect better from academics specialising in the study of 'the social', yet debates about movement activism have largely been focused through the concepts of interests, identities and recognition. So it is to these debates that I now turn.

From 'Interests' to 'Identities'

The last 30 years or so have witnessed a major shift in intellectual focus across the whole of the humanities and the social sciences. This is often described as the 'cultural turn' and is associated with the rise to prominence of post-structuralism and post-modernism as forms of intellectual analysis. A break from the previous intellectual hegemony was long overdue and as I have already said, they were – in part at least – a direct response to the struggles of the so-called NSMs (see Chapter 5). But these shifts of intellectual focus have major implications for how human rights and struggles for human rights are analysed. At the heart of many of these debates has been the concept of identity.

Emancipation? Self-subjugation? Homogenisation and Exclusion?

This section looks at the three most prominent ways in which the relationship between human rights and identity has been analysed.

Emancipation?

Ideas of emancipation have been, and remain, central to many movement struggles. Certainly they lay at the heart of the activism of the so-called NSMs. The key understandings and assumptions involved here are that oppressions are rooted in, or worked through, particular social categories such as women, ethnic groups, indigenous peoples, lesbians and gays. People in such categories suffer oppression as a consequence of being seen and treated in their category terms. Put another way, such people have a negative identity ascribed to them and are then 'othered' as a consequence of existing relations and structures of power. Movement actors take up these ascribed identities, reconstructing and articulating them positively as a collective identity through which movement activism is facilitated. For example, the articulation of the slogan 'black is beautiful' or the re-appropriation of terms like 'queer' and 'dyke' by gay men and lesbians are examples of the way in which negative identities as categories of oppression are inverted to become positive identities, something to be celebrated. Thus, struggles for rights and human rights around such social categories have important dimensions which are about validating and legitimating these positively reconstructed identities. Put another way, emancipatory potentials here cannot be understood simply in instrumental or institutional terms because they are necessarily embedded in much wider social processes. Moreover, in this sense, rights claims have an important psycho-social element, an attempt to build a particular form of 'power-to' – self-esteem – as a rights bearing subject. This is almost entirely overlooked in the human rights literature.[3]

Self-subjugation?

Arguments that struggles for rights rooted in identities can be self-subjugating rather than emancipatory has been developed in two very different ways. The first is based on an argument that the oppression and subordination of a particular social category (for example, women) is not in fact rooted in that category but rather flows from another, more fundamental, form of oppression. Thus, it can then be argued that struggles based on a particular identity are diversionary and perpetuate subjugation by focusing on the wrong target. This sort of argument was developed from many different standpoints and, in the 1970s and 1980s, it led to much agonising and fraught debate over 'hierarchies of oppression' amongst movement activists and academics (see Ramazanoglu 1989). The second approach is more complex, involving arguments that the very attempt to appropriate an oppressed identity and use it in a positive way perpetuates oppression of people in that category. This form of argument, regularly developed in post-structuralist analyses, is typically constructed in terms of the analysis of discourse. Below I look at one example by way of illustration.

Wendy Brown is a post-structuralist and feminist political theorist whose work in the 1990s was widely acknowledged (Bhambra and Margree 2006). In *States of Injury: Power and Freedom in Late Modernity*, Brown (1995) offers what looks like a sophisticated and compelling account of identity-based struggles in the United States in the 1980s and 1990s. She claims that what drives identity politics can be understood through Nietzsche's concept of *ressentiment*, '…the moralising revenge of the powerless, "the triumph of the weak as weak"' (Brown 1995:66–7). Further, she argues that the characteristics of late-modern secular societies expand the conditions for the production of *ressentiment*. Thus, she argues, 'the late modern liberal subject', starkly accountable yet dramatically impotent, 'quite literally seethes with *ressentiment*' (Brown 1995:69). Enter, she says, politicised identity:

> In its emergence as a protest against marginalisation or subordination, politicised identity thus becomes attached to its own exclusion both because it is premised on this exclusion for its very existence as identity and because the formation of identity at the site of exclusion, as exclusion, augments or 'alters the direction of the suffering' entailed in subordination or marginalisation by finding a site of blame for it. But in so doing it installs its pain over its unredeemed history in the very foundation of its political claim, in its demand for recognition as identity. (Brown 1995:73–4)

Brown moves on to ask about the consequences 'of installing politicised identity in the universal discourse of liberal jurisprudence?' In other words, '[w]hat is the emancipatory force of rights claims on behalf of politicised identities in late-twentieth-century North American political life?' (Brown 1995:96). Identifying a range of paradoxes about rights she argues:

> …rights necessarily operate in and as an ahistorical, acultural, acontextual idiom: they claim distance from specific political contexts and historical vicissitudes, and they necessarily participate in a discourse of enduring universality rather than provisionality or partiality. Thus, while the measure of the political advocacy requires a high degree of historical and social specificity, rights operate as a political discourse of the general, the generic, and universal. (Brown 1995:97)

In a manner very close to some of the arguments presented in this volume, she notes that while rights may operate as an indisputable force of emancipation at one moment in history, at another time they may become a regulatory discourse, a means of obstructing or co-opting more radical political demands. This paradox, she says, is captured in part by Nietzsche's insistence that 'liberal institutions cease to be liberal as soon as they are attained' (Brown 1995:98). But rather than explore institutionalisation as a social process, Brown simply assumes that human rights emerged 'as a means of privileging an emerging bourgeois class' relying on a fallacious argument of simultaneous emergence (Stammers 1999a:996). Thus, she says, rights '…emerged both as a means of protection against arbitrary use and abuse by sovereign and social power and as a mode of securing and naturalizing dominant social powers – class, gender, and so forth' (Brown 1995:99).

Interrogating the works of Karl Marx and feminist legal scholar Catherine McKinnon, she then asks whether 'rights affixed to identities partly function to imprison us within the subject positions they are secured to affirm or protect?' (Brown 1995:120). Drawing from Foucault, she answers:

> post-Marxist theory permits us to understand how rights pervasively configure political culture... and discursively produce the political subject... it also permits us to grasp the way in which disciplinary productions of identity may become the site of rights struggles that naturalise and thus entrench the powers of which those identities are the effects. (Brown 1995:120)

She is particularly critical of McKinnon who, she says '...seeks to encode the "experience" or "subject position" of a fiction called "women" in the timeless discourse of the law' (Brown 1995:132). This claim of law being a timeless discourse is important to Brown's framework and I come back to it later in this chapter. Overall, though, Brown's position is summed up in this passage:

> As a regulatory fiction of a particular identity is deployed to displace the hegemonic fiction of universal person, we see the discourse of rights converge insidiously with the discourse of disciplinarity to produce a spectacular impotent mode of juridical disciplinary domination. (Brown 1995:133)

Make no mistake, Brown's work raises a whole range of critical questions for movement activists and analysts of human rights. In particular, she warns of the

> ...profoundly antidemocratic elements implicit in transferring from the relatively accessible sphere of popular contestation to the highly restrictive sphere of juridical authority the project of representing politicised identity and adjudicating its temporal and conflicting demands. (Brown 1995:133)

Nevertheless, it is important to be clear about the boundaries of Brown's analysis. Firstly, she does specify that she is looking at contemporary identity claims in the context of the legal system of the United States. Yet, whilst appearing to avoid the trap of universalising the American experience, Brown nevertheless implies wider applicability through her reliance on general concepts developed by Nietzsche, Marx and Foucault. Secondly, her focus on liberal jurisprudence and the legal system means that other important parts of the story are left almost entirely unexplored. Most importantly here, there is no concrete analysis of movement activism at all. The motivations of social movement actors are simply inserted into her argument through her appeal to Nietzsche. Moreover, her focus on discursive construction leaves other dimensions of actors' agency at the stage door of the post-structuralist spectacle – tethered, as it is in her account, to the concept of *ressentiment*.

Yet Brown specifically opens up the possibility that the motivation for movement activism could be based on something other than *ressentiment*. She counterposes *ressentiment* to what she calls 'collective liberation through empowerment' and the possibility of 'self-affirming action'. But she apparently sees no sign of these. Indeed, she seems entirely oblivious to the fact that self-affirming action and understandings of collective liberation through empowerment are usually considered to be key aspects of the construction of collective identities in social movements (Della Porta and Diani 1999). If she was aware of these possibilities, she certainly chose to ignore them. Talking about her reading of identity politics early on in the book, she notes:

> ...identity politics concerned with race, sexuality, and gender will appear not as a supplement to class politics, not as an expansion of left categories of oppression and emancipation, not as an enriching augmentation of progressive formulations of power and persons – *all of which they also are* – but as tethered to a formulation of justice that reinscribes a bourgeois (masculinist) ideal as its measure. (Brown 1995:59, my emphasis)

But if they 'also are' what is the point of an analysis that not only entirely avoids any meaningful engagement with them but also goes on to cast serious doubt on the existence of such possibilities?

Wendy Brown's work is illustrative of a number of general problems found in some post-structuralist accounts of the relation between identity and human rights. Despite apparent intellectual sophistication, such accounts often re-introduce the very intellectual devices they criticise (for example, binary oppositions, homogenisation and essentialism) and are sometimes discursively structured towards assumptions of despair, impossibility and futility. Interestingly, this tendency towards pessimism is also a strong feature of structuralist Marxism (see Chapter 7; Stammers 1999b:74–5; Eschle and Stammers 2004:337–8).

Homogenising and Exclusionary Potentials

I have already looked at these potentials in the discussion of the liberalisation and nationalisation of natural rights in Chapter 4. Both the institutionalisation of supposedly universal natural rights into citizenship rights within particular jurisdictions homogenised 'the people' who were to benefit from citizenship rights whilst excluding all those not regarded as citizens. The issue of identities being essentialised and fixed in law is central and arguments around these sorts of questions come from a wide range of perspectives. For example, within early second wave feminism, 'black and third world feminists' (Eschle 2001:11–12) crucially challenged the construction of the category 'women' as privileging white, middle class, heterosexual women – both homogenising the category women into a particularly narrow form and effectively excluding the majority of women in the world (Eschle 2001; Dobrowolsky 2001:60).

In contemporary debates about human rights the importance of this issue is most clearly expressed in respect of cultural rights. Indeed, some argue that the very attempt to think about cultural rights tends to push advocates towards homogenised and essentialised view of identities and culture because, in many popular conceptions '...the group is defined by a singular and distinctive culture and that cultures are discreet, clearly bounded and internally homogenous, with relatively fixed meanings and values' (Cowan, Dembour and Wilson 2001:3). This, already essentialist, understanding is then accentuated if claims for cultural rights are instantiated in law because – in pursuit of generalisable principles – law tends to essentialise social categories and identities. Thus, Cowan, Dembour and Wilson argue that the essentialisation of culture is inherent in the making of claims for cultural rights. Unlike Wendy Brown, however, they recognise the field of law as complex, contested and fluid (Cowan, Dembour and Wilson 2001:6).

Adam Kuper (2003) goes further, suggesting that '[f]ostering essentialist ideologies of culture and identity may have dangerous political consequences' (Kuper 2003:25). He seeks to debunk what he sees as myths which inform campaigns for indigenous peoples' rights, arguing that the 'rhetoric of the indigenous peoples movement rests on widely accepted premises that are nevertheless open to serious challenge' (Kuper 2003:22) because they can feed into a dangerous exclusivity. He warns that 'a drift to racism may be inevitable where so-called cultural identity becomes the basis for rights' (Kuper 2003:24). Kuper's argument also clearly resonates with important elements of the debates about nationalism and self-determination in the human rights literature and as discussed in Chapters 3 and 4 above. Furthermore, if the idea of cultures as unities is a fantasy (Chanock 2002:41), then what should we make of demands for cultural rights? On the one hand, such demands are premised on defending particular practices and ways of life from the depredations of power, on the other, the institutionalisation of rights sediments constructions of culture and identities in ways that are often homogenising and exclusionary. So are there any ways to resolve these difficulties?

Strategic Essentialism?

One way through such dilemmas is to acknowledge explicitly that identities, cultures and law are all social constructions and, as such, are to some extent always contested, contestable and in flux. The reproduction of particular structures of identity and culture and law require social actors to reproduce them. They can also be transformed but that does not mean that 'anything goes' (see Chapter 1). Existing structures of identities, culture and law have a huge impact on the possibilities for reconstruction. In other words, rights institutionalised as law do, indeed, construct and sustain a degree of sedimentation. Yet, at the same time, that sedimentation is not 'fixity', it remains socially contingent. Law is not the 'timeless discourse' claimed by Wendy Brown.

There has been some interesting work which has explicitly looked at the strategic deployment of identities and the possibilities of utilising a 'partial, porous essentialism' in connection with rights struggles. Dobrowolsky (2001) analysed aboriginal women's struggles in Canada from the 1960s to the 1990s and – in contrast to the view that 'dominant rights discourses shape social movement pursuits and outcomes' (Dobrowolsky 2001:80) – found that more weight needs to be given to the potential of movement actors and their agency in constructing identities and right discourses. Aboriginal women's mobilisations show the promotion of a shared, albeit shifting, collective identity that emphasises commonality but is also open to difference. This does not mean complete formlessness but rather what Dobrowolsky sees as a contextual or strategic essentialism in which identity is related to context and allows activists to stress different aspects of identities according to the axis of oppression at issue in particular situations (Dobrowolsky 2001:81–2).[4]

Another interesting example is Mary Bernstein's (1997) analysis of the strategic uses of identity in lesbian and gay movements. While, in my view, Bernstein employs an overly mechanical model (to explain interactions between movement organisations, opposition to such movements and the role of state actors) she nevertheless suggests a tripartite division of identity that is helpful in terms of thinking about the relationship between collective identity in social movements and the role of identity in rights claims. She specifies identity:

- for *empowerment*, where activists must draw on an existing identity or construct a new collective identity in order to create and mobilise a constituency;

- as *goal*, where activists may challenge stigmatised identities, seek recognition for new identities, or deconstruct restrictive social categories as goals of their collective action;
- as *strategy* which can be deployed at the collective level as a political strategy aimed at cultural or instrumental goals. (Bernstein 1997:536–9)

All three of these ways of thinking about identity capture aspects of expressive activism and the last moves us well beyond the often assumed oppositional polarity between strategy and identity. But most importantly, such an approach to the social construction of identities stresses the point that identities are always 'in process' or 'becoming'.

So, perhaps, what is most interesting about the deployment of identities in rights claims is not so much the dangers of self-subjugation but, rather, what such claims tell us about the continuing persistence of oppressive relations and structures of power. So, for example, the significance of the continued use of the category 'women' is less that women may be imprisoning themselves in an oppressive discourse but rather more a reflection of the continuing oppression of the women around the world through the organisation of power around sex and gender. A praxis of strategic essentialism in relation to identity and rights seems able to capture the emancipatory potential of the use of the category 'women' without rejecting the claim that homogenisation and exclusion are often a consequence of the institutionalisation of identities through rights.

Clearly connected to this is the question of the immutability of law. While law can be claimed to be fixed and timeless, this claim is crucially inaccurate. Indeed, once we recognise that law is itself contestable, the arguments against embedding identities in law starts to look a lot weaker. Perhaps, therefore, we need to connect our understandings of oppression, identity and law in a different sort of way. Such an approach would both recognise that identities are sedimented by law but also that law itself is transformable within the broader potential fluidity of social relations in general. Such an approach would recognise that, ultimately, what fixes identities is not so much rights as law, but rather the extant relations and structures of power and the ways rights are institutionalised within those relations and structures. We are back to the paradox of institutionalisation.

From Identity to Recognition

The conceptual vehicle many theorists have settled on to make the necessary links between social struggles and identities is the concept of recognition. What is important about such work is the way in which recognition has also been related to human rights. So this section examines some elements of these debates, hopefully without disappearing entirely into the thickets of social and political theory.

Some Hegelian Perspectives in Brief

In 1984, Lewis Hinchman suggested some advantages of a Hegelian perspective on human rights compared with those of liberal political theory. He argued that it develops a more plausible account of the origin and meaning of rights than we find in the highly abstract and reductionist constructs of Hobbes and Locke. Moreover, he says, Hegel's account is entirely consistent with the notions of freedom and dignity which today plays so great a role in our common sense approach to rights. Hinchman noted that Hegel's philosophic project rested on the belief that we pursue knowledge, at least in part, to find out who we are (Hinchman 1984:18). Hegel's grounding of human rights is not, he says, to be found in the *Philosophy of Right* because this text already presupposes self-conscious persons who can recognise each other as selves (Hinchman 1984:19). Better, says Hinchman, to look in the *Phenomenology of Spirit* or *Philosophy of Mind* because the achievement of mutual recognition depends, crucially, on the possibility of transcending relations of power and domination. Although not a track pursued by Hinchman himself, this simple point is provocative. If we understand contemporary struggles for human rights as struggles for recognition, then one implication of this is that human society has not yet transcended the conditions of power and domination identified in Hegel's famous account of the master/slave relation. In other words, to think of struggles for human rights as struggles for recognition seems to demand not so much a focus on philosophy or law but on an analysis of contemporary configurations of power and an acknowledgement that, in many respects, these remain barbarous.

Belden Fields' (2001, 2003) recent work on rights and recognition supports this latter point and adds further developments from a broadly Hegelian perspective. Belden Fields argues that the core values of human rights emerge out of struggles against domination and these core values are liberty, equality and solidarity. Each of them, he says, requires social recognition which entails an important affective element. Thus, he argues:

> ...human rights require much more than an aggregation of citizens possessing merely formal/legal rights under positive law... it must also entail an affective element that permits individuals to express solidarity and empathy with others who are not members of the same political entity and who are not subject to the same positive law. This affective capacity, along with higher analytical and creative capacities, is part of what makes human beings unique amongst the species and is an essential part of what makes human rights possible and obligatory. (Belden Fields 2001:48)

In a not dissimilar vein, Costas Douzinas (2000) argues that the recognition implied by human rights goes much further than the respect and self-respect involved in ordinary legal rights. The fact that human rights have extended to new groups and expanded to novel areas of activity indicates, he argues, their deeply agonistic character. Thus recognition, he says, cannot be based on any universal characteristics of law, rather on continuous struggle (Douzinas 2000:287–8):

> Every new right-claim is a fighting response to dominant social and legal relations, at a particular place and time, a struggle against the injuries and harm they inflict; it aims to negate inadequate forms of recognition for individuals and groups and create more complete and nuanced types.

Human rights claims are, negatively, a reaction to the multiple offences and insults of power.... (Douzinas 2000:292–3)

None of these authors puts social movements at the centre of their analysis of human rights, but each of them links human rights to a struggle against oppressive power through the concept of recognition. Social movements come much closer to centre stage in a recent exchange between Nancy Fraser and Axel Honneth.

The Fraser–Honneth Exchange

Many of the issues central to this chapter were interrogated by Fraser and Honneth (2003) in *Redistribution or Recognition? A Political–Philosophical Exchange*. They both examine the relationships between interests, identity and recognition and their interconnections within the political, economic and cultural domains of the social. Both are also concerned with the role and impact of social movement struggles and the domains of justice and rights.

Both agree that recognition is crucial for any analysis of the contemporary era but that its relation to redistribution remains under-theorised. Redistribution, they say, was 'central to both the moral philosophies and the social struggles of the Fordist era' but 'struggles over religion, nationality, and gender are now inter-imbricated in ways that makes the question of recognition impossible to ignore' (Fraser and Honneth 2003:2). They argue that an adequate understanding of justice requires the relation between redistribution and recognition to be fully analysed and understood, but neither accepts the economistic reduction of recognition to a mere epiphenomenon of distribution. However, beyond these points, agreement ceases. Whereas Honneth understands recognition as the fundamental moral category within which issues of redistribution can be subsumed, Fraser rejects this subsumption, casting '... the two categories as co-fundamental and mutually irreducible dimensions of justice' (Fraser and Honneth 2003:3).

Several important aspects of Nancy Fraser's analysis are consistent with the approach taken here. She argues against explanations and interpretations of 'the social' rooted in binary polarities and rejects reductively economistic or culturalist analyses. Furthermore, she is concerned to identify forms of ideas and practices that can lead to substantive social transformation. Most interestingly, like Melucci and Cohen and Arato, she believes that social movements have a key role to play in processes of transformation.

She begins her analysis by arguing that many struggles over the last decades have been influenced by 'folk paradigms of justice'[5] through which redistribution became equated with class politics and recognition equated with identity politics. In contrast, she argues that '...virtually all real-world axes of subordination can be treated as two-dimensional' (Fraser and Honneth 2003:25) encompassing elements of both redistribution and recognition. Her account of contemporary capitalist society relies on a distinction between class and status. She argues that both of these terms denote socially entrenched orders of subordination (Fraser and Honneth 2003:48) locating class in the field of economic relations and status in the sphere of cultural relations. From there, Fraser then explicitly shifts the meaning of the term recognition away from self-realisation and self-identity (see below), reconceptualising it as a matter of justice in what she calls the 'status order' of society.

At the heart of her proposals to tackle injustice is the notion of participatory parity. She sees this as an evaluative standard, a norm which can straddle the dimensions of distribution and recognition and which can act as a standard for both warranting claims and evaluating proposed remedies for injustice (Fraser and Honneth 2003:37–8). In particular, Fraser argues that claims for recognition aim 'to deinstitutionalise patterns of cultural value that impede parity of participation and to replace them with patterns that foster it' (Fraser and Honneth 2003:30). This norm of participatory parity must, she says, be applied dialogically and discursively, through democratic processes of public debate (Fraser and Honneth 2003:43). To move in this direction she calls for a political strategy of 'non-reformist reform', combining attempts to reform existing structures with a more radical thrust of substantive transformation which attacks injustice at its roots (Fraser and Honneth 2003:72–82). Stressing that strategic questions have to be answered pragmatically – not via *a priori* assumptions laid down by philosophers and theoreticians – she argues that the task of developing an integrated strategy for change is a project for an emerging counter-hegemonic bloc of social movements (Fraser and Honneth 2003:86). While Fraser does not specifically deal with human rights, her entire project is focused on overcoming entrenched forms of oppression and subordination through movement struggles at the level of social praxis.

Axel Honneth combines criticisms of Fraser with his own proposals. Arguing that struggles around redistribution should be understood as a sub-species of struggles for recognition, he suggests '...subjects perceive institutional procedures as social injustice when they see aspects of their personality being disrespected which they believe have a right to recognition (Fraser and Honneth 2003:132). Recognition is of central importance today not, says Honneth, because it expresses the objectives or goals of the so-called NSMs, but because it has proved to be the appropriate tool for categorically unlocking the social experiences of injustice. He claims that a '...moral experience that can be meaningfully described as one of disrespect must be regarded as the motivational basis of all social conflicts' (Fraser and Honneth 2003:157). In contrast to Fraser's emphasis on the notion of parity of participation, Honneth argues 'the purpose of social equality is to enable the personal identity formation of all members of society... enabling individual self realisation' (Fraser and Honneth 2003:176). This, he says, constitutes the real aim of the equal treatment of all subjects.

Underlying his arguments is a specific historical claim about the development of what Honneth calls the capitalist recognition order and its differentiation into three social spheres: love, law and achievement. These spheres have been institutionalised within capitalist society and struggles for recognition comprise contestations around such institutionalisation. Within this formulation, rights are located in the sphere of law and Honneth argues that – in so far as law has to mediate in respect of the other spheres of recognition – any questioning of existing ways of life will lead to the conclusion that an expansion of individual rights is required, since the conditions for respect and autonomy cannot be adequately guaranteed under the normative principles of love or achievement (Fraser and Honneth 2003:189). For example, talking of the rise of workers' movements and the struggles for economic and social rights, Honneth argues:

> ...it was the modern legal order, with its inherent claim to equal treatment, that saw to it that the...appropriation of resources by structurally advantaged groups could be considered legitimate. But it was also precisely this principle of equal legal treatment that can be mobilised in countless social struggles... especially by the working class, to establish social rights... the emergence of the welfare state can perhaps best be understood as the penetration of the principle of equal legal treatment into the previously autonomous sphere of social esteem. (Fraser and Honneth 2003:149)

Honneth's emphasis on long-term historical development makes him critical of Fraser's argument that there has been a significant shift in the nature of social struggles, from a focus on interests to a focus on identities. In contrast, he asserts a continuity of focus on both interests and identity once translated into his spheres of recognition. He notes that the desire for recognition had already marked the social protests in emerging forms of capitalist society and that historians such as E.P. Thompson have shown that, in terms of motivational sources for resistance and protest, peoples' experience of the violation of their understandings of honour was often of much more importance than material interests (Fraser and Honneth 2003:131). More generally, Honneth argues that '[t]he moral vocabulary in which 19th century workers, groups of emancipated women at the beginning of the 20th century, and African Americans in big US cities in the 1920s articulated their protests was tailored to registering social humiliation and disrespect' (Fraser and Honneth 2003:135). Honneth accuses Fraser of introducing a potentially theoretically unbridgeable chasm between symbolic and material aspects of social reality, arguing that through the lens of his theory of recognition, the relation between the two can be seen as the historically mutable result of cultural processes of institutionalisation. Furthermore, he implies Fraser has made these errors because she has idealised the struggles of the so-called NSMs.[6]

I have dwelt on the work of Fraser and Honneth because each of them identifies issues and forms of analysis that are crucial to understanding the relationship between human rights and social movements. The emphasis given to recognition is an important corrective to the previously strong disciplinary and ideological tendencies to focus on material interests. But more importantly, both stress the necessity of transforming norms and values embedded *within* existing institutional structures if meaningful and substantive social change is to be achieved. Fraser's emphasis on the role of social movement struggles is clearly germane, as is Honneth's emphasis on historical continuity in struggles for recognition.

Yet, at the same time, there are elements in their respective contributions which are very much at odds with the approach taken here. Despite her argument that subordination almost always involves issues around both redistribution and recognition, Fraser does come close to re-introducing the binary separation between interests and identities at another level when she seems to argue that redistribution is an economic issue and recognition a cultural issue. Moreover, Honneth is right in suggesting that Fraser's argument relies too much on a separation between old and new forms of struggle. That said, despite his emphasis on historical continuity, Honneth's apparently individualistic re-formulation of the concept of recognition leaves little space for grasping the importance of collective and solidaristic social movement action as contributing to transformative social change that was such a feature of his earlier work.[7]

The Expressive/Instrumental Dynamic

So what are the advantages of switching to a terminology of expressive and instrumental dimensions of movement activism?

What does this terminology capture or explain that is not adequately captured or explained by looking at activism in terms of interests, identities or recognition or some combination of them? There are several points to consider.

The first is that it allows us to incorporate the possibility of altruistic, 'other-centred' movement activism. Most of the arguments examined in this chapter share an assumption that movement activism is focused on the needs or desires of an individual or collective actor, on an 'I' or a 'we'. Analyses that rely on the categories of interests, identity and recognition therefore effectively preclude the possibility of explaining solidarity with an 'other'. One exception discussed above was Belden Fields who emphasised 'social recognition' that entails an empathetic and solidaristic element extending to others beyond a 'we the people' of a particular polity (Belden Fields 2003:86–90). In social movement studies, Melucci has specifically discussed altruistic activism (Melucci 1996:166–70) and other analysts have argued that the expressive dimensions of social movement activism typically have an outwardly directed aspect, an aspect which proposes alternative norms, values and ways of being and living in the world. While such alternatives are not always proffered in a spirit of empathy or solidarity, the possibility that they can be should not be ignored. Put another way, the possibility that 'universal' understandings of human rights in historical movement struggles have contained an orientation of empathy and solidarity with 'the other' should certainly not be lost because of terminological inadequacy.

The second key point is that the usage of 'expressive' and 'instrumental' allows us to incorporate the strategic aspect of movement activism so that means/ends relations can potentially be examined as they should be, not simply as abstract principles but as real social relations and processes. Analyses that rely on the categorisations of interests, identity and recognition tend to preclude this possibility by focusing largely on the 'ends' of interests, identity and recognition, often assuming the relationship between means and ends is unproblematic. There is a clear connection here with what, in Chapter 4, I called 'the organisational question' and the general lack of attention it receives. As far as human rights are concerned, we can again point to the disciplinary and ideological proclivities in the human rights literature. So, for example, debates in political philosophy and political theory are overwhelmingly concerned with 'ends'. Means, strategy and tactics are simply not their domain. In fact, the problem goes much wider. Studies of social movements also sometimes ignore 'means'. For example, Manuel Castells (1997:69–71), drawing directly from the work of Alain Touraine, uses a framework for examining social movements which categorises them in terms of identity, adversary and goals. 'Ends' here are most clearly represented in terms of the goals of the movement. But there is no obvious conceptual space for exploring 'means' as a fundamental aspect of movement activism. So, the usage of expressive and instrumental dimensions provides the conceptual space within which the impact of organisation and strategy can be added into the mix. In my view, this provides a much more useful framework through which the link between social movements and human rights can be analysed because it incorporates a way of analysing the 'organisational question' and the paradox of institutionalisation.

This brings me to the third point. The tendency to separate interests and identities into a binary polarity is so strong in the existing literature that it is almost impossible to use these terms without implying that polarity. True the distinction between 'expressive' and 'instrumental' still contains moments of separation and difference, but the fact that these terms are introduced here as being in dynamic interaction offers the possibility that recognition of this dynamism can be retained at the heart of their meaning. But then the question arises as to what further work can be done to elaborate this dynamism? This is especially important if questions of means and strategy are to be taken seriously. For example, is instrumental activism better focused towards the institutional world and expressive activism better oriented towards the everyday world? Is it the case that, strategically, instrumental activism is likely to be most useful in terms of transforming aspects of the institutional world whilst expressive activism is likely to be most useful with respect to seeking to transform norms, values and ways of living and being in everyday worlds? These are big questions which, as Fraser argues, simply cannot be answered abstractly, in an *a priori* way by philosophers and theorists. But we can now at least pose them as questions. Potentially, they fundamentally shift ways of thinking about the relationship between social movement struggles and human rights. Certainly, this dynamic framework disrupts the usual assumption that instrumental activism is solely about means and expressive activism solely about ends. When social movements make concrete demands in respect of human rights claims, they straddle instrumental and value-rational action in the Weberian senses discussed above. In other words, substantive claims in respect of norms, values and ways of living/ being in everyday worlds are necessarily embedded in such claims. Similarly, as we saw above, expressive forms of activism can also have important strategic dimensions.

In work with Catherine Eschle (Eschle and Stammers 2004; Stammers and Eschle 2005), we have argued that – in the contemporary world – the instrumental demands of social movements are potentially strengthened by the instrumental activism of 'their' more formally structured movement organisations engaged in the institutional world. Conversely, the expressive dimensions of activism by social movement organisations are potentially strengthened by their articulation through the informal social movement networks into the everyday world, potentially connecting to and stimulating more diffuse, long-term shifts in public cultures and social processes (see also Figure 1.3 in Chapter 1).

Finally, it is important to stress that this expressive/instrumental dynamic has long historical and wide geographical application. As we have seen, most of the debates examined in this and the previous chapters have assumed a fundamental shift from old to new, from interests to identity. But, because my understanding of the relation between the expressive and the instrumental is dynamic, we are able to see it as both historically continuous whilst – at the same time – being differently configured in different trans-historical and trans-cultural settings.

Conclusion

A central argument of this book is that an important originating source of human rights is to be found in social movement struggles against power. This chapter has explored this in detail in terms of what I have called the expressive/instrumental dynamic of movement activism. It is within the crucible of this dynamic that key ideas and practices of human rights have been socially constructed. This, by itself, demonstrates the crucial relevance of the pre-legal 'moment' of creativity and construction of human rights. But attention to this dynamic also illustrates the continuing importance of non-legal dimensions of human rights not only in terms of further creativity and construction around norms, values and ways of living and being in the world but also in terms of the concrete social demands of social movements and the strategies they deploy to achieve them.

This chapter has also raised important questions around the extent to which rights claims can be understood as a form of 'strategic essentialism', a proposal that identities are always in the process of 'becoming', and an argument that law is neither timeless nor immutable but rather subject to contestation and transformation. So, while law certainly sediments identities, inclusions, exclusions and concepts, this sedimentation should never be understood as 'fixity', as historically permanent. The content and structure of my discussion has also tried to situate my overall analysis of the link between social movements and human rights in terms of some key examples of recent intellectual debates. In particular, my discussion of Wendy Brown's work and the exchange between Nancy Fraser and Axel Honneth indicates the relevance of my analysis to central contemporary debates within social and political theory. One key issue which has been bubbling through the last two chapters is the extent to which we are living in a substantively 'new' world. For much of the last two decades this possibility has been examined through the concept of globalisation. So the next chapter will examine analyses of human rights and social movements in the context of globalisation.

7

ANALYSES OF GLOBALISATION AND HUMAN RIGHTS

This chapter brings us to contemporary history so we are necessarily looking at a moving target. We can nevertheless identify significant continuities with key themes developed throughout this volume. Indeed, through the understanding of globalisation employed here, the history of human rights itself can be seen as an aspect of much longer-term globalising trajectories. That human rights are intimately tied up with recent forms of globalisation is widely accepted but the nature of that link and how it should be interpreted is a matter of deep dispute. One key issue is how to interpret and analyse the evidence that contemporary social movements all around the world are constructing, reconstructing and deploying claims to human rights in order to challenge a wide variety of forms and spatial configurations of power (see for example, Rajagopal 2003; Kabeer 2005; Newell and Wheeler 2006; Ackerly 2008). Is it possible that contemporary social movements are uniquely placed to expose the complexities of relations and structures of global power when compared to the structures of institutionalised politics? Some commentators seem to think so, arguing that we are witnessing the emergence of a 'movement of movements' through which challenges to power are being connected in significantly new ways. Could it even be the case that Nancy Fraser's 'counter-hegemonic bloc of social movements' referred to in the last chapter is in the process of construction?

Not so according to other commentators, many of who appear to remain in the thrall of my metaphorical mirrors. Key proponents of human rights continue to privilege the importance of civil and political rights, and many more focus on the key role of elite actors – including actors in large (I)NGOs – developing the human rights agenda in a purely institutionalised direction, with an emphasis on the construction of international law and the role of state duties.[1] On the other hand, critics often condemn the efforts of social movements and (I)NGOs to progress a human rights agenda on the interconnected grounds that engagement with the institutional world cannot bring about positive social change and that human rights can only serve to sustain existing relations and structures of power. Between the utopian optimism of some human rights activists and the deep pessimism of many critics lie a series of largely unexamined issues and questions posed by, and implicated in, the paradox of institutionalisation discussed in Chapter 4.

This chapter looks at these various issues through the lens of globalisation. The first section therefore briefly explores relevant issues in debates about globalisation. The second then looks at the relationship between human rights and globalisation, offering brief historical reflection before engaging with the arguments of both optimists and pessimists. The final section examines the rise of the so-called 'movement of movements', looking at the use of human rights in this latest wave of activism and how these developments have been conceptualised.

On Globalisation

It is not the purpose of this section to try to settle the many arguments about globalisation (see Held et al. 1999; Rosenberg 2000, 2005; Cox 2005). But it is important to locate the key lines of debate around this question and to identify the orientation adopted here. I agree with Held et. al. (1999) that the most helpful way of starting to assess these debates is to distinguish between those arguments which claim that globalisation has a monocausal origin and is a unidirectional set of processes and those which claim that globalisation has multicausal origins and is a multi-directional set of processes. These sorts of arguments also connect directly to: how one understands and analyses power; the so-called 'agency-structure problem', and the nature of 'the social'; all of which were discussed in Chapter 1.

Typical of the arguments based on monocausal origin and unidirectional processes are those of neo-liberals and some Marxists who see globalisation as structurally driven by economic or technological imperatives and by those (from a variety of disciplinary and ideological positions) who understand cultural forms of globalisation to be homogenising, usually assuming this to mean the imposition of 'western values' all around the world. Such processes are celebrated or denounced depending on the stance of commentator, but that is not the point here. Rather, it is to contrast these types of arguments with those which understand globalisation processes having multicausal origins and multidirectional effects.

Multicausal accounts recognise the complex historical interplay between economic, political and cultural factors in shaping globalisation and also recognise that effects can be equally complex and contradictory. Thus, for example, cultural forms of globalisation are typically seen as both homogenising and fragmenting in highly complex ways. One cultural theorist, Roland Robertson, has argued that contemporary globalisation needs to be understood as 'the universalisation of particularity and the particularisation of universality' (Robertson 1992:100) which – ugly as it may be – has a special relevance to the key debates in the human rights literature around 'universal' and 'particular'. Multicausal analyses suggest that globalisation processes should be understood as the intensification of interconnectedness and the stretching and deepening of social relations around the world, with impacts and outcomes that are uneven, complex and unpredictable. Nevertheless, such accounts also typically hold that globalisation processes are leading to substantive social change. Thus such accounts are often described as 'transformationalist' (see Held et al. 1999:7–10). It is important to stress that, in contrast to most monocausal/unidirectional explanations, multi-causal/multidirectional accounts do not ontologically privilege a particular domain of the social, nor do they assume that 'power over' is simply reproduced through time. Critics often argue that such accounts fail to grasp the deep asymmetries of power in the world. But, in my view, this argument is misplaced. Indeed, such accounts of globalisation are usually particularly careful to explain that complex interactions are necessarily suffused with power. What they do not assume is how that power 'cashes out' in the complexity of any particular historical or spatial conjuncture. It should be clear that such transformationalist explanations of globalisation are consistent with my broader theoretical approach (see Chapter 1).

Two other specific issues in the globalisation debate need to be noted here because of the potential impact on human rights praxis. The first of these is the extent to which globalisation is a new phenomena and represents an epochal shift in social relations. Associated debates and questions were examined in the last two chapters and here, again, I would argue that it is important that we do not overemphasise the importance of discontinuity to the extent that we cannot also see historical continuity. Held et al. have argued that social processes with globalising trajectories have an historical provenance stretching back before the 'modern era' (Held et. al. 1999:414–24) and the implications of this point will be examined in a moment. Yet at the same time, the acceleration of globalisation since the end of the Second World War appears to be resulting in substantive and qualitative shifts in social relations – cultural, political and economic. So, the second specific issue is the extent to which globalisation may be transforming the nature and capacities of nation states around the world. Given that the nation state has been typically seen as the principal duty bearer in respect of human rights, any such shifts would clearly have major implications, not least the extent to which anyone could rely on the international human rights institutions being able to take on duties to protect human rights effectively.

Human Rights as Globalisation

The history of human rights depicted in this volume begins in a period classified by Held et al. as 'Early Modern Globalisation', lasting from about 1500 to 1850. Held et al. make no reference to the rise of natural rights except in so far as they mention the 'first national revolutions' in North America and France. While this period of history corresponds to the emergence and rise of 'European modernity', the authors are careful not to suggest that the two are synonymous (Held et al. 1999:414–36).

In the context of the understanding of globalisation set out above, it is clear that the historical development of natural and human rights discussed in previous chapters can be understood as aspects of globalising processes. But the translations and reconstructions of natural rights in struggles against slavery and colonialism discussed in Chapters 2 and 3 also make clear the importance of distinguishing between dominant forms of European power on the one hand and the history of human rights on the other. For example, although Linebaugh and Rideker (2000) use the term globalisation to mean 'globalisation from above', their work is all about examining the network linkages of 'struggles from below'. In particular, their chapter on *'The Divarication of the Putney Debates'* takes us from London in the 1640s to Naples, Ireland, Barbados, the River Gambia and Virginia in the period up to 1776, then to nineteenth-century debates in Germany on the future of Marxism and social democracy and, finally, to the Pan African Congress in Manchester in 1945. The authors say that among the delegates to this latter gathering were students of the Putney Debates, '…who saw their significance within a history of the struggle against slavery and empire' (Linebaugh and Rideker 2000:108). Indeed, Linebaugh and Rideker conclude their work by arguing that '[t]he globalizing powers have a long reach and endless patience. Yet the planetary wanderers do not forget, and they are ever ready from Africa to the Caribbean to Seattle to resist slavery and restore the commons' (Linebaugh and Rideker 2000:353). In their view, it is those planetary wanderers who – historically – have been the key disseminators of understandings of natural and human rights in what many today would describe as 'globalisation from below'.

In *Colonialism in Question,* Fredrick Cooper takes a similar sort of stance. He assumes globalisation to be a linear concept which both claims 'newness of that which is not new at all' and exhibits the same deep ethnocentrism as the concepts of modernity and modernisation (Cooper 2005:10). Yet, he too wants to rescue an appreciation of historical agency 'from below' from both orthodox Eurocentric historiography and what he sees as the excesses of some post-colonial theory. With regard to the latter he argues:

> ... resistance might be celebrated or subaltern agency applauded, but the idea that struggle actually had effects on the course of colonisation is lost in the timelessness of colonial modernity. The Haitian revolution – and especially the possibility that the Haitian revolution actually affected the meanings of citizenship or freedom in Europe and the Americas – is as strikingly absent in prominent postcolonial texts as in conventional narratives of European progress. The result is the ownership of notions like human rights and citizenship is conceded to Europe – only to be subjected to ironic dismissal for their association with European imperialism. (Cooper 2005:16)

Like Linebaugh and Rideker, he argues that human rights are a product of struggle, reflecting the labours of '...unnamed ex slaves, dependent labourers, and colonised peasants who revealed the limits of colonial power and defined alternative modes of living and working in the crevices of authority' (Cooper 2005:21). Again, this is an historical account of what many today would call 'globalisation from below'.

Contemporary Globalisation and International Human Rights

Critics and proponents of both contemporary globalisation and contemporary international human rights certainly agree that the latter is deeply implicated in the former. Indeed, if it is accepted that an accelerated phase of globalisation began around 1945 then, at the very least, the establishment of the international human rights system positively correlates with that. Moreover, as has already been discussed in previous chapters, the international human rights system has become a focus for a wide range of social action, whether as state and inter-state practices or the activism of

(I)NGOs and social movements. Proponents and critics of human rights also usually share a view of the globalising aspects of human rights in terms of universalisation. For proponents this is a positive development, for critics a negative one. But, beyond this simplistic and unhelpful dichotomy, more complex areas and issues can be identified. Although the construction of international human rights law has been an elite-driven and highly institutionalised process, it has nevertheless – as I argued in Chapter 4 – created some sort of 'concrete universal' of human rights which, despite its limitations, is open to challenge, contestation and transformation.

Even if it is clear that human rights are an important aspect of globalisation, that does not mean that other aspects of globalisation sit easily with, or support, human rights. Whilst noting that human rights appears to have acquired the status of a global ideology, Tony McGrew suggests that contemporary globalisation is associated with a set of growing disjunctions between the global diffusion of human rights and the social, political and economic conditions necessary for their effective realisation (McGrew 1998:194). Indeed, he argues that wider processes of globalisation present a number of important challenges to human rights including the fact that existing asymmetries of power in the global politics of rights means that the human rights system is all too likely to reflect western interests. He also points to a major contradiction between, on the one hand, the flows and connections of contemporary mobilisation and activism around human rights by social movements and (I)NGOs and, on the other, the orthodox normative discourse of human rights, largely couched in the language of an international society of states.

This ambiguity and complexity is also identified by Richard Wilson (1997) although in a somewhat different register. He suggests that arguments against human rights from cultural relativists are being increasingly undermined by the globalisation of cultural, economic and political processes. Referring to the key role of global networks of human rights activism in disseminating human rights praxis, he argues that nearly all the world's people now live in an environment of legal pluralism through the sustained interaction between local, national and transnational legal norms. Thus, he says, globalisation cannot simply mean the same thing as westernisation and, therefore, '[t]he universality of human rights (or otherwise) thus becomes a question of context, necessitating a situational analysis' (Wilson 1997:12).

The emphasis by McGrew and Wilson on the key role of social movements and (I)NGO activism relates to a substantive change over the last 60 years when compared to the first half of the twentieth century. Even if NGO actors were influential in the originating discussions and debates that led to the drafting of the UN Charter and the Universal Declaration of Human Rights (see Chapter 4) the overall number of NGOs involved was tiny. Since then, there has been a veritable explosion of a range of social activism around human rights. One (albeit very inadequate) indicator of this is the number of NGOs granted consultative status with the UN Economic and Social Council. This stood at 41 in 1948, had risen to nearly 500 by 1968 and, by 1992, had risen to over 1000 (Korey 1998:2). There are at least many hundreds of movements, associations, and (I)NGOs worldwide whose activism is oriented to, or by, human rights. Jackie Smith argues that human rights 'remains the major issue around which the largest number of TSMOs [transnational social movement organisations]...organize, and a consistent quarter of all groups work principally on this issue' (cited in Tarrow 2005). Yet Keck and Sikkink make the point that '...as recently as 1970, the idea that the human rights of citizens of any country are legitimately the concern of people and governments everywhere was considered radical' (Keck and Sikkink 1998:79). But whilst this explosion of activism around human rights tells us something, it is far from obvious what that something is.

Firstly, we need to be aware of the connections and differences between (I)NGOs and social movements. A major problem in much of the literature is that social movements are conceptually conflated with (I)NGOs (Stammers and Eschle 2005:50–52). This is of considerable importance especially since so many critics believe (I)NGOs are necessarily incorporated into existing structures of power, losing any emancipatory potential they may have once had. Then we need to think about how different forms of activism may be interlinked. In particular, we need to consider how movement activism in the 'everyday world' might be either supported or threatened by (I)NGO activism in the 'institutionalised world' and vice versa.

A bulletin of the UN Non-Governmental Liaison Service of 1998 neatly illustrates the potential connections. The bulletin notes '…a growing perception that economic and social rights are increasingly being eroded by the momentous disruptions brought about by economic globalization' (UN Non-Governmental Liaison Service 1998:1). Reporting on various meetings and seminars, the bulletin notes that globalisation is associated with rising income inequalities and that 'top-down' forces often call for liberalisation policies which favour powerful private economic interests and account for many of the negative features of globalisation. It says there is a need to ensure that key transnational actors, including the international financial institutions and transnational corporations, fulfil their duties with respect to all human rights. In discussing how this might be achieved, a special rapporteur to the human rights sub-commission is cited as contrasting 'top-down' approaches with 'bottom-up' forces of globalisation: 'These [latter] forces, he said, are 'globalising social aspirations and human rights standards' and fostering global alliances of civil society groups across different sectors, which are demanding changes in national, regional and global economic institutions and processes' (UN Non-Governmental Liaison Service 1998:4).

At the human rights sub-commission in 1998, many NGO interventions had apparently raised the issue of the then proposed Multilateral Agreement on Investment (MAI). The sub commission's resolution acknowledged the '…widespread protests by civil society against the agreement' and stated the sub commission was:

> …concerned about the possible human rights implications of the [MAI] and particularly about the extent to which the Agreement might limit the capacity of States to take proactive steps to ensure the enjoyment of economic social and cultural rights by all people, creating benefits for

a small privileged minority at the expense of increasingly disenfranchised majority. (UN Non-Governmental Liaison Service, 1998:5)

We will probably never know the extent to which an effective linkage between movement activism in the everyday world and (I)NGO activism in the institutional world helped to scupper the MAI, but these sorts of linkages deserve much more attention than they usually receive. I come back to this issue in Chapter 8.

The contrast between 'top-down' and 'bottom-up' approaches is often also described in terms of globalisation from above (hereafter GA) and globalisation from below (hereafter GB). The origins of this distinction may lie in the early work of Richard Falk (for example, Falk 1987) and it is certainly helpful in terms of transcending the limits of monocausal and unidirectional accounts of globalisation. Most importantly, it recognises that social activism outside of the main spheres of institutionalised structures of power can both have agency and articulate an agenda which has a globalising trajectory.

Human rights as GA and GB were specifically analysed by Nikhil Aziz in an interesting and early contribution to debates about recent globalisation and the connection to human rights (Aziz 1995). He argues that these two aspects of globalisation stand in a dialectical relationship to one another but, whereas GA can be understood as homogenising and hegemonic in trajectory and intent, GB is inherently pluralistic and 'non hegemonic'. Aziz identifies political, economic and cultural dimensions of GA and GB and, with respect to the latter, argues that it is manifested in the form of a variety of transnational social movements that have wide-ranging concerns grounded in a notion of human community based on unity in diversity. He argues that these worldwide movements organised around such issues as the 'environment, human rights, women's issues, peace and justice, universal literacy and liberation from oppression' are similar to earlier socialist and communist movements in so far as their concern is with the elimination of political, economic and social inequalities. He continues:

Globalisation from below thrives on diversity and promotes the spread of power through grassroots transnational alliances, networks and coalitions...

Globalisation from below involves mass participatory democracy and grass-roots movements open to and searching for new political visions and alternative forms of governance and development. (Aziz 1995:13)

Much of this sounds familiar. Aziz's account here closely parallels accounts of the so-called New Social Movements, especially when he argues that the methods and strategies of these movements are distinct from socialist and communist movements because they seek a non-violent as opposed to violent revolution and generally abjure power in the sense of not seeking to seize control of the state (Aziz 1995:12).

Aziz argues human rights are an integral part of globalisation. In the case of GA, human rights become another weapon in the arsenal of western countries in the efforts to bring recalcitrant Third World nations to heel. In contrast, GB implies an expanded and open understanding of human rights and offers the possibility of a unified focus for social movement struggles. Calling for a dialogue between western intellectual traditions and those from other cultural and religious frameworks, Aziz sees the possibility of human rights being reconstructed so as to make them much more genuinely universal and able to challenge multiple forms of power and domination. For Aziz this clearly includes the relations and structures of power embedded within Third World societies, for example, patriarchal power. But he makes the important point that a critique of such power needs to come from within such cultures, not be imposed from the outside. Although the contrast between GA and GB is an advance on monocausal and unidirectional accounts of globalisation, the nature of the relationship between them remains unclear. Aziz's claim that GA and GB stand in a dialectical relationship requires development and explanation. Without these, his advocacy of GB is too uncritical and utopian (see Eschle and Stammers 2004:338–9).

Certainly grasping the complexities of the relation between GA and GB is no easy task but one clear link would be via the paradox of institutionalisation discussed in Chapter 4. At the same time, as Aziz and many others have made clear, there is persistent and substantive evidence that powerful western states use human rights as instruments of their foreign policy (for example, Bartholomew 2006) and convincing analyses of how human rights have been used to sustain the interests of corporate capital and operate culturally as a form of western imperialism.[2] Unfortunately, many critics conclude from this latter evidence that there is no complexity to analyse. They assume that any and all attempts to engage with the existing international system are doomed to failure.

Critics of Contemporary Activism

Transnational Struggles: 'Resistance Is Futile'

In *Global Civil Society and its Limits,* Laxer and Halperin specifically argue that '...global social movements cannot be the main vehicle for the achievement of human rights' (Laxer and Halperin 2003:15) and, more generally, they reject suggestions that transnational activism can have any significant transformative potential. They argue that proponents of GB have been effectively seduced by an ideological campaign which they call 'globalism', the purpose of which is to facilitate the further globalisation of capital. They claim that, through buying into aspects of this ideology, many who oppose corporate globalisation inadvertently help to promote it and that 'the chimera of global civil society drags such struggles on to the enemies' ground, where opposition forces cannot compete'. In other words, at the global level, the balance of forces is weighed so heavily in favour of existing relations and structures of power that transnational activism is doomed to fail. Their proposed solution is 'reinvigorated national challenges at the level of the state and the citizen-people', a return to nationally based and nationally oriented struggles. While recognising the importance of transnational solidarity, they argue that 'the mobilizations, mass participation, the focus and the framing of issues must be primarily national and local' (Laxer and Halperin 2003:2)

In a not dissimilar vein, though in the context of discussing the dominance of neo-liberal versions of human rights, Tony

Evans recognises that movements are being organised to resist further globalisation in many regions of the world. But he warns that optimistic analyses of the transformative capacity of social movements are 'failing to take full account of the social and economic power of capital'. Thus, he argues, optimistic radicals offer 'a distorted view of the emancipatory possibilities associated with transnational associational movements' (Evans 2001:425). He concludes:

> ...the protection of human rights, particularly economic and social rights, cannot be achieved through mechanisms associated with state, international law, and the idea of the international citizen [and that] civil society reflects the narrow self-interest of those in a structural position to take full advantage of the conditions of globalisation, to the exclusion of the many. (Evans 2001:431)

This persistent theme – that transnational resistance is futile – is usually underpinned by assumptions derived from reductionist Marxism, even though sometimes presented in post-modernist garb. Such assumptions come in a variety of guises: about the nature of civil society; about the nature of rights; about the nature of contemporary social movements and the nature of (I)NGOs. They are often linked together to build what the authors consider to be a damning critique.

A good example of this process at work is to be found in Pasha and Blaney's (1998) influential paper, 'Elusive Paradise: the promise and peril of global civil society'. They begin by arguing, quite rightly, that it is crucial to acknowledge the contradictory features of associational life to be found in 'global civil society'. They note associational life contains fundamental inequalities as well as movements to redress inequality and, beyond that, a range of seemingly incommensurable identities and values. Without dismissing the possibility that 'transnational associational life' could hold some potential as a force for global democratisation, the bulk of their argument takes on a deeply pessimistic tone. It is their underlying assumptions that drive that pessimism. On the nature of (global) civil society, they simply reassert the view that the anatomy of civil society is to be found in political economy, entirely ignoring any evidence or arguments that there might be rather more to it than that. They claim that '[t]he norms of behaviour demanded of members of civil society are dedicated to preserving this economic, cultural and ideological marketplace' (Pasha and Blaney 1998:423). While this is indeed what is often demanded of groups seeking connections and engagement with the institutional world, they take no account of any radical activism which explicitly seeks to subvert such a marketplace. Social movements are portrayed and dismissed as largely 'middle class' and 'post-industrial' (Pasha and Blaney 1998:422). No mention is made of any grassroots movements from the global south and no assessment is made of, for example, the Zapatistas or any other radical movements. Their argument about rights displays a similar narrow lineage. They argue that rights *constitute* members of societies as individuals: stabilising and sustaining social practices supportive of such individuality largely on the basis of 'exchange and contracts in the market' (Pasha and Blaney 1998:421). Neither associational or collective rights, nor economic and social rights – not to mention historical struggles for these – are acknowledged as meaningful or significant.

NGOs in the Service of Imperialism?

The above examples are unusual in that they explicitly focus on movement activism. The vast bulk of the critical literature targets (I)NGOs, stressing the dangers and realities of co-option, assimilation and bureaucratisation. Although often producing highly negative assessments, much of this literature nevertheless gives the benefit of the doubt to (I)NGO actors, in so far as it depicts them as unwitting villains or victims in these processes. For example, in a chapter entitled 'Human Rights: The Trojan Horse of Recolonization', Esteva and Prakash argue that the latest breed of 'developers and globalisers' are the new promoters of human rights who encourage local populations to challenge local and customary authorities. Thus, '...it comes to pass, more and more, that under the benign banner of human rights, indigenous and other non-modern communities suffer unprecedented forms of repression, of suffering and power abuses' (Esteva and Prakash 1998:114). They argue that, '[e]ven with the best intentions of preventing power abuses, global quests to universalise human rights are counter-productive' (Esteva and Prakash 1998:137). In other words, while attempting to protect people from one kind of abuse, (I)NGOs perpetuate another kind: a cultural domination that is unprecedented in its destruction of what they call the human pluriverse, with its diverse interpretations and understandings of what constitutes 'the good life' in communal and cultural terms. Condemning each of the twelve points of the platform of the 1995 Beijing Women's Conference as signifying cultural imperialism (Esteva and Prakash 1998:117–19) they offer what they claim to be a Gandhian understanding of 'liberation without modern states or human rights' (Esteva and Prakash 1998:114).

Esteva and Prakash certainly raise a range of important questions and critiques of human rights as they are currently institutionalised. But a closer look at their arguments reveals their conception of human rights to be a very limited and traditional one. As noted in Chapter 2, they assume that human rights are bourgeois rights, solely the rights of possessive individuals that emerged with the rise of capitalism in the west. There is no reference to workers' rights or collective rights, nor to the use of rights discourses by anti-imperialist movements and indigenous peoples' movements around the world. But that said, even Esteva and Prakash do not entirely reject the possibility that human rights could be reconstructed so as to serve a more positive purpose, nor do they directly challenge the conscious motives of the many tens of thousands of people around the world working for a vast range of (I)NGOs. Not everyone is so generous.

In a vitriolic polemic, Petras and Veltmeyer (2001) not only depict (I)NGOs as being in the service of imperialism but also claim local (I)NGO leaders are little more than self-serving parasites living off the backs of the poor: 'NGO leaders can be conceived of as a kind of neo-comprador groups...trading in domestic poverty for individual perks' (Petras and Veltmeyer 2001:129). In structural terms, the authors argue, '...the proliferation of NGOs reflects the emergence of a new petit bourgeoisie...' and that globalist rhetoric '...provides a cover for a kind of ersatz "internationalism" devoid of anti-imperialist commitments. In short, this new petite bourgeoisie forms the "radical wing" of the neo-liberal establishment' (Petras and Veltmeyer 2001:138). These sorts of claims are altogether too crude and simplistic, but even these authors still pose questions that should not be ignored. For example, one of their sub-headings 'NGO Structure: Internally Elitist and Externally Servile' (Petras and Veltmeyer 2001:132) pithily points to real problems in what I called 'the institution-alisation of activism' (see Chapter 4). Particularly important in this respect is their connected argument that the activities of large western (I)NGOs have destroyed and displaced organised leftist movements in the south by co-opting their intellectual strategists and organisational leaders (Petras and Veltmeyer 2001:132–3). I would argue that, here, we are back to the wider implications of the paradox of institutionalisation and how we should understand relations and structures of power in the world today.

To sum up this section, there are a wide range of important critiques which identify many aspects of human rights praxis as being deeply problematic in the context of processes of accelerated globalisation. These include matters of fundamental political, economic and cultural concern, all of which bring us back to the extent to which human rights can serve to sustain extant relations and structures of power. None of these, I would suggest, should be dismissed out of hand. Yet many of these critiques rely on narrow and impoverished understandings of human rights. Reductionist accounts of rights attached to, or constituting, western 'egoistic man' pursuing his own self interest are linked to an equally reductionist account of (global) civil society whose anatomy is said to be found in political economy. Even when these accounts avoid rejecting human rights altogether, they overwhelmingly emphasise their negative dimensions. But not all contemporary radicals, Marxist or otherwise, do this. So let me now turn to look at some examples of contemporary social movement activism and some quite different sorts of accounts of the relationship between human rights and globalisation.

The Rise of a 'Movement of Movements'?

It would be impossible in the confines of this chapter to give even a summary account of the way in which understandings of human rights are used by social movements all around the world today (for some broader coverage see O'Brian et al. 2000; Rowbotham and Linkogle 2001; Edwards and Gaventa 2001; Cowan et al. 2001; Rajagopal 2003; Kabeer 2005; Tarrow 2005; Newell and Wheeler 2006). Instead, I focus on this specific topic partly because it has stimulated animated debate but also because – if it were the case that a counter hegemonic bloc of social movements is emerging – then the human rights praxis of this movement of movements will be of fundamental importance to the strategic direction of these movements and to their chances of achieving substantive and transformative social change.

The Contemporary Constellation of Critical Social Movements

Prior to the 'Battle of Seattle' in 1999, virtually all scholarship which commented on the relationship between social movements, globalisation and human rights used the concept of the New Social Movements as their reference point (see Chapter 5). I referred to it in respect of the work of Aziz, and we can see it at work in the accounts of some of the critics just discussed. However, since 1999, a new focus has emerged with the apparent rise of contemporary critical social movements. In Chapter 5, I argued that there were significant continuities between these contemporary movements and the so-called NSMs, but that there was also a key difference in that the problem of economic power was re-emphasised – most often in terms of a critique of capitalism and/or corporate power. The importance of this is twofold.

Firstly, activism previously focused on areas such as the environment, the oppression of women, indigenous peoples and human rights now appears to have constructed linkages and networks around the issue of the negative impacts of economic globalisation. These linkages cover a huge spectrum of both institutionalised activism – associated with large (I)NGOs, such as Greenpeace, Oxfam or Amnesty International – and non-institutionalised activism more typically found in the protests against the G8/WTO. Put another way, this 'movement of movements' appears to encompass entities as different as Oxfam, Friends of the Earth, the anarchist 'black bloc' and the so-called 'clown army' (on the latter see Maeckelbergh 2007). What is more, activists appear to be increasingly and explicitly recognising the imbrication and multi-layering of different relations and structures of power all around the world. At the same time, perhaps precisely because of this recognition, there is also broad agreement about the need to struggle for basic economic and social rights as a consequence of the predations unleashed by neo-liberal economic globalisation.

Secondly, on this topic it is especially important to acknowledge the tendency for academic analysis to lag behind social praxis. While several of the critiques published in the late 1990s took the so-called NSMs as their reference point, since 'anti-capitalism' has come to the fore some Marxist analysts have started to take a more optimistic stance. Underlying this, of course, is the hope that some sort of counter-hegemonic bloc could be constructed, a bloc perhaps capable of instigating a broader, sustained, attack on global capitalism. Whether more critics of human rights might follow suit remains to be seen. So, what are important elements of this movement of movements?

In some respects the struggles of the Zapatistas looks closest to classic revolutionary insurgency. Moreover, it is often claimed that it was their '*encuentros*' that acted as a catalyst for the mobilisation and organisation of the direct action wing of contemporary critical movements in the form of groups such as People's Global Action – one of the key networks involved in mobilising opposition to the Multilateral Agreement on Investment and the G8/WTO. Yet at the heart of the Zapatistas struggle are demands for the recognition the rights of the indigenous people of Chiapas. The Zapatistas have been explicitly positive about the potentials of human rights activism and their declarations and communiqués resonate with key aspects of the history of natural rights. For example, their 'First Declaration of the Lacandon Jungle' in January 1994 begins:

> We are a product of 500 years of struggle: first against slavery, then during the War of Independence against Spain led by insurgents, then to avoid being absorbed by North American imperialism, then to promulgate our constitution and expel the French empire from our soil....

Citing article 39 of the Mexican constitution, the Declaration continues:

> National Sovereignty essentially and originally resides in the people. All political power emanates from the people and its purpose is to help the people. The people have, at all times, the inalienable right to alter or modify their form of government. (EZLN 1994a)

Thus, in terms highly reminiscent of the US Declaration of Independence, the Zapatistas declared war on the Mexican state. Their second declaration, some six months later, called for democracy, justice and freedom and included the claim '...our path sprang out of the impossibility of struggling peacefully for our elemental rights as human beings' (EZLN 1994b). Later declarations developed a much more specific emphasis on the rights of indigenous peoples (EZLN 1996, 1998).

Many have argued that the Zapatistas have articulated a quite different approach to achieving their objectives (Holloway and Pelaez 1998; Klein 2001), one which eschews traditional approaches to socialist revolution. In particular, they appear to position themselves specifically between traditional understandings of reform and revolution. They also recognise oppressive power as multi-faceted and interlinked and see global civil society as a crucial space for transformative action. Certainly, they have explicitly sought to build linkages with radical social movement activism around the world.

Despite their globalist aspirations, the Zapatistas remain locally based with a specific focus on indigenous peoples' rights in Chiapas. The World Social Forum (WSF) process is clearly something else altogether. Arguably, it is the entity through which a 'movement of movements' has most clearly taken shape and is beginning to establish institutional forms. The Forum was initiated by the Brazilian Workers' Party as an oppositional 'mirror' to the World Economic Forum, but a whole range of activism has coalesced around this process since the first meeting in 2001. It has also generated important regional fora such as the African Social Forum and European Social Forum. Clearly all these processes and events involve a vast range of movements and (I)NGOs with very diverse orientations in terms of goals, organisation and ideology. At the same time, it is clear that among many activists there is a strong commitment to establishing a different way of working. The 'Charter of Principles' of the WSF[3] contains some very unusual statements when compared to both traditional revolutionary and reformist programmes and manifestoes. Points ten to twelve give a flavour of this and also identify the importance of human rights.

10. The WSF is opposed all totalitarian and reductionist views of economy, development and history and to the use of violence as a means of social control by the state. It upholds respect for Human Rights, the practices of real democracy, participatory democracy, peaceful relations, equality and solidarity, among people, ethnicities, genders and peoples, and condemns all forms of domination and all subjection of one person by another.

11. As a forum for debate, the WSF is a movement of ideas that promotes reflection, and the transparent circulation of the results of that reflection, on the mechanisms and instruments of domination by capital, on means of actions to resist and overcome that domination, and on the alternatives proposed to solve the problems of exclusion and social inequality that the process of capitalist globalisation with its racist, sexist and environmentally destructive dimensions is creating internationally and within countries.

12. As a framework for the exchange of experiences, the WSF encourages understanding and mutual recognition amongst its participant organisations and movements, and places special value on the exchange among them, particularly on all that society is building to centre economic activity and political action on meeting the needs of people and respecting nature, in the present and for future generations. (WSF Charter of Principles, June 2001, cited in Sen et al. 2004:70–71)

The WSF process is attempting to build networks of oppositional activism, construct effective strategies for global resistance and achieve some degree of social transformation. Human rights are central to at least some of those networks and to debates about appropriate strategies. For example, Gina Vargas, Peruvian feminist and member of the WSF International Council has argued '[t]he WSF is a space for the affirmation, amplification and construction of rights in the global arena. It is a space for widening democratic, subjective and symbolic horizons' (in Sen et al. 2004:228). Fisher and Ponniah's (2003) collection of documents from the 2002 World Social Forum includes a 'conference synthesis on economic, social and cultural rights' organised under the auspices of 'The Dignity and Human Rights Caucus'. A consensus was achieved on highlighting the following three proposals:

1. The establishment of a permanent forum on economic, social and cultural rights, in the broad context of trade, financial and international justice;
2. The declaration of the primacy of human rights so as to overcome the unacceptable gap between economic globalisation and human rights;
3. Generate broad support for the draft Optional Protocol to the International Covenant on Economic, Social and Cultural rights. (Fisher and Ponniah 2003:311)

Apparently led by a number of INGOs, what is specifically interesting about these proposals is how they strategically attempt to connect the grassroots mobilisations underpinning much of the WSF process with aspects of the institutionalised international human rights system. While it might be tempting to simply argue that here is a straightforward example of activism seeking to straddle the everyday and institutional worlds, there is more to it than that. Unsurprisingly, within the WSF there are major differences of view around the nature and legitimacy of human rights, the relationship between 'western values' and 'universal values', and the relation between 'reform' and 'revolution'. Indeed,

Fisher and Ponniah identify these as three of five key debates running through the WSF (Fisher and Ponniah 2003:9).

Picking up the same theme, Boaventura de Sousa Santos has argued:

> ...the social struggles that find expression in the WSF do not adequately fit either of the ways of social change sanctioned by western modernity: reform and revolution. Aside from the consensus on nonviolence, its modes of struggle are extremely diverse and appear spread out in a continuum between the poles of institutionality and insurgency. (in Sen et al. 2004:235)

Examining what I have pointed to as continuity between the so-called NSMs and contemporary critical social movements, de Sousa Santos also notes that one of the political novelties of the WSF is its very broad conception of power and oppression (Santos 2006). But we can see further continuity here too – that much longer history of social movement struggles against arbitrary power and privilege and 'old wrongs'.

In briefly discussing the Zapatistas and the WSF above, I do not pretend to have even scratched the surface of their complex relations to human rights, let alone be able to convey the depth and texture of many other contemporary social movement struggles. It is nevertheless clear that these two examples have captured the imagination of many commentators and it is to some examples of these that I now turn.

Conceptualising Contemporary Critical Activism: 'Resistance is Fertile!'

Of particular interest here is the shift in position of some previously pessimistic scholars. For example, following 'Seattle', Stephen Gill (2000) published a short piece ruminating on the possible emergence of what he called 'the postmodern prince'.[4] While still emphasising an economic driver of social relations, he considered the possibility that contradictions in the global political economy were creating an organic crisis leading to the emergence of a 'worldwide movement that can perhaps be best understood in terms of new potentials and forms of global political agency' (Gill 2000:137). Suggesting that such a movement was beginning to take concrete form, he explains his depiction of a 'postmodern prince' in terms of breaking with the modernist myth of the mass democratic party as the political structure of salvation. Rather, he says, the movement takes a non-institutionalised, multiple and capillary form. In conclusion he argues:

> Global democratic collective action today cannot, in my view, be understood as a singular form of collective agency, for example a single party with a single form of identity. It is more plural and differentiated, as well as being democratic and inclusive. The new forms of collective action contain innovative conceptions of social justice and solidarity, of social possibility, of knowledge, emancipation, and freedom. The content of their mobilising methods includes diversity, oneness of the planet and nature, democracy and equity. (Gill 2000:140)

Leslie Sklair takes the above themes and connects them directly to human rights. In a radical shift from his previous position, he now argues that 'the globalisation of human rights is the logical and substantive link between cooperative democracy and socialist globalisation' (Sklair 2002:306). What is more, he argues that it is precisely struggles for human rights which can provide a focal point for the wide range of critical movement activism in the contemporary world.

Brecher, Costello and Smith (2000) argue that the key aspect of the vision of what they call 'globalisation from below' is drawn from the international discourse on human rights and that this vision goes well beyond the constricted concept of human rights as civil and political rights. Referring to declarations agreed in and around recent UN conferences, they argue that the human rights dimensions of these declarations '...have gone a long way towards establishing a broad global consensus on what the world needs, one that is profoundly at odds with the realities of globalisation from above' (Brecher, Costello and Smith 2000:64). Their own draft programme puts human rights standards centre stage (Brecher, Costello and Smith 2000:Ch.6).

Noam Chomsky – that most trenchant critic of the way human rights have been used and abused in the contemporary world – sums up the point neatly. Talking about the place of the economic and social provisions of the UN Declaration and other international human rights conventions in the United States, he argues that existing standards are only meaningful 'insofar as popular struggle over many years has given them substance' (in Evans 1998:51). This book has argued that this is, indeed, a key part of the history of human rights. Is it also the future of human rights?

Conclusion

I have argued that monocausal/unidirectional accounts of globalisation are too simplistic and that multicultural/ multidirectional accounts are better able to grasp the complexity of the processes involved. Human rights praxis is, and arguably has been for a long time, an important aspect of globalisation. But its meaning is often contested in the familiar terms of my metaphorical mirrors. There is, however, a significant and growing literature which sees some elements of human rights praxis as an important aspect of 'globalisation from below'.

Contemporary critical social movements, many with clear anti-capitalist and anti-imperialist credentials, use human rights in a way that has much in common with their historical usage in terms of struggles against arbitrary power and privilege. Indeed perhaps it is precisely these (themselves globalising) movements that are best able to grasp and articulate the multidimensionality of power as it operates and functions globally today. Is it then these movements that are also the best placed to continue and develop struggles for human rights on a world scale? The next and final chapter examines some of the implications of the arguments in this book for the future of creative human rights praxis.

8

RENEWING THE CHALLENGE TO POWER

The first few years of the twenty-first century have seen human rights plunged into a crisis of actuality and a crisis of legitimacy. On one level, the crisis of actuality is plain to see – gross human rights violations are being directly perpetrated by a wide range of social actors all around the world – but mass human rights violations are also being generated structurally, as a consequence of contemporary institutional configurations of global and local power. These are often not understood as human rights violations at all and, in this sense, kept largely hidden from view. The crisis of legitimacy is, in significant part, a product of the caricatures proffered in much of the human rights literature. Though historically always controversial, these caricatures now so misrepresent human rights that their legitimacy is being rapidly and dangerously stripped away. So deep is this crisis of legitimacy that even some advocates of human rights are now asking *Can Human Rights Survive?* (Gearty 2006). The continuing dismissal of human rights and human rights activism by supposedly radical theorists is especially worrying. Scholarly cynicism is a dangerous potion when mixed with the bleak realities of the crisis of actuality.

In my view, the best chance of human rights surviving as a positive force in the world is for human rights praxis to be re-connected to its long-term historical trajectory identified in this study; that is, as a challenge to arbitrary power and privilege. This challenge needs to be at the forefront of all forms of human rights praxis, not just those forms arising from social movement struggles. In other words, as John Vincent (1986:102) once put it, human rights must remain subversive to be effective and legitimate. But reference to subversion poses some curious questions. How can any social order embrace and endorse its own subversion? How could subversion be institutionalised, in the sense of embedding the possibility for the abolition or substantive transformation of societal institutions in those very institutions themselves? Interestingly, there is the hint of an answer that has been persistently raised in movement struggles around human rights.

From the American Declaration of Independence to the Zapatista rebellion in Chiapas, power has been understood as legitimate only to the extent that it is serves the interests of the people. The people, it has regularly been claimed, have an absolute right to challenge and transform illegitimate and unjust power as they see fit. Leaving the difficulties of defining 'the people' to one side here, we can then ask how the organisation of 'power to' can be constrained from morphing into 'power over' given the problems of institutional power discussed in Chapter 4. Then there is the further question of the extent to which 'power over' can itself be justified as necessary for the proper governance of a community.

At the heart of attempts to provide non-violent answers to these questions have been ideas and practices of democracy, typically organised and institutionalised as a form of political power. But given that power is institutionalised economically and culturally as well as politically, the immediate question that follows is whether political democracy could ever be sufficient to effectively constrain all other forms of social power? Furthermore, despite appearing to share the common objective of constraining power, democracy has often been seen as having an uncertain and ambivalent relation to human rights (for example, Beetham 1999). So perhaps it is necessary to reformulate my earlier questions and to ask how subversion could be democratically institutionalised and, more broadly, what might be involved in institutional democratisation. In the context of these questions we can then also consider whether social movements might have a particular role to play in such processes.

At the end of this chapter I will reflect briefly on these very big questions, arguing that understandings of democracy are in urgent need of reconfiguration if creative human rights praxis is to be able to renew the challenge to power. But before turning to these, I want to contextualise them, firstly by looking at the contemporary crises of human rights in more detail and secondly by exploring how creative human rights praxis might be re-oriented so as to challenge power more effectively.

The Contemporary Crises of Human Rights

Rather than produce a long list of human rights horrors for the first decade of the twenty-first century, what I want to do here is consider them in the context of the contours of the historical and social analytic framework developed in this study. One historical point that immediately flows from making this connection is that the terrible events of the twentieth century, often understood as the basis for the international human rights system, are paralleled by equally horrendous events of previous centuries, notably the genocide, slavery and gross economic exploitation perpetuated by the European powers and their colonists in the Americas, Asia and Africa over the last 500 years. Thrown on to an even broader historical canvas, a good case could probably be made to show that the entire history of human civilization has been marked by repeated barbarisms. One could reasonably infer from this that the twenty-first century is in danger of continuing that pattern, especially if human rights praxis loses its capacity to challenge power effectively.

Analysing Contemporary Human Rights Abuse

I argued in Chapter 5 that, once movement struggles around human rights are re-located alongside broader historical struggles against oppression, we can then see a range of 'old wrongs' organised through five sites of power which have trans-historical and trans-cultural reach and impact. Looking at contemporary human rights abuses across these five sites of power can, I think, provide some important insights.

Political Power: Outside and In

While much of the human rights literature has been oriented towards looking at the 'inside' of political power, that is within the nation state, a historical perspective makes it clear that many of the most gross violations of human rights have occurred as a consequence of the extension of political power 'outside' its supposed community/nation. Variously understood as empire, colonialism and imperialism, it has a long history, instances of empire being found in ancient civilisations of the Americas and in Asia and the Middle East. Its 'modern' form has been rightly associated with the rise of European power, including the power of European colonialists in the Americas and elsewhere.

The contemporary projection of political power by the United States and other western states is generating a wide range of human rights abuses. At the same time these are being systematically identified and challenged by a range of movements and organisations, including leading (I)NGOs such as Amnesty International and Human Rights Watch. So perhaps a good case can be made to show that the combination of a globalising human rights culture and globalising media is making it more difficult for powerful states to emulate their historical predecessors than would otherwise be the case. Nevertheless, regardless of how it is conceptualised, 'Empire' remains a key form of power to be contested and transformed (Hardt and Negri 2000; Bartholomew 2006). Existing state-centric forms of institutionalised human rights offer virtually no protection against powerful predatory states. The current and possible future global dominance of the United States (for example, Nye 2002:Ch.1) means that recent abuses by that state, together with the peculiar and narrow understanding of human rights prevalent in that country, and their attempts to rewrite international human rights law as they see fit, all bode ill for the future of human rights. It certainly has some of the hallmarks of the totalising desire and arrogance of imperial power through the ages.

At the same time, all around the world, the 'inside' of state power also remains highly problematic. Whether we look at the authoritarian trajectory of the Russian Federation, the continuing persistent violations of human rights in China, state-led persecution of homosexuals in many African and Asian states, the impact of the Patriot Act in the United States, restrictions in other western countries claimed to be necessary because of the so-called 'war on terror' – all of these make it clear that internal state power remains a major threat to human rights. Moreover, the expert management of the political field through cultural manipulation and the acquisition and deployment of advanced surveillance and control technologies has developed the potential power of Leviathan in directions that not even Machiavelli and Hobbes could have dreamt about.

Economic Power: Local and Global

The organised and systematic exploitation of peoples based on the control of economic resources also has a very long history. However, in its modern – largely capitalist – form, the accomplishment of such exploitation was globalised and embedded as the dominant structural logic of economic relations in the industrialising cultures and their empires by the end of the nineteenth century. Workers and socialist movements in the industrialised countries sought to challenge such power but, as discussed in Chapter 4, these challenges were effectively nationalised. This left whole swathes of the world's population vulnerable to relations and structures of economic power. Economic predation was often organised politically as imperialism and colonialism until the middle of the twentieth century, but the processes of political decolonisation quickly revealed the crucial role of economic power in a globalising world. In the latter half of the twentieth century the abuse of economic power was often characterised by local people being driven off the land so that local landowners and large corporations could create vast cash crop monocultures (for example, Shue 1980). By the beginning of the twenty-first century, the abuse of economic power can additionally be characterised in terms of sweatshop labour being organised in export processing zones specifically established to avoid the regulation of the terms and conditions of labour (ILO 2007). A combination of the behaviour of transnational corporations and the international financial institutions together with the extant structural logic of the global economy have wrought havoc in communities all around the world. Accelerating economic globalisation supported by a virulent neo-liberal economic ideology and the rapid deployment of advanced information and computing technologies has resulted in a vast growth in global inequality and a huge increase in absolute poverty (Pogge 2002; Felice 2003; UNDP 2003, 2005).

Ethnicity

Despite patchy progress in the latter half of the twentieth century, oppression and exclusion organised and perpetrated around ethnic difference remain an enormous problem around the world. Over the last 20 years, the world has witnessed terrible examples of genocide and ethnic cleansing, Rwanda, the Balkan wars and Darfur being only the most obvious examples. Perhaps even more sinister is the extent to which forms of such oppression and exclusion are often mundanely and routinely perpetuated structurally through all sorts of social institutions. Brysk and Shafir (2004) have highlighted the plight of migrant workers and refugees who face discrimination and persecution via varied intersections of cultural, political and economic power. Some analysts of globalisation have warned we should only expect such problems to deepen dramatically as ontological insecurity, together with broader anxieties and uncertainties, are fostered by globalisation while those very same processes are also bringing different ethnicities together in an increasing mobile and shrinking world (Giddens 1999). Such circumstances are ripe for exploitation by demagogues and xenophobes.

Sex and Gender: The Backlash

Albeit very unevenly, considerable progress was made around the world in the twentieth century to combat forms of oppression and exploitation organised around sex and gender. In particular, women's movements successfully forced a range of issues on to the agendas of governments and international institutions. So much so that some have claimed that women's issues have been successfully 'mainstreamed', especially through the international institutions. Yet not only are such claims vigorously contested (Carbet 2004; Goetz 2006) but patriarchal power also remains deeply embedded throughout most societies and cultural formations. Moreover, a significant backlash against gains achieved through women's struggles is taking place around the world. Some commentators have again argued that the upsurge in male violence around the world from the early 1990s needs to be understood through the lens of globalisation (Giddens 1999). The rise of the fundamentalist regimes such as the Taliban in Afghanistan, the systematic use of rape as a tool of war in the Balkans (MacKinnon 1993), the trafficking of women for the sex industry all make the threat clear enough. But, again, it is also important to stress the extent to which the exploitation and oppression of women operates in thoroughly mundane and routinised ways in both institutional and everyday settings. For example, despite the governments of India and China banning the use of sex-selective technologies, strongly embedded cultural attitudes in the everyday world perpetuate the problem of Asia's 'missing women' (Das Gupta 2005).

While lesbian, bisexual, gay and transgender movements have made some limited progress in a few societies, homosexuality and other sexual orientations face severe discrimination, repression and violence in many others. As discussed in Chapter 5, LBGT movements have been the least successful of the so-called NSMs. Heterosexism remains deeply embedded in the everyday world and receives crucial support and nourishment from a wide range of institutions, especially religious organisations.

Control of Information and Knowledge

The achievement of mind control has often been desired, but much less regularly achieved. Nevertheless, historically, the control of information and knowledge has always been a key source of power and a source of human rights abuses. From the latter half of the nineteenth century there was a strong tendency to assume that this form of power was merely an adjunct to political or economic power. In the academic world, Foucault's historical work on the power/knowledge nexus was a timely reminder that such a subsumption was too simplistic. The contemporary dynamics of globalisation, the rise of mass media and the information technology revolution demonstrate that, while political and economic interests certainly try to harness the control of information and knowledge to their own purposes, this site of power has its own dynamics and arguably should be seen as a crucial site of power in its own right.

My longer historical and trans-cultural perspectives are important here because they show, for example, that the origins, development and institutionalisation of world religions have largely been based on attempting to effect such control. Adherents of this or that religion or sect are expected to accept the framework or interpretations offered as 'certain truth' – as faith. If many Enlightenment thinkers assumed that the growth of scientific knowledge would gradually secularise social relations, they made a bad mistake. In the context of the anxieties and uncertainties of globalisation, there has been both a resurgence of religious belief and the rise of a range of religious and other fundamentalisms. One common feature of such fundamentalisms is their attempt to exercise strategic control over the dissemination of information and knowledge in ways that protect or validate particular assertions of 'certain truth'.

Mass media outlets independent of state control select and shape information and knowledge that is delivered to mass publics according to a range of criteria that comprises the structural logic of the media world. While this logic can reflect existing economic and political interests and generate a bias towards the status quo, a whole range of other cultural, technical and competitive dynamics are involved in that shaping and selection (Downing, Mohammadi and Sreberny 1995; Ginsburg, Abu-Lughod and Larkin 2002; Nightingale and Ross 2003) In recent decades, there have been important instances of the mass media apparently facilitating significant transformative change (for example in Eastern Europe in 1989) and in effectively bringing down otherwise powerful governments and corporations.

At the moment, the extent and depth of the information technology revolution that began in the last decades of the twentieth century cannot be easily assessed. But it has qualitatively transformed flows of information and knowledge. Spatial barriers to flows across such networks have been largely removed for those linked to global computer networks. Many influential commentators have argued for some years that the control of information and knowledge is not just a site of power in its own right, but is becoming the key site of power in the contemporary world. Manuel Castells (1996) describes the rise of 'the network society' in 'the information age' and earlier Alain Touraine (1981) had depicted the emergence of a 'programmed society' – a society controlled by a technocratic elite in which information and knowledge supplanted material production as the key source of social power. However analysed and assessed, this is a feature of the contemporary world that cannot be ignored.

Our 'Runaway World': Dangers and Possibilities

Since the articulations of human rights in the seventeenth century, the world has changed almost beyond recognition and so has the nature of power. Yet in other ways it looks frighteningly familiar – perhaps even more threatening and dangerous. If we come back to the relationship between 'power to' and ' power over' examined in Chapter 1, there can be no doubting that human capacity to develop, organise and systematise 'power to' has increased enormously. Furthermore, in a myriad of ways such 'power to' has supported and enhanced the quality of life for millions of people around the world. Since the seventeenth century we have seen the development and rise of sophisticated political, economic and cultural institutions which many argue are the hallmark and the key achievements of 'modernity'.

Yet, working from the simple proposition that the development of 'power to' necessarily brings with it the threat of 'power over', it also becomes clear that the dangers of 'power over' have also increased enormously over that same timescale. In other words, without forgetting the gross human rights violations of earlier historical periods, we can say that the threats have also changed dramatically. The last 60 years have witnessed the latest qualitative step-change as a consequence of the dual dynamics of globalisation and the information revolution. 'Power over' organised in and through the five sites identified pose enormous threats in the contemporary world.

Proponents of human rights would no doubt point to the emergence of the international system of human rights as one explanation of why such enormous threats have not been actualised to the extent that they could be. Indeed, central to my analysis of human rights is the view that they can indeed be used to limit and constrain 'power over'. Yet, in the context of our 'runaway world' (Giddens 1999) can human rights be made 'fit for purpose'? Is it possible for human rights to renew the challenge to power?

For this to be possible human rights praxis has to be broadly understood and regarded as legitimate amongst peoples around the world. Unfortunately, right now, that is clearly not the case because key elements of institutionalised human rights praxis and the failings of intellectual work on human rights have combined together in ways that have led to a deep crisis of legitimacy.

Delegitimising Human Rights

This brief section reiterates some of the relevant themes developed in this book. The first part looks at the failures of institutionalised human rights praxis, the second focuses on the limits of much academic work on human rights.

Failures of Institutionalised Human Rights Praxis

Here I want to re-emphasise some outcomes of the negative side of the paradox of institutionalisation. At the heart of this, in geo-political terms, is the use and abuse of human rights by powerful states to legitimate their foreign policy interests and the structures of the international political and economic institutions. This can take us back to critiques like those of Noam Chomsky (1978) but even strong advocates of human rights have recognised the same point. In Chapter 4 I noted that Jack Donnelly accepts that the shape of the existing inter-state system seriously disrupts and distorts the potential of human rights (Donnelly 2003:168–71). In *Can Human Rights Survive?* Conor Gearty talks of the damage done to the emancipatory power of human rights by being deployed as a rationale for military action (Gearty 2006:14).

The problem of the use and abuse of human rights by powerful states is compounded by the state-centrism of the international system as a whole and the close link between human rights and nation states. There is still an extremely strong tendency to assume that, for all practical purposes, duties correlative to human rights rest with states and this is structurally perpetuated by the fact that the UN is an organisation of states. Treaties, declarations and conventions are agreed and signed up to by 'states parties' and so it is those entities that have obligations under international instruments. This means there is a fundamental problem in allocating correlative duties to non-state actors even when it is clear that such duties should also be ascribed elsewhere, for example, to transnational corporations according to contemporary campaigns challenging the contemporary abuse of economic power (Corporate Watch 2007).

The overwhelming focus on human rights as law results in them being increasingly understood as nothing other than a form of 'legal instrumentalism' (Riles 2006). Conor Gearty calls this a 'crisis of legalism' (Gearty 2006:Ch.3). This emphasis on law (including such an emphasis by (I)NGOs and social movements) means that the expressive dimensions of human rights and human rights activism discussed in Chapter 6 tends to be ignored. Arguably, this puts the proverbial cart before the horse, in so far as human rights as law should be about reflecting the broader 'expressive' project of building a human rights culture from below across the whole of social relations. From a 'top-down' position it could no doubt be argued this is wrong and that law is a 'gentle civiliser' (Koskenniemi 2004). Yet even rudimentary historical reflection makes it clear that such an uncritically positive view of law is unsustainable. On the contrary, law has often been deeply and systematically implicated in the enforcement of oppressive forms of power throughout much of human history.

These aspects can be brought together in terms of thinking about the bureaucratisation of human rights, processes whereby law and politics are brought together in institutional structures that operate procedurally, technocratically and in other ways that tend to hollow out the emancipatory and expressive dimensions of human rights. Without dismissing the positive benefits of the international human rights system, there is clearly a major problem with a reduction of human rights praxis to a praxis that is organised through and oriented towards institutionalised structures of power. In Chapter 4, I cited Philip Allott arguing that 'the reality of the idea of human rights has been degraded..... they were turned into bureaucratic small change [and] became a plaything of government and lawyers'. One might add to Allott's comments that it also makes them susceptible to other forms of power, perhaps best illustrated by the way transnational corporations have sought to capture human rights for their own use (Grear 2003). Such attempts are predatory in a dual way, seeking to use human rights to legitimate their own power whilst, at the same time, undermining their legitimacy. In sum, the failures of institutional human rights praxis involve working through '...how the term "human rights" has come to be abused by the powerful, as a means of legitimising the exploitation both of peoples and of the world's natural resources' (Gearty, 2006:60).

The Corrosive Distortions of the Mirrors

The extent to which the realities of human rights praxis are distorted in much of the specialist academic literature was summed up by my metaphor of the hall of mirrors. Here I want to emphasise the extent to which these distortions corrode the legitimacy of human rights and activism around human rights. The failure to engage properly with the connection between human rights and social movement struggles and the complexity and ambiguity of the paradox of institutionalisation mean that key aspects of human rights are missing from 'the story of human rights' and/or stripped bare of any analytical meaning. This in turn, leads to an inability to be able to interrogate properly the relationship between human rights and power. Scholarly naïveté on this point is shared by proponents and critics. For uncritical proponents power is not an issue in the story of human rights. For uncritical critics, human rights can be nothing other than the handmaiden of power. Overly simplistic assumptions and the rejection of ambiguity and complexity are the hallmarks of such analyses. Given the dominance and impact of these distorting stories of human rights, it is little wonder that their legitimacy is so readily called into question.

Underlying these problems is a very narrow and impoverished operationalisation of the concept of social practice. Partly a direct consequence of the boundaries of the disciplines of philosophy and law, the only forms of social practice that are often recognised and analysed in the mainstream literature is the theoretical work involved in the construction of 'ideas' and, then, the 'practices' of law. The rest of social practice, social relations and social power often disappear altogether. For example, in a recent volume *The Legalization Of Human Rights*, the editors make it clear that they wish to question the assumption that there is a simple division of labour between the 'foundational', theoretical perspective on human rights and the legal one (Meckled-Garcia and Cali 2006:12). While they argue that '...the relationship between international human rights law and human rights moral theory is not simply reducible to the latter giving practical effect of the former' (Meckled-Garcia and Cali 2006:25) no other forms of social practice ever put in an appearance. In other words, their interrogation never transcends the internal relationship between the theoretical and the legal. Some of the other essays in this volume do offer a wider understanding of the sociality of human rights (see especially, Kapur 2006) but the editors' position typifies the problem I am identifying. 'Theory' and 'law' are the stuff of human rights, there is little else to think about.

In terms of possibilities for emancipation and social transformation, this reduction of social practice to theory and law becomes a potent disabling force when mixed with the contemporary scholarly fashion for cynicism and irony amongst social analysts who often see themselves as radical critics. In Chapter 6 I discussed the work of the feminist post-structuralist scholar, Wendy Brown, who explicitly avoids a broader discussion of relevant social practices in order to sustain her focus on theory and law and to enable her to depict the motivation of movement actors through Nietzsche's concept of *ressentiment*. Interestingly, a direct parallel to this intellectual sleight of hand can be found in the work of Marxist philosopher and social theorist Alex Callinicos. In an introductory textbook on social theory, Callinicos (1999) questions the extent to which post-structuralist and post-colonialist theorists such as Michel Foucault and Edward Said have transformed the conceptual structures of social theory. He argues:

> The idea, for example, that the various forms of oppression are irreducibly plural, and represent distinct sites of struggle which cannot somehow be incorporated (as orthodox Marxists would claim) into an all embracing movement centred on the working class can be formulated in terms that derive directly (post-structuralism) or indirectly (Weberian historical sociology) from Nietzsche's doctrine of the will to power. (Callinicos 1999:265)

This is a book on social theory, so Callinicos is right to point to threads of theoretical connection. But there is something else going on here as well because – just like liberal, Marxist and poststructuralist theorists in the field of human rights – Callinicos appears to privilege theory as a form of social practice. The suggestion that the possible existence of plural sites of power, oppressions and struggles can all be reduced to and analysed through Nietzsche's concept of the will to power seems as ludicrous as Brown's suggestion that the motivation of movement actors can be understood through Nietzsche's concept of *ressentiment*.

I am not saying that Nietzsche's work has nothing to tell us about power and human rights. But I am arguing that the history of struggles for human rights cannot be grasped through reading the work of any particular theorist, whether Locke or Nietzsche and whether regarded as saint or sinner. Theories of human rights and human rights law are clearly important dimensions of their subject matter. But the widespread assumption that they are the totality of what human rights are – the totality of the social praxis of human rights – has had disastrous consequences.

Re-orienting Creative Human Rights Praxis

The story of human rights set out in this book is offered as an indicative rather than conclusive account. But, to the extent there is merit in the overall analysis, the implications for the future construction of creative human rights praxis are clear enough in general terms. Human rights praxis should focus on effectively challenging the 'old wrongs' arising from the five sites of trans-historical and trans-cultural forms of power identified above. As a key part of this, analyses of human rights also need to focus on the expressive dimension of human rights, both in terms of the empowerment of the oppressed and in terms of reconstructing local and global cultures of human rights that are fully embedded in the institutional and everyday worlds.

The analysis here also provides some quite different ways of thinking about the 'is' and the 'ought' of human rights. For example, given human rights are both about challenging existing forms of 'power over' and creating new forms of 'power to' (thus necessarily engaged in the creations of new configurations of social power more generally) does this mean that human rights praxis should always be oriented towards a general, macro-level strategy of minimising 'power over' whilst maximising 'power to'? What forms would such a strategy have in particular and concrete circumstances and how could it be operationalised? What I have called the paradox of institutionalisation clearly throws up enormous questions about strategy and the relationship between means and ends. While not novel in suggesting that human rights must somehow sustain their emancipatory and subversive potential, this work has nevertheless opened up different sorts of questions regarding institutionalisation and institutionalised forms of human rights. Historically, understandings of human rights have often been institutionalised as a consequence of violence and revolution. Further, the process of institutionalising human rights as law seeks to remove them from social contestation – sedimenting them within positive law and its supposed timeless majesty. Yet, as we have seen, sedimentation is not fixity and the paradox is, well, paradoxical. Below, these points are explored in a little more detail, firstly by reflecting on how they might impact on a range of actors and issues before coming back to questions relating to institutionalisation and law.

Actors and Issues

Actors

The relevance of the above points will clearly impact very differently depending on the position of actors in the institutional and everyday worlds. Grassroots movement actors involved in largely non-institutionalised activism around human rights always face a range of key strategic questions. Two key questions at the instrumental end of my expressive/instrumental continuum are, firstly, whether claims and demands should be couched in terms of achieving legal change and, secondly, the extent to which movement actors should be engaged with the institutional world and, if so, on what terms. At the expressive end of my continuum are questions regarding the inclusive or exclusive orientations of attempts to construct or reconstruct identities, norms and values. More generally, movement actors would need to consider whether proposed alternative ways of becoming and being in the world are compatible with any local and global human rights cultures.

Actors in (I)NGOs are more likely to be engaged with the institutional world, campaigning for and around human rights. While there is a vast range of (I)NGOs, these actors are potential interlocutors between non-institutionalised movement activism and the actuality of human rights abuses on the one hand, and institutional structures, in particular institutionalised human rights systems. Actors in some of these entities will see themselves as being involved in specifically human rights organisations and have a focus on achieving legal change. Others will see themselves as involved in other types of movements (for example women's movements, indigenous peoples' movements) with a human rights aspect to their activism. Actors in these latter movements are less likely to have an entirely legalistic focus (see Estévez 2008). While some of these (I)NGOs will have emerged directly from social movements and others will contextualise their history in terms of social movement struggles, others may make no connection to social movements at all.

Regardless of these important differences, actors in all of these organisations will face the ambiguities and complexities of the paradox of institutionalisation, whether internally in terms of their own organisation or externally in terms of their engagement with the institutional world. Some (I)NGO actors are acutely aware of this. For example, in 'Learning From Experience: Activist Reflections On "Insider-Outsider" Strategies', Anne Carbet (2004) asks whether insider strategies are a good use of energy, whether participation legitimises illegitimate institutions and whether activist agendas are being co-opted and watered-down by institutional bureaucracies. She also warns of the danger of institutionalised actors becoming disconnected from grassroots activism. Actors in (I)NGOs need to be very clear about their strategies and the extent to which their practices are oriented towards challenging power. They need to ensure and sustain links of communication and accountability to any social movements from which they have emerged and to any broader constituencies they seek to or claim to represent.

Professional human rights practitioners are most likely to be fully enmeshed in the paradox of institutionalisation. Their work for state, international or other institutions, including large human rights (I)NGOs, will often be deeply compromised by the broader interests of their institutions, entanglements within organisational hierarchies and organisational drift towards bureaucratisation, instrumentalism and procedural rationality. All of this is very likely to pull such actors away from the sorts of substantive values and challenges posed by movement struggles. Yet, if we cannot live without institutions, these sorts of tensions will be ever-present and need to be much more directly addressed. Relevant tasks for such institutional actors would involve recognising the legitimacy of movement struggles and trying to ensure that their institutional work supports rather than impedes such struggles. More importantly, these actors are potentially well placed to find pathways through which the institutionalisation of subversion could take place within their own institutional structures. Put another way, they could have a key role to play in processes of institutional democratisation.

Human rights scholars are also important actors in the field of human rights. At first sight the challenge facing them looks straightforward – to escape from the hall of mirrors! Yet this is no easy task for some of the reasons discussed in Chapter 1. It would involve recognising and acknowledging the limitations of one's own discipline and be willing to accept the sanctions such dissidence might bring. It would involve addressing three central weaknesses in the existing scholarly literature: the lack of a proper 'long history' of human rights able to locate human rights in broader accounts of struggles against oppression; the reduction of the sociality of human rights to 'theory' and' law', and the tendency to assume that human rights should be a process of 'top-down' elite construction. All of these involve acknowledging the processes of 'bottom-up' agency in the historical and social construction of human rights. In academic terms, this means recognising the importance of developing a non-Eurocentric historical sociology of human rights which embeds a concept of creative agency from below at its core.

Issues

Here I focus on particular issues where specific weaknesses in the existing human rights literature are indicated or where a different sort of answer is suggested to the familiar answers of that literature. As mentioned above, while there is substantive discussion of the 'internal' problematic of state power in the human rights literature, existing discussions of the externalisation of political power has been largely delimited by the specificities of nineteenth- and twentieth-century colonialism and struggles against it. Thus, while there is a significant human rights literature on the notion of a people's right to self-determination, there is very little on the human rights implications of the various other ways in which political power can be externalised. While notions of a people's right to self-determination can be used to challenge the legitimacy of both political power externalised as military intervention and political interference in a country's internal affairs, this argument often quickly collapses into a state-centric argument about the sovereignty of nation states. But this fails to capture the myriad of ways in which political power can be externalised leading to sustained and systemic violations of human rights. While political opposition to contemporary forms of 'Empire' are legion and activists have used existing civil and political rights to challenge systematic violations perpetrated following the invasions of Afghanistan and Iraq, there remains an urgent need to reconstruct human rights in ways that more effectively address the externalisation of political power.

There are major problems with the way in which economic power is conceptualised and located in existing human rights praxis. It remains the case that many believe human rights have nothing to do with economic power. Steiner and Alston note, for example, that examination of 'globalisation, development and human rights', takes us far from the traditional focus of human rights involving, as it does, consideration of economic analysis and the responsibility of non-state actors (Steiner and Alston 2000:1306). While liberal approaches to human rights are undoubtedly responsible for this state of affairs, the proposed solutions to the abuse of economic power coming from the reformist and revolutionary traditions of the left offered fundamentally statist solutions. These became hegemonic by the end of the nineteenth century and persist to this day. In particular, the social democratic tradition has directly and significantly impacted upon contemporary constructions of human rights. This arises from a double dynamic. Firstly, correlative duties to economic rights were constructed as state duties. Secondly, those state duties were then constructed in such a way that it was not so much the duty of the state to prevent human rights violations occurring but rather to 'mop up' after violations of basic human rights had occurred. This dynamic significantly blunts direct challenges to relations and structures of economic power. The analysis in this book suggests human rights need to be re-oriented to achieve a direct focus on economic power. While many on the left doubt the efficacy of demands that corporations and international economic institutions respect human rights, contemporary movement struggles against corporate power are beginning to shift the agenda, the adoption of the UN Norms on the responsibilities of transnational corporations (OHCHR, 2003) being one sign of such a shift.

I argued in an earlier paper (Stammers 1995) that duties in respect of economic and social rights could be reconstructed in terms of a general 'duty of care' being made proportional to power. Such an approach is potentially translatable into a legally enforceable framework. The notion of a duty of care is embedded in many legal systems that have roots in the English common law tradition and these jurisdictions have potential purchase on some of the world's largest and most powerful corporations. Moreover, such a notion of a duty of care proportionate to power can function at the expressive level, at the level of 'common sense', in so far as publics around the world might readily agree that powerful corporations have a much greater duty to avoid violations of human rights than individual persons in the street or field. Interestingly, this sort of reconstruction would replicate the trajectory of early claims for natural rights. These were not simply a philosophical or moral appeal for states to behave better; they were dimensions of broader social movement challenges to arbitrary power and privilege. None of this is to say that the state is unimportant, nor that the state should not seek to protect economic and social rights. Rather, it is simply to say that states should not be regarded as the endpoint in terms of duties to respect human rights, rather as part of a broader social dynamic.

Configurations of power are never static even when they are deeply embedded. So, for human rights to challenge power effectively, any shifts in the configuration of power needs to be understood and taken into account. Many analysts now argue that major shifts have taken place around the control of information and knowledge in the contemporary world. One aspect of this is the global rise over the last 60 years of radio and television with their enormous capacity to select, transmit and interpret information and knowledge. Then there are the more recent but very rapid developments in computer-based communication and information technologies. Critical analyses of the relationship between 'power to' and 'power over' in these fields are essential but, from a human rights point of view, we should now be asking whether – as a site of power – the control of information and knowledge has become much more important and independent than it was say 60 or 100 years ago? Most discussions involving human rights and the mass media have revolved around preserving 'freedom of information' (with the mass media being seen as a bulwark against the abuse of political power) but my argument here implies that human rights need urgent reconstruction so as to challenge effectively the abuse of power by the mass media. Also connected, via debates about globalisation and the rise of 'the information age', is what to do about the worldwide rise of religious and other fundamentalisms with a consequent resurgence and deepening of attempts to control, shape and limit flows of information and knowledge in accordance with the tenets of particular belief systems. Historically, relations and structures of power organised around religious beliefs have been a major factor in the history of oppression in virtually all societies. Indeed, while in recent decades people of many faiths have been at the forefront of struggles for human rights, the longer history of the development of human rights was, in part at least, a challenge to such forms of religious power.

There are also a range of fields of knowledge production emerging which are likely to impact across all five main sites of power, thus shifting the pattern of their configuration. The biotechnology revolution has the potential to change some of the fundamental terms of human existence. Genetic manipulation, fertility and reproductive technologies plus new diagnostic and microsurgical techniques are all threatening to transgress traditional understandings of the boundaries between life and death. It is even claimed by some that the revolution in computing and artificial intelligence will, within just a few decades, pose fundamental questions about sentience and the boundaries between human and machine intelligence. Last but not least, it is clear that the impacts of climate change will have the most dramatic, if not catastrophic, effects on human life across the planet. Overall, my argument here is a simple one. Struggles for and around human rights always needs to keep an eye on what is moving, what is shifting in terms of power. This is one key reason why we cannot simply take a particular list of human rights and claim it to be timeless.

One issue that frequently comes up in discussions of human rights is that of proliferation and the extent to which proliferation devalues human rights. Upendra Baxi is interestingly ambivalent on this issue, suspecting that criticism of undue proliferation is often really about suppressing 'the authorship of the violated' (Baxi 2002:68). Baxi is almost certainly right on this point, yet – at the same time – the tendency to try to mediate the entirety of social relations through constructions of human rights may well serve to devalue and discredit them. The argument in this book suggests potential limits around meanings of human rights. I have argued that, historically, the creative agency of social movements has been a key originating source of human rights. Could we say, therefore, that – in the absence of such agency – human rights cannot or should not be created? This brings us back to the question of what Baxi calls 'representational power' discussed in Chapter 4. As noted previously, whilst altruism has been an important aspect of human rights constructions and there is not necessarily a problem in speaking on behalf others, at the same time there is also a long standing recognition of authoritarian and abusive potential in claiming to work on behalf of, or protect the rights of, others. Perhaps, therefore, we should simply acknowledge that some forms of social obligation should be constructed in terms of duties, not in terms of human rights. Yet the difficulties and complexities involved can be illustrated by reference to the

UN Convention on the Rights of the Child (CRC). Freeman has pointed out that there has been an active children's rights movement since at least the middle of the nineteenth century (Freeman and Veerman 1992; Freeman 1996) but, significantly, this movement has almost entirely comprised adults not children. The CRC did not emerge as a consequence of struggles by children themselves. Further, and following the historically anomalous pattern of the 1948 UN Declaration, the CRC arose from a process that was largely institutionalised from the outset. That said, it appears that in some important ways the CRC has acted as a catalyst for the self-organisation of some working children in movements and organisations in the global south (Liebel, Overwien and Recknagel 2001), prompting some scholars to consider what role children's activism might play in the more general quest for social transformations (Liebel 2003). To the extent that young social actors are able to construct movements and generate creative movement praxis, then activism around rights seems entirely consonant with the analyses offered in this volume. Yet, it seems to me that it could also be argued that children's movements and organisations are most likely to emerge when children are forced by their circumstances to act as if they were adults, for example by having to work or having to take on household and family responsibilities when their parents are missing. So, is this the exception that proves the rule? Given the dangers of representational power, especially when combined with the difficulties posed by the paradox of institutionalisation, we might ponder whether many children might not be better served by an institutional regime clearly couched in terms of parental, community and societal duties rather than in terms of rights which, especially in the case of children rights, can be so easily be hijacked by adults?

General histories of social movement struggles also show that movement actors have often assumed that the best way of overcoming and/or constraining one form of 'power over' is through the application or substitution of another form of 'power over'. Put another way, attempts to empower the oppressed have often been constructed in such a way as to lead to the emergence of another form of power over. So, for example, the traditional socialist strategy for constraining economic power was the application of state power. Likewise, one liberal solution to limit the dangers of state power was to venerate the virtues of 'free' economic power in a market. Finally, as we have seen, struggles against colonialism came to be premised on setting up new post-colonial nation states, sometimes with highly abusive consequences. Again, this has important ramifications for thinking about the future of human rights. Currently, the way many green activists call for the application of state power to deal with the environmental crisis is sometimes too uncritical and displays an authoritarian edge. Furthermore, as we have already seen, there is already a major problem of state-centrism in respect of human rights and this certainly implies that social movements need to work carefully around how they construct demands in respect of correlative duties.

Inside the Paradox: Institutionalisation and Law

There has been a clear and general historical trajectory for social movement praxis to demand that the constructions of human rights be instantiated as constitutional provision and positive law. This can be understood as attempts to reconfigure extant relations and structures of power positively. Yet, once institutionalised, human rights become ambiguous with respect to power. What are the implications of this? If the paradox of institutionalisation is indeed an inherent feature of institutions *per se*, yet we accept that human flourishing requires the creation and sustaining of social institutions, then we have to find ways of living with the paradox. This means both recognising that institutions and law are necessarily suffused with power but that they are also susceptible to transformation. This is a process/praxis approach to institutions and law which both rejects reductionist and essentialist arguments and recognises that institutions and the law exist within wider contexts of social relations including contestation, struggle and social transformation.

While institutions and law may be contested and transformed, historically it was the case that the institutionalisation of human rights established a range of historical exclusions which became deeply sedimented and proved very hard to reverse. Furthermore, this problem has not disappeared. Current state-centric approaches to human rights and the emphasis given to citizenship rights as an expression of human rights continues to construct important categories of exclusion. In recent work, Alison Brysk has asked who has a 'right to rights' in an examination of the exclusionary nature of citizenship in an age of globalisation and migration. She argues '…what we see … is a political culture in which universal personhood continues to be subordinated to citizenship as a basis for rights' (Brysk, 2002: 21). She concludes by arguing for the importance of recognising the political vocabulary enunciated in the natural rights revolutions and the UN declaration so that such rights become genuinely universal and cosmopolitan – rewriting the ancient idea of a citizen of the world in a way that it is universal but diverse. This, she claims, is the central theoretical and practical challenge of our age. Upendra Baxi talks about the logics of exclusion and inclusion and he seems to see the UNDHR and subsequent social movement struggles as having succeeded in generating a logic of inclusion. I have tried to show in this book that this logic of inclusion – a universalist dimension of movement praxis – has a much longer history. That said, Baxi's argument is consistent with my claim that the international human rights system that began in 1948 established a 'concrete universal' of human rights which could then be opened up to challenge, contestation and transformation.

To the extent that one finds commentary on struggles from below in the human rights literature, this is usually couched either in utopian terms or else posed at such a level of generality that very little concrete assessment of possibilities or outcomes can be made. What is more, such discussion typically focuses on the political and/or legal systems. In this book I have argued that social movement praxis around human rights is much wider and deeper than can be expressed solely in political and legal terms. In particular, what I described as the expressive dimension of human rights activism is partly about building up a human rights culture built on understandings of threats posed by various forms of power. So it is important not to assume that all activism around human rights must, of necessity, become enmeshed in the paradox. In this connection, one theme that does recur in some of the literature is the link between struggles for human rights and the nature of democracy. For example, Etienne Balibar (1994:19) says that the 'politics of the rights of man' can be nothing other than forms of struggle that, as such, necessarily take us to the boundaries and limits of democracy. Baxi also suggests an important link between human rights and the invention of forms of participatory governance without developing the point in detail (Baxi 2002) and Leslie Sklair now sees human rights as the logical and substantive link between what he calls co-operative democracy and socialist globalisation (Sklair 2002:Ch.11). Points such as these bring us back to the question of the relation between human rights and social change and what role, if any, democratisation could play in addressing the difficulties of the paradox of institutionalisation and in facilitating substantive social transformation.

This, in turn, brings us back to what I described at the beginning of this chapter as the subversion of institutions and the institution-alisation of subversion. Historically, the subversion of institutions has often involved the use of violence and armed conflict. But, nowadays, many activists would see a resort to violence and armed conflict as incompatible with a commitment to human rights. While this is no doubt partly explained by the commitment of some activists to the legitimacy of existing institutions and 'rule of law', it is also clear that a whole range of social movements actors from the 1960s onwards have sought to eschew violence and armed struggle. This was clear with many of the so-called NSMs and, significantly, a commitment to non-violence has been incorporated into the charter of principles of the World Social Forum. Even in the most militant wings of contemporary critical movements, there is much debate about the legitimacy of particular tactics and whether they constitute violence (see Gilly 2003). In terms of movement history, this commitment to non-violence combined with militant, active civil disobedience can be traced back to the struggles for *swaraj* in India and Gandhi's conceptualisation of *satyagraha* which was then re-articulated by sections of the black civil rights movement in the United States who took their lead from Martin Luther King. Put another way, by looking at recent developments in human rights from the perspective of social movement struggles, a commitment to non-violence has a distinctly non-Eurocentric origin. It offers a specific continuity with that aspect of the history of human rights which identifies that the subversion of existing institutions is necessary but offers it in such a way that violence and armed struggle might be avoided. Furthermore, over the last 60 years or so, not all movement struggles have needed to subvert existing institutions in order to achieve some degree of success. So perhaps the need to resort to militant active civil disobedience could be reduced if the possibilities for substantive transformation could themselves be institutionalised – we are back to the institutionalisation of subversion. What might this involve?

Human Rights and Institutional Democratisation

Reconstructing Human Rights: The Limits of Existing Proposals

Over the last 15 or 20 years many proponents of human rights have adopted an increasingly social democratic tone summed up best, perhaps, by the slogan used by United Nations at the time of the 50th anniversary of the UNHDR 'all human rights for all'. That said, contestation around the legitimacy of different categories of rights has not disappeared. Indeed, among proponents, this contestation now takes place between neo-liberal and social democratic approaches to human rights. One unfortunate consequence of the dominance of the rhetoric around this contest is the difficulty in being able to perceive the distinction between social democratic and more radical, movement oriented, approaches to human rights. One way of examining this distinction is to look at the extent to which there is a 'movement dimension' in current proposals for reconstructing human rights.

Wholly Intra-institutional

Under this heading are proposals whose frame of reference is purely the reform of international law through the work of the existing international institutions or that appear to assume that human rights can be transformed through theoretical enquiry without reference to transforming institutional structures or the processes required to deliver such transformation. These sorts of proposals are intra-institutional by default.

William Felice (2003) focuses on the place of economic and social human rights in world politics in *The Global New Deal*. Using Amartya Sen's capability approach to establish what individuals need for adequate functioning, Felice considers how economic and social rights might be reconstructed so as potentially to overcome structural violence and oppression. With this laudable goal in mind, his proposals focus attention on the rights of the poor, women and ethnic minorities and on finding ways of sustaining the environment and peace and security. Yet, Felice does not specify who or what he thinks has the agency to develop and then instantiate his prescriptions, nor does he even raise this question in general terms. There is certainly no discussion of the role of either (I)NGOs or social movements in the reconstruction of human rights. The implication must be that Felice believes his proposals could be implemented through the existing international institutional set up. But he does not explain how he thinks this might happen. In other words, his study lacks any strategic dimension – instead appearing to assume that some sort of global social democratic regime will emerge from the existing inter-state system.

A more traditional political theory approach to the same sorts of issues is offered by Thomas Pogge (2002) in *World Poverty and Human Rights*. He clearly identifies key aspects of world poverty, poses crucial questions about causation and calls for the substantive reform of understandings of human rights that, in some ways, parallel arguments in this volume.[1] While his proposals are directed towards the reconstruction of international institutions in order to make them compatible with human rights, there is again no consideration of the agency that might bring such changes about. So, despite his apparently radical analysis, Pogge's work ultimately seems to rely on an appeal to western elites to behave in a better, more moral, way. The fact that he suggests that the best hope for the global poor 'may be our moral reflection' (Pogge 2002:26) indicates that his strategic cupboard is bare in terms of practical ways of constructing challenges to power.

Some Space for (I)NGOs?

Some recent proposals do suggest that (I)NGOs have a role to play in the development of human rights but few of these either critically examine the concept of (I)NGOs or the relationship between (I)NGOs and social movements (see Stammers and Eschle 2005). More importantly, many of these approaches remain 'top-down' in the sense that it is assumed human rights developments are processes which are, or should be, elite driven. This usually means that the existing international political and legal set up is seen as the appropriate arena for the development of human rights. It is within this context that large and powerful western (I)NGOs are often included as elite actors. For example, in *The Power of Human Rights: International Norms and Domestic Change*, Risse, Ropp and Sikkink (1999) study the impact of ideas and norms in international politics. While they acknowledge that the 'international human rights regime' has been framed as a consequence of particular struggles (such as the struggle against apartheid in South Africa) the ideas and norms they focus on are those already expressed in the International Bill of Rights. In other words, they sidestep the necessity of assessing the importance of the creation of human rights norms through bottom-up struggle, turning their study into a 'top-down' examination of the implementation of existing international norms. This is neatly captured by the chapter title 'The Socialisation of International Human Rights Norms into Domestic Practices'.[2] Grassroots movement actors appear in this study but only as bit-part players, supporting transnational network pressure on a violating state. In fact, local activists are seen as essential for the embedding of international human rights norms into domestic practices through processes of habituation and institutionalisation, processes which are seen in wholly positive terms. What the authors call a 'global human rights polity' is a transnational advocacy network including (I)NGOs such as Amnesty International and Human Rights Watch, but otherwise comprising intergovernmental organisations and the leading western states.

Maybe Space for Movements?

Despite the tendency to focus on (I)NGOs, there is a little work which explores the role of social movements in the reconstruction of human rights, or which at least points to the potential relevance of such an exploration. But, even with this work, we need to keep our critical faculties engaged because such work often drifts either towards the sort of top-down approaches I have just described, or else adopts an idealised, utopian, view of the transformative potentialities of social movements (see Eschle and Stammers 2004).

Richard Falk is one of the most important and influential authors to look at the relationship between social movements and human rights in the contemporary world. Over many years he has produced detailed analyses of both the role of social movements and human rights in the potential transformation of 'world order'. Yet the trajectory of his work also features the two weaknesses just described. His earlier work on social movements draws heavily from NSM theory and, as a consequence, rather assumed that movements and (I)NGOs were the new transformative agents in global politics, pursuing an increasingly settled and progressive agenda of 'new politics' based on non-hierarchical methods and forms of organisation (Falk 1987). In contrast, some of his later work has become much more focused on the reform of international law and how that might facilitate the achievement of global justice. Indeed, in *Human Rights Horizons: The Pursuit Of Justice In A Globalising World*, Falk (2000) gets close to many quite traditional orientations to human rights regarding economic power (for example, assuming that it is the role of states and NGOs to 'mop up' human rights violations after they have occurred) and tending to focus on the political realm and on civil and political rights.

That said, Falk's work remains some of the most important in terms of trying to link human rights to movement struggles. For example, in one book chapter (in Brysk 2002), he contrasts human rights discourses in terms of 'above' and 'below' and notes a concern and commitment to a much more substantive form of democracy in discourses from 'below'. He argues that the conceptual differences in these two prevailing human rights discourses are of fundamental importance and that the subaltern discourse combines critique of hegemonic structures with a commitment to a just world order so as to enable all peoples to achieve material, social and spiritual dignity. In terms of specific positive proposals, he argues that there is a positive law foundation for extending the full sweep of the subaltern discourse on human rights contained within what he calls 'the sleeping provisions' of Article 25 (1) and 28 of the Universal Declaration of Human Rights.

In the previous chapters, I have mentioned the work of Nikhil Aziz (1995) and Leslie Sklair (2002) who have identified the relationship between social movements and human rights as being important for thinking about achieving substantive social change. We have also seen that Upendra Baxi (2002), Balakrishnan Rajagopal (2003) and Costas Douzinas (2000) have all identified social movements as key creators and defenders of human rights. Indeed, like Aziz and Sklair, all of these authors appear to see social movements as the potential agents of substantive social change. Yet, while suggestive, their arguments remain underdeveloped. None of them has spelt out in any detail either what substantive issues contemporary movements should be tackling or what strategic approaches they should be taking.

Towards Institutional Democratisation

In the concluding chapter to *The Transformation of Democracy*, Tony McGrew notes that 'Globalisation presents modern democratic theory with a daunting task: how to reconcile the principle of rule by the people with a world in which power is exercised increasingly on transnational, or even global scale' (McGrew 1997:231). But it is not just democratic theorists who face such a daunting task. Arguably, social movement activists are faced with the combined task of reconstructing the praxis of democracy and the praxis of human rights at one and the same time.

The Limits of Liberal Democracy

Much exploration of the relationship between human rights and democracy has focused on the nature of the relationship between liberal understandings of human rights and liberal understandings of liberal democracy (Beetham 1999; MacPherson 1977). Given that I have argued for the need to transcend liberal understandings of human rights, the reader will not be surprised to hear that I also believe it is necessary to transcend both the limited forms of democracy in 'actually existing' liberal democracies and also liberal understandings of what democracy is. As a set of political institutions, liberal democracy has been heavily criticised, critics typically pointing out that 'imperfect competition' gives structural advantage to powerful (usually economic) interests within the polity. More generally, liberal democracy has also long been criticised for its limited, procedural character, and the extent to which formal political equality obscures asymmetries of power in social relations more generally. The general terms of these sorts of critiques are my starting point, but here I want briefly to explore two somewhat different issues: firstly, specific aspects of substantive practices of democracy and how they could be operationalised and then, secondly, the relationship between a reconstructed praxis of human rights and a praxis of substantive democracy.

There are a myriad of theories and schematics for developing and deepening democratic governance. While many of these are directed towards achieving meaningful democracy within nation states, others address the question of democratic global governance. Below I focus on the latter because these have often explicitly linked democratising processes to the development and achievement of reconstructed versions of human rights. Falk's work discussed above is a prominent and important example. Yet a review of the literature on global governance reveals two things. Firstly, again, many of these proposals are conceptualised at such a level of generality or abstraction that it is difficult to assess what they might amount to in terms of social practices. They rarely address the question of how proposals would be operationalised and what impact their implementation might have on their retention of meaningful democratic credentials. The sorts of issues raised by the critique of institutional power examined in Chapter 4 are rarely taken into account. Secondly, when we look at that small minority of proposals that are more precise and detailed in terms of their operationalisation, we find that these are typically rooted in assumptions of the necessity of top-down governance and the legitimacy of elite rule.

Perhaps the most important and best known, apparently quite radical, set of proposals are those first elaborated by David Held (1995). Yet, in contrast to some of his earlier writings, social movements rarely appear in his substantive work on cosmopolitan democracy, *Democracy and the Global Order*. They are instead subsumed within a much broader and diverse field of self-regulating associations and groups in civil society. In fact, as Tony McGrew notes (1997:253), Held's model gives centrality to law and public authorities as the necessary conditions for the establishment of a more democratic world. So, what Held advocates as cosmopolitan democracy is, as Molly Cochran puts it (2002:519), 'top-down institutionalisa-tion'. Despite the apparent radicalism of Held's model there is no substantive engagement with the general problematic of institutional power. Rather, he seems to side step the paradox of institutionalisation by stitching his apparently radical proposals into Schumpeterian cloth within which elite rule is accepted as both inevitable and benign. Supporters of Held's model have rejected such critiques (see Archibugi 2004) and Molly Cochran has sought to rescue cosmopolitan democracy by attempting to develop and incorporate a pragmatic bottom-up perspective via the work of James Bonham and John Dryzek, emphasising the democratic potentials of 'international public spheres' (Cochran 2002). While work of this sort is potentially more capable of grasping the creative praxis of social movements, it remains oriented to working through tensions in existing meta-theoretical frameworks rather than engaging with that praxis.

Bridging the Institutional and Everyday Worlds

Neither specific proposals for the reconstruction of democratic global governance nor more general calls for deliberation, participation and struggles from below effectively engage with the general problematics of institutional power and the organisational question which I have called the paradox of institutionalisation. Nor, for that matter, do many political parties or movements take these questions seriously. As noted in Chapter 4, across most of the ideological spectrum, the bulk of social activists have simply accepted what they see as the inevitability of elite rule and oligarchy. Put another way, representation as hierarchy is assumed to be the pinnacle of democratic praxis as if it is hardwired into our very psyches.[3] Yet the existence of social movements and the identification of their capacity for creative social praxis points in other directions. So is it possible that social movements might be able to contribute something quite specific to the praxis of both human rights and democracy?

My suggestions here are tentative and speculative but they do point in directions that remain largely unexamined in the literatures on human rights and democracy. They involve re-examining topics familiar in the democratic litany: deliberation, participation, rep-resentation, dialogue, communication, agonism, but looking at them through a lens able to grasp the creative praxis of social movements and the breadth and depth of the network relations key to understanding social movements as social movements. There are two key, interrelated, points here. The first is the way in which social movements and 'their' organisations have a particular capacity to straddle the institutional and everyday worlds (see

Chapter 1). The second is the potential for constructing democratic praxis within social movements and between social movements and 'their' organisations. From here, it could be possible to identify forms of social praxis and strategic possibilities for achieving social change which neither assumes top-down governance nor the complete abolition of the institutional world as it currently exists. In other words, through their capacity to straddle the institutional and everyday worlds it may be possible to generate practices of mediation and accountability which could address some of the problems identified in the critique of institutional power. Bearing in mind that social movements are not organisations, 'not even of a peculiar kind' (Diani 2000:166) they necessarily retain much more open forms of collective association than is the case with formally structured organisations. Furthermore they are inherently diverse in terms of ideologies, organisation and goals and cannot be 'disciplined' in the manner of political parties. Through these underlying facets of their form and the expressive/instrumental dynamic discussed in Chapter 6, social movements potentially offer ways for communicating concerns from the everyday world to the institutional world via 'their' (I)NGOs. Further, from the perspective of those embedded in the structures of the institutional world, the existence of social movement networks offers the opportunity for forms of communication and dialogue that have the potential to transcend the often perceived illegitimacy of top-down decision making and 'education from above' (Stammers and Eschle 2005:60–61; Cochran 2002:527–9).

Historically, social movements have been important sites for the creation of forms of democratic praxis and movements themselves have been the sites of struggles for democracy. While (I)NGOs are always likely to be routinely subjected to the pressures of the paradox of institutionalisation, could 'democratised links' between the informal networks of movement activism and 'their' movement organisations help to inoculate (I)NGOs from these dangers? Put more broadly, could democratised relations within social movements help to arrest the dynamic of the drift from 'power to' to 'power over' in institutionalised settings?

Democratising 'the Social'

Most discussions of democracy and the democratisation of institutions are focused solely on the political sphere. All of the various proposals discussed in this chapter have been of this type. Yet it is clear that the problems of the paradox of institutionalisation are phenomena that are manifested across all spheres of the social: the economic and cultural, as well as the political. Social movements are social and they create movement. Their sociality and their movement can go in any direction, positive or negative. Movements can be fascistic and genocidal and, even when movements formulate demands in terms of human rights, that does not – of itself – preclude the institutionalisation of exclusion. Yet, historically, movements that have constructed and struggled for human rights have typically challenged arbitrary power and privilege, and not just politically. In other words, social movement struggles around human rights have contained a dimension which points towards democratising all forms of social relations, in the sense that both democracy and human rights share the objectives of limiting and constraining 'power over'.

This, it seems to me, is the key. Institutional democratisation cannot be restricted to the democratisation of political institutions, it must involve processes that seek to limit and constrain 'power over' throughout social relations whilst acknowledging that we need institutions to generate social 'power to'. Yet, while the history of social movement praxis around human rights demonstrates this trajectory, this history has been lost in the hall of mirrors. If the analytic link between human rights and social movements can be properly recognised then perhaps the creative praxis of social movements – 'the secret of fire' as Peter Waterman (2005:78) has put it – will once again become clear.

NOTES

Chapter 1

1. Here I am using the terms 'realist' and 'idealist' in their philosophical sense not in the way these terms are used in International Relations. I say in part a realist underpinning because, as Sayer notes with respect to 'critical realism', it can only be partly naturalist because there must always be an interpretive or hermeneutic element in social science (Sayer 2000:17). This work also has a short but useful discussion of tendencies towards philosophical idealism in post-structuralist and post-modernist approaches to social enquiry (Sayer 2000:68–72).

2. The labelling and boundaries of disciplines are themselves highly tendentious. For example, while International Relations (IR) is often seen as a sub-discipline of Politics, a significant number of IR scholars see IR as a separate discipline. Politics as a discipline is often divided into its 'normative' and 'explanatory' wings, with the latter being understood as Political Science. Here I follow this latter distinction by including 'normative political theory' within what I call the philosophical approaches, reluctantly adopting the usual term 'Political Science' to denote explanatory approaches.

3. Although there is an explicitly 'social constructionist' strand of normative political and philosophical theorising. For example, see Morton (2007); Ackerly (2008).

4. However, the historical commitments to cultural relativism within anthropology (although see Cowan, Dembour and Wilson 2001) and to structuralist or systems–theoretic analyses in sociology (Turner 2006) are important orientations within these disciplines which may explain any earlier reluctance to take the study of human rights seriously.

5. For a starting point into these debates see the short, but classic, works by Carr (2001) and Elton (2002); then also, E.P. Thompson (1978); W. Thompson (2000); D. Thompson (2001: Parts III & IV); Cooper (2005).

6. My focus on political ideologies reflects the dominance of their impact on the human rights literature since 1948 which has been largely secular in orientation. Religious ideologies were of great historical importance in shaping early ideas and practices of human rights and have continued to be of significance. Yet, until very recently,

discussion of religion in the mainstream literatures has tended to be subsumed into the broader debate about cultural relativism.

7. There are of course enormous debates about the categorisation of political ideologies. For straightforward and consolidated introductory discussion see Goodwin (2007); Heywood (2007).

8. 'Realist' here as used in the International Relations literature (Bayliss and Smith 2005:Ch.7)

9. There is vast and disparate literature on 'the agency–structure problem'. Entry points include Hay (1995); Bartky (1995) and Wendt (1987). For more detailed consideration see E.P. Thompson (1978); Giddens (1979, 1984); Cohen (1989); Sayer (1992); Sztompka (1993: Chs13–15); Collier (1994) Layder (1994); Archer (1995); Tucker (1998).

10. There is of course also a huge literature on power. Work that has helped inform this study include Lukes (1974, 1977, 1986, 2005); Foucault (1980, 1982); Honneth (1991); McNay (1992); Hindess (1996); Haugaard (1997); Stewart (2001). See also the special issue of Political Studies Review (Political Studies Association 2006) for commentary on Lukes recent reformulations where he also now concludes that 'power over' is best seen as a subset of 'power to' (Lukes 2005:69–74).

Chapter 2

1. There is a philosophical debate about the extent of continuity between ideas of 'natural' and 'human' rights. See Tuck (1979); Finnis (1980); Waldron (1984, 1987).

2. Even scholars of a social liberal/social democratic persuasion such as Jack Donnelly and Micheline Ishay make this sort of claim. Indeed, Ishay's account of the history of human rights relies on a conflation of 'the enlightenment', 'liberalism' and existing 'western civilization' (Ishay 2004:64–6).

3. Foucault's detailed account of a public execution at the beginning of Discipline and Punish is an exemplary illustration (Foucault 1977). See also Hunt's account of the torture and execution of Jean Calas which may have prompted Voltaire to write his 'Treatise on Toleration' (Hunt 1996:7; Voltaire ([1763] 2000). In respect of slavery, Robin Blackburn notes '[T]he liberty the slave aspired to would be that of freedom from unremitting toil, from daily abuse and from being at the continual command of another' (Blackburn 1988:55). See also Turner (2006) on embodiment and vulnerability.

4. Richardson's usage of 'liberalism' in this paper appears to encompass virtually all traditions of western political thought including socialism

and Marxism. So, perhaps in a manner not dissimilar to Ishay (see note 2) perhaps Richardson is effectively conflating 'liberalism' with 'enlightenment' or 'modernist' thought.

5. The second paragraph of the United States' Declaration of Independence of 1776 reads:

> We hold these truths to be self evident, that all men are created equal; that they are endowed by their Creator with certain unalienable rights; that among these are life, liberty, and the pursuit of happiness. That, to secure these rights, governments are instituted among men, deriving their just powers from the consent of the governed; that, whenever any form of government becomes destructive of these ends, it is the right of the people to alter or to abolish it, and to institute a new government, laying its foundations on such principles, and organising its powers in such form, as to them shall seem most likely to effect their safety and happiness.

While the first sentence of this paragraph is very well known and widely quoted in the human rights literature, the second sentence receives much less attention.

Chapter 3

1. Locke and Marx are usually depicted as arch-antagonists in the human rights literature. But there is a significant link here in their respective derivations of 'property rights' and 'value' from the mixing of labour with natural resources. Interestingly, Tully has pointed out that Locke was seen by some as the father of modern socialism in the nineteenth century, not just in Britain but also in France and Germany (Tully 1993:97).

2. Freeman (1995:40) makes an interesting connected point when he argues that 'Liberal individualism has traditionally failed to recognize its own dependence on the assumption that nation states have collective rights'.

3. A Google search 'Cherokee Constitution, 1827' offers various versions, some of which do not include Article 1 which specifies the boundaries of Cherokee land.

4. Wolpert (1993:Ch.15) argues the annexation of Oudh in 1856 was one catalyst of the insurrection. But he also points to policies affecting a whole range of cultural issues and traditions apparently designed to undermine Hindu and Muslim religious practices, including the legal prohibition of sati in 1829. Wolpert argues that the final straw was the smearing of new rifle cartridges with 'animal fat and lard'.

Given that Hindu and Muslim soldiers were supposed to bite the tips off cartridges before loading them, this act of 'incredible stupidity' entirely alienated them, prompting mass disobedience.

5. While stressing the necessity of liberation from colonial rule, '[o]n another level, the call for swaraj represents a genuine attempt to regain control of the 'self' – our self-respect, self-responsibility, and capacities for self-realization – from institutions of dehumanization' (Swaraj Foundation 2007; see also Prasad, 1985; Pinto 1998).

Chapter 4

1. For example, Veblen defined institutions as 'settled habits of thought common to the generality of men' or from a more recent, rational choice perspective, 'any form of constraint that human beings devise to shape human interaction'. Moving in part towards the way institutions are understood in this volume, Hall defines institutions as 'the formal rules, compliance procedures and standard operating practices that structure the relationship between individuals in various units of the polity and economy' (all cited in Kariithi 2001).

2. There are of course exceptions. As well as work identified in Chapter 4, Richard Falk has pointed to the complexities that need to be explored in *Human Rights Horizons* (Falk 2000:13, 20) and Bryan Turner has made the 'precariousness of institutions' a central theme in his discussion of vulnerability and human rights (Turner 2006).

Chapter 5

1. A classic case study would be the emergence and development of what is now the German Green Party (see Mayer, Ely and Schatzschneider 1998).

Chapter 6

1. The introductory chapter of the volume edited by Risse, Ropp and Sikkink (1999) *The Power of Human Rights: International Norms and Domestic Change* seems to replicate this tradition. It deals with similar sorts of issues as this chapter (for example, the 'diffusion of norms') but does so from an entirely different, 'top-down', starting point. This is well illustrated by the title of their introductory chapter, 'The socialization of international human rights norms into domestic practices'.

2. In the context of the discussion of Weber's work in this chapter, Riles appears to use legal instrumentalism so as to cover Weber's concepts of instrumental action and formal rationality.

3. There are exceptions. The most well known is probably Joel Feinberg but his comments were unfortunately couched in unreconstructed sexist terminology (see Kiss, 1997). Note also that this psycho-social element cannot simply be reduced to either 'passive victim' or 'possessive individual'. Rather, it focuses on a vulnerable social self-seeking protection from 'power over' via individual and/or group empowerment. See also Turner (2006).

4. Post-colonial theorist Gayatri Chakravorty Spivak is generally credited with coining the term 'strategic essentialism', but Dobrowolsky specifically mentions Diana Fuss as her inspiration for the use of this term (Dobrowolsky 2001:81).

5. It is very curious that the people Fraser cites as contributors to the construction of these 'folk paradigms' are all eminent theorists and philosophers: Iris Marion Young, Richard Rorty and Brian Barry (Fraser and Honneth 2003:15). This raises the question of what tactical or strategic role these 'folk paradigms' play in the construction of Fraser's overall argument. Does it, for example, connect to her tendency to ascribe interests and identities to 'old' and 'new' social movements respectively as critiqued in Chapter 5?

6. Honneth argues there is a danger of reducing social suffering and moral discontent to just that part of it already visible in the public sphere, put there by publicity-savvy organisations that have already crossed the threshold of mass media attention (Fraser and Honneth 2003:115). Honneth may be making the common error of conflating social movements with high profile (I)NGOs such as Amnesty International or Greenpeace, or else assuming that social movements only exist when 'visible' in the public sphere? Contrast this with Melucci's (1989) arguments on the importance of movement networks submerged in everyday life.

7. There appears to have been a fundamental shift in Honneth's understanding of recognition. In influential earlier work, especially in *The Struggle for Recognition* (Honneth 1995) he identified love, law and solidarity as the three spheres of recognition. However, in this later rendition, solidarity is replaced by achievement. Both Belden Fields and Douzinas, whilst critical of aspects of this earlier work, nevertheless saw it as an important step forward in understanding the relationship between struggles for recognition and human rights because of the connection made between law and solidarity. It is doubtful that these authors would be sympathetic to Honneth's new specification of recognition.

Chapter 7

1. These various emphases are often inter-connected. See, for example, Gathii and Nyamu (1996).
2. The now somewhat dated volume by Chomsky on Human Rights and US foreign policy (Chomsky 1978) remains compelling reading. For a different way into these issues, a document from the British government's Department for International Development 'Realising Human Rights for Poor People' is worth careful scrutiny. At first sight it appears very positive, focusing on economic and social rights, emphasising participation and democratic government from below. But buried at its heart is a 'market fundamentalism' through which the realisation of human rights is ultimately filtered (DFID 2000).
3. Jai Sen has pointed out that there are two different versions of the charter. (Sen et al. 2004:72–3).
4. This was republished as the last chapter of his *'Power and Resistance in the New World Order'* (2003) in which, it seems to me, Gill attempts to reconcile this now more optimistic stance with his earlier, more pessimistic, position taken, for example, in 'Globalization, Market Civilization and Disciplinary Neo-Liberalism' also in this collection but first published in 1995.

Chapter 8

1. He proposes a reorientation of human rights so as to make them claims against coercive social institutions, to move away from the purely juridical approach to human rights and to ground human rights in terms of protecting the weak and vulnerable.
2. What is more, without actually denying the importance of economic and social rights, in an all too typical slippage, they focus on those 'classic' civil and political rights: the right to life, freedom from torture and freedom from arbitrary arrest and detention.
3. It is indeed 'naturalised' by long-standing dominant streams of thinking which assume hierarchy to be the key feature of 'the natural order'.

BIBLIOGRAPHY

Abbink, J. de Bruijn, M. and van Walraven, K. (eds) (2003) *Rethinking Resistance: Revolt and violence in African history*, Boston/Leiden, Brill.

Abeysekera, S. (2003) Report of speech to *Feminist Organizing for a Global Future* at http://www.cwgl.rutgers.edu/globalcenter/vienna10/nov17event.html, last accessed April 2007.

Ackerly, B.A. (2008) *Universal Human Rights in a World of Difference*, Cambridge, Cambridge University Press.

Ackerman, P. and DuVall, J. (2000) *A Force More Powerful: A Century of Nonviolent Conflict*, New York, St. Martin's Press.

Adam, B. (1995) *The Rise of a Gay and Lesbian Movement*, revised edition, New York, Twayne Publishers.

Allott, P. (2001) *Eunomia: New Order for a New World*, Oxford, Oxford University Press.

Alvarez, S. (1999) 'Advocating Feminism: The Latin American Feminist NGO "Boom"' in *International Feminist Journal of Politics* 1(2)181–209.

Amnesty International (2007) Web pages of Amnesty International at http://www.amnesty.org/, last accessed April 2007.

Anaya, S.J. (2004) *Indigenous Peoples in International Law*, New York, Oxford University Press.

Anderson, B. (1991) *Imagined Communities*, revised edition, London, Verso.

Arblaster, A. (1984) *The Rise and Decline of Western Liberalism*, Oxford, Blackwell.

Archer, M. (1995) *Realist Social Theory: The morphogenetic approach*, Cambridge, Cambridge University Press.

Archibugi, D. (2004) 'Cosmopolitan Democracy and its Critics: A Review' in *European Journal of International Relations* 10(3)437–73.

Avineri, S. (1968) *The Social and Political Thought of Karl Marx*, Cambridge, Cambridge University Press.

Aziz, N. (1995) 'The Human Rights Debate in an Era of Globalization' in *Bulletin of Concerned Asian Scholars*, Oct/Dec. 1995, 9–16.

Bailyn, B. (1967) *The Ideological Origins of the American Revolution*, Cambridge, Mass. Harvard University Press.

Baker, K.M. (1990) *Inventing the French Revolution*, Cambridge, Cambridge University Press.

Balibar, E. (1994) *Masses, Classes, Ideas: Studies on Politics and Philosophy Before and After Marx*, New York, Routledge.

Bartholomew, A. (2006) *Empires Law: The American imperial project and the 'war to remake the world'*, London, Pluto Press.

Bartky, S.L. (1995) Agency: what's the problem? In Gardiner, J.K., *Provoking Agents: Gender and agency in theory and practice*, Urbana, University of Illinois Press, pp.178–93.

Baxi, U. (2000) 'Human Rights: Suffering between movements and markets' in Cohen, R. and Rai, S. (eds) *Global Social Movements*, London, Athlone Press.

— (2002) *The Future of Human Rights*, Oxford, Oxford University Press.

Bayliss, J. and Smith, S. (2005) *The Globalisation of World Politics: An introduction to international relations*, 3rd edition, Oxford, Oxford University Press.

Beetham, D. (1995) 'What Future for Economic and Social Rights?' in *Political Studies*, 43 (Special Issue) 41–60.

— (1999) *Democracy and Human Rights*, Cambridge, Polity Press.

Belden Fields, A. (2001) 'Underlying Propositions for Grounding a Holistic Conception of Human Rights' in Stammers, N. (ed.) *Papers in Social Theory 6: Rights, Movements, Recognition*, Brighton, Warwick social theory centre/Sussex centre for critical social theory, pp.32–58.

— (2003) *Rethinking Human Rights for the New Millennium*, New York, Palgrave Macmillan.

Bernstein, M. (1997) 'Celebration and Suppression: The Strategic Use of Identity by the Lesbian and Gay Movement' in *American Journal of Sociology*, 103(3)531–65.

Bhambra, G.K. and Margree, V. (2006). 'Reappraising Identity Politics: The Need for a "Tomorrow"', *Journal of the Interdisciplinary Crossroads*, 3(3)493–512.

Blackburn, R. (1988) *The Overthrow of Colonial Slavery 1776–1848*, London, Verso.

— (2007) *The Rise and Fall of Slavery in the Americas*, London, Verso.

Blaut, J.M. (1999) 'Marxism and Eurocentric Diffusionism' in Chilcote, R. (ed.) *The Political Economy of Imperialism: Critical Appraisals*, Boston, Kluwer, pp.127–40.

Boggs, C. (1986) *Social Movements and Political Power*, Philadelphia, Temple University Press.

Booth, K. (1999) 'Three Tyrannies' in Dunne, T. and Wheeler, N. (eds) *Human Rights in Global Politics*, Cambridge, Cambridge University Press, pp.31–70.

Bradley, G. (2005) 'The New Global Order? Empire, New Social Movements and the Zapatistas Movement' in *Western Journal of Graduate Research,* 12(1)27–50, Society of Graduate Students, University of Western Ontario.

Brecher, J., Costello T. and Smith, B. (2000) *Globalization From Below*, Cambridge, Mass., South End Press.

Brems, E. (1997) 'Enemies or Allies? Feminism and Cultural Relativism as Dissident Voices in Human Rights Discourse' in *Human Rights Quarterly*, 19(1)136–64.

Brown, W. (1995) *States of Injury: Power and Freedom in Late Modernity*, Princeton, New Jersey, Princeton University Press.

Brubaker, R. (1984) *The Limits of Rationality: An essay on the social and moral thought of Max Weber*, London, Allen and Unwin.

Brysk, A. (ed.) (2002) *Globalization and Human Rights*, Berkeley, University of California Press.

Brysk, A. and Shafir, G. (2004) *People Out of Place: Globalization, Human Rights and the Citizenship Gap*, London, Routledge.

Buck-Morss, S. (2000) 'Hegel and Haiti' in *Critical Inquiry*, 26:821–65.

Buechler, S. (2000) *Social Movements in Advanced Capitalism*, Oxford, Oxford University Press.

Bunch, C. (1993) 'Feminist Visions of Human Rights in the Twenty-First Century' in Mahoney, K.E. and Mahoney, P. *Human Rights in the Twenty-First Century: A Global Challenge*, London/Dordrecht, M. Nijhoff, pp.967–77.

— (2003) Report of speech to *Feminist Organizing for a Global Future* at http://www.cwgl.rutgers.edu/globalcenter/vienna10/nov17event.html, last accessed April 2007.

Burns, J.H. (1990) 'The Idea of Absolutism', in John Miller (ed.) *Absolutism in Seventeenth Century Europe,* Basingstoke, Macmillan, pp.21–42.

Calhoun, C. (1993) '"New Social Movements" of the Early 19th Century', *Social Science History,* 17(3)385–427.

Callinicos, A. (1999) *Social Theory: A Historical Introduction*, Cambridge, Polity Press.

Campbell, J. (2004) *Institutional Change and Globalization*, Princeton, New Jersey, Princeton University Press.

Carbet, A. (2004) 'Learning from Experience: Activist Reflections on "Insider-Outsider" Strategies' in *Spotlight* No.4, December 2004, Toronto, The Association for Women's Rights in Development (AWID).

Carozza, P. (2003) 'From Conquest to Constitutions: Retrieving a Latin American tradition of the idea of human rights' in *Human Rights Quarterly* 25(2)282–313.

Carr, E.H. (2001) *What is History*, 2nd edition, Basingstoke, Palgrave Macmillan.

Carroll, P.N. and Noble, D.W. (1988) *The Free and the Unfree: A New History of the United States,* 2nd edition, Harmondsworth, Penguin Books.

Carter, A. (1990) 'On individualism, collectivism and interrelationism', *Heythrop Journal,* XXXI: 23–38.

Castells, M. (1983) *The City and the Grassroots*, London, Arnold.

— (1996) *The Information Age, Vol. 1: The Rise of Network Society,* Oxford, Blackwell.

— (1997) *The Information Age, Vol. 2 The Power of Identity*, Oxford, Blackwell.

Chanock, M. (2002) '"Culture" and human rights: orientalising, occidentalising and authenticity' in Mamdani, M. (ed.) *Beyond Rights Talk and Culture Talk*, New York, St.Martin's Press, pp.15–36.

Cheah, P. (1997) 'Posit(ion)ing Human Rights' *Public Culture,* 9:233–66.

Cherokee Constitution (1827) at http://www2.volstate.edu/cbucy/History%202030/Documents/Cherokee%20Constitution-Doc52.htm, last accessed April 2007.

Chief Tecumseh (1810) *Tecumseh To Governor Harrison At Vincennes 1810* at http://www.civics-online.org/library/formatted/texts/tecumseh.html, last accessed April, 2007.

Chomsky, N. (1978) *Human Rights and American Foreign Policy*, Nottingham, Spokesman Books.

Clark, A. (1995) *The Struggle for the Breeches: Gender and the making of the British working class,* Berkeley, University of California Press.

Clark, J. and Diani, M. (1996) *Alain Touraine*, London, Falmer Press.

Cochran, M. (2002) 'A Democratic Critique of Cosmopolitan Democracy: Pragmatism from the Bottom-Up' in *European Journal of International Relations* 8(4)517–48.

Cohen, I.J. (1989) *Structuration Theory: Anthony Giddens and the Constitution of Social Life,* New York, St, Martin's Press.

Cohen, J. and Arato, A. (1992) *Civil Society and Political Theory,* Cambridge, Mass., MIT Press.

Cohen, R. and Rai, S. (eds) (2000) *Global Social Movements*, London, Athlone Press.

Cole, G.D.H. (1953) *An Introduction to Trade Unionism*, London, George Allen and Unwin.

260 HUMAN RIGHTS AND SOCIAL MOVEMENTS

Collier, A. (1994) *Critical Realism: An introduction to Roy Bhaskar's philosophy*, London, Verso.

Constitution of Liberia (1847) at http://onliberia.org/con_1847 orig.htm, last accessed April 2007.

Cooper, F. (2005) *Colonialism in Question: Theory, knowledge, history*, Berkeley, University of California Press.

Corporate Watch (2007) Corporate Watch web pages at http://archive. corporatewatch.org/index.htm, last accessed May 2007.

Cowan, J. (2006) 'Culture and Rights after "Culture and Rights"' *American Anthropologist,* 108(1)9–24.

Cowan, J., Dembour, M-B and Wilson, R. (2001) *Culture and Rights: Anthropological Perspectives*, Cambridge, Cambridge University Press.

Cox, M. (ed.) (2005) 'Debate: Rosenberg and Globalization' in *International Politics* 42(3)352–99.

Cranston, M. (1973) *What are Human Rights*, New York, Taplinger.

Crook, S., Pakulski, J. and Waters, M. (1992) *Postmodernization: Change in advanced society*, London, Sage.

Dalton, R. and Kuechler M. (1990) *Challenging the Political Order: New Social and Political Movements in Western Democracies*, Cambridge, Polity Press.

D'Anieri, P., Ernst, C. and Kier, E. (1990) 'New Social Movements in Historical Perspective' *Comparative Politics*, 22: 445–58.

Darnovsky, M., Epstein, B. and Flacks, R. (eds) (1995) *Cultural Politics and Social Movements*, Philadelphia, Temple University Press.

Das Gupta, M. (2005) 'Explaining Asia's missing women: A look at the data' in *Population and Development Review*, 31(3)529–35.

Davis, G.F., McAdam, D., Scott, W.R. and Zald, M.N. (2005) *Social Movements and Organization Theory*, Cambridge, Cambridge University Press.

de Jong, W., Shaw, M. and Stammers, N. (eds) (2005) *Global Activism, Global Media*, London, Pluto Press.

Delamotte, E., Meeker, N. and O'Barr, J. (eds) (1997) *Women Imagine Change: A Global Anthology of Women's Resistance From 600 BCE to present*, New York, Routledge.

Della Porta, D. and Diani, M. (1999) *Social Movements: An Introduction*, Oxford, Blackwell Publishers.

Della Porta, D. and Kriesi, H.P. (1999) *Social Movements in a Globalizing World* Basingstoke, Macmillan.

Dembour, M. (2006) *Who Believes in Human Rights: Reflections on the European Convention*, Cambridge, Cambridge University Press.

Dershowitz, A. (2004) *Rights from Wrongs: A Secular Theory of the Origins of Human Rights,* New York, Basic Books.

DFID (2000) *Realising Human Rights for Poor People,* Department for International Development, London, October 2000.

Diani, M. (2000) 'The Concept of Social Movement' in Nash, K. (ed.) *Readings in Contemporary Political Sociology,* Oxford, Blackwell, pp.155–76.

Dobrowolsky, A. (2001) 'Identity and Rights Reclaimed' in Stammers, N. (ed.) *Papers in Social Theory 6: Rights, Movements, Recognition,* Brighton, Warwick social theory centre/Sussex centre for critical social theory.

Donini, A. (1996) 'The Bureaucracy and the Free Spirits: Stagnation and Innovation in the Relationship Between the UN and NGOs', in Weiss, T.G. and Gordenker, L. (eds) *NGOs, The UN and Global Governance,* Boulder, Lynne Rienner, pp.88–92.

Donnelly, J. (2003) *Universal Human Rights in Theory and Practice,* 2nd edition, Ithaca, Cornell University Press.

— (2006) 'The virtues of legalization' in Meckled-Garcia, S. and Cali, B (eds) *The Legalization of Human Rights,* London, Routledge, pp.67–80.

Douzinas, C. (2000) *The End of Human Rights,* Oxford, Hart Publishing.

Downing, J., Mohammadi, A. and Sreberny, A. (eds) (1995) *Questioning the Media: A Critical Introduction,* London, Sage.

Doyle, W. (1999) *Origins of the French Revolution,* 3rd edition, Oxford, Oxford University Press.

Dubois, L. (2004) *Avengers of the New World: The Story of the Haitian Revolution,* Cambridge, Mass., The Belknapp Press.

Dunne, T. and Wheeler, N. (eds) (1999) *Human Rights in Global Politics,* Cambridge, Cambridge University Press.

Edwards, M. and Gaventa, J. (2001) *Global Citizen Action,* London, Earthscan.

Eley, G. and Hunt, W. (1988) *Reviving the English Revolution,* London, Verso.

Elliott, J. (1998) *The Fate of Reason: Max Weber and the Problem of (Ir)rationality* at http://www.unc.edu/~elliott/docs/weber.pdf, last accessed May 2007.

Elton, G.R. (2002) *The Practice of History,* 2nd edition, Oxford, Blackwell.

Eschle, C. (2001) *Global Democracy, Social Movements and Feminism,* Boulder, Westview Press.

Eschle, C. and Stammers, N. (2004) 'Taking Part: Social Movements, INGOs and Global Change' in *Alternatives,* 29(3)333–72.

Escobar, A. and Alvarez, S. (1992) *The Making of Social Movements in Latin America,* Boulder, Westview Press.

Esteva, G. and Prakash, M.S. (1998) *Grassroots Postmodernism*, London, Zed Books.

Estévez, A. (2008) *Human Rights and Free Trade in Mexico: A Discursive and Sociopolitical Perspective,* Basingstoke, Palgrave Macmillan.

Evans, T. (ed.) (1998) *Human Rights Fifty Years On: A Reappraisal,* Manchester, Manchester University Press.

— (2000) 'Citizenship and Human Rights in the Age of Globalization' in *Alternatives,* 26(1)415–38.

Eyerman, R. and Jamison, A. (1991) *Social Movements: A cognitive approach*, Cambridge, Polity Press.

EZLN (1994a) *First Declaration of the Lacandon Jungle,* translation in English at http://www.struggle.ws/mexico/ezlnco.html, last accessed May 2007.

— (1994b) *Second Declaration of the Lacandon Jungle,* translation in English at http://www.struggle.ws/mexico/ezlnco.html, last accessed May 2007.

— (1996) *Fourth Declaration of the Lacandon Jungle,* translation in English at http://www.struggle.ws/mexico/ezlnco.html, last accessed May 2007.

— (1998) *Fifth Declaration of the Lacandon Jungle,* translation in English at http://www.struggle.ws/mexico/ezlnco.html, last accessed May 2007.

Falk, R. (1987) 'The Global Promise of Social Movements: Explorations at the edge of time' in *Alternatives,* 12(2)173–96.

— (2000) *Human Rights Horizons*, London/New York, Routledge.

Felice, W. (2003) *The Global New Deal*, Lanham, Rowman and Littlefield.

Finnis, J.M. (1980) *Natural Law and Natural Rights*, Oxford, Oxford University Press.

Fischer, S. (2004) *Modernity Disavowed: Haiti and the cultures of slavery in the age of revolution*, Durham N.C., Duke University Press.

Fisher, W.F. and Ponniah, T. (eds) (2003) *Another World is Possible: Popular Alternatives to Globalization at the World Social Forum*, London, Zed Books.

Fontana, B. (1992) 'Democracy and the French Revolution' in Dunn, J. *Democracy: The Unfinished Journey 508BC to AD 1993*, Oxford, Oxford University Press.

Foran, J. (ed.) (2003) *The Future of Revolutions: Rethinking Radical Change in the Age of Globalization*, London, Zed Books.

Foucault, M. (1977) *Discipline and Punish: The birth of the prison*, Harmondsworth, Penguin.

— (1978) *The History of Sexuality: An introduction,* Harmondsworth, Penguin.

— (1980) *Power/Knowledge*, edited by Colin Gordon, Brighton, Harvester Press.

— (1982) 'The Subject and Power' in Dreyfus, H.L. and Rabinow, P. *Michel Foucault: Beyond structuralism and hermeneutics*, Chicago, University of Chicago Press, pp.208–26.

Fraser, N. and Honneth, A. (2003) *Redistribution or Recognition: A Political–Philosophical Exchange*, London, Verso.

Freeman, M. (1995) 'Are there Collective Human Rights' in *Political Studies*, 43 (Special Issue) pp.25–40.

— (2002) *Human Rights*, Cambridge, Polity Press.

— (2005) 'The Historical Roots of Human Rights Before the Second World War' in Smith, R. and van den Anker, C. (eds) *The Essentials of Human Rights*, London, Hodder Arnold, pp.151–4.

Freeman, M.D.A. and Veerman, P. (eds) (1992) *The Ideologies of Children's Rights* Dordrecht, Nijhoff.

Freeman, M.D.A (ed.) (1996) *Children's Rights: A Comparative Perspective*, Aldershot, Dartmouth.

Friends of the Earth (2007) Web pages of Friends of the Earth UK at http://www.foe.co.uk/ and Friends of the Earth USA at http://www.foe.org/index.html, last accessed May 2007.

FoEI (2004) Friends of the Earth International, *Our Environment, Our Rights: Standing up for People and the Planet*, August 2004, Amsterdam.

Gathii, J. and Nyamu, C. (1996) 'Reflections on the United States-Based Human Rights NGOs' Work on Africa' in *Harvard Human Rights Journal*, 9:285–96.

Gauchet, M. (1989) 'Rights of Man' in Furet, F. and Ozouf, M. *A Critical Dictionary of the French Revolution*, Cambridge, Mass., The Belknapp Press.

Gearty, C. (2006) *Can Human Rights Survive?* Cambridge, Cambridge University Press.

Geggus, D.P. (2002) *Haitian Revolutionary Studies*, Bloomington, Ind., Indiana University Press.

German Social Democratic Party (1891) 'The Erfurt Programme (1891)' translated by Thomas Dunlap, *German History in Documents and Images*, German Historical Institute, Washington, DC (www.german-historydocs.ghi-dc.org).

Giddens, A. (1979) *Central Problems in Social Theory*, London, Macmillan.

— (1984) *The Constitution of Society: Outline of the Theory of Structuration*, Cambridge, Polity Press.

— (1999) *Runaway World: How Globalisation is Reshaping Our Lives*, London, Profile.

Gill, S. (2000) 'Toward a Postmodern Prince?' in *Millennium: Journal of International Studies*, 29(1)131–40.

— (2003) *Power and Resistance in the New World Order*, Basingstoke, Palgrave Macmillan.

Gilly, A (2003) 'Globalization, Violence and Revolutions: Nine Theses' in Foran, J. (ed.) *The Future of Revolutions: Rethinking Radical Change in the Age of Globalization*, London, Zed Books, pp.107–24.

Ginsburg, F.D., Abu-Lughod, L. and Larkin, B. (eds) (2002) *'Media Worlds: Anthropology on New Terrain'*, Berkeley, University of California Press.

Glendon, M.A. (2001) *A World Made New: Eleanor Roosevelt and the Universal Declaration of Human Rights*, New York, Random House.

Goetz, A.M. (2006) 'Gender Equality in the Work of the UN: Where are the Accountability Systems?', Paper for the Women's Foreign Policy Group meeting held at UN Headquarters, New York, 3rd May 2006. Available at http://datemembersclicks.com/site/wfpg/Anne_Marie_Goetz_Transcript.pdf, last accessed October 2007.

Goodwin, B. (2007) *Using Political Ideas*, 5th edition, London, John Wiley.

Grant, W. (1985) 'Insider and outsider pressure groups' in *Social Studies Review*, September.

Grear, A. (2003) 'A tale of the land, the insider, the outsider and human rights' in *Legal Studies*, 23(1)32–65.

Greene, J.P. (ed.) (1979) *The Re-interpretation of the American Revolution 1763–1789*, Westport, Connecticut, The Greenwood Press.

Greenpeace (2007) web pages of Greenpeace UK at http://www.greenpeace.org.uk/ and Greenpeace International at http://www.greenpeace.org/international/, last accessed April 2007.

Guha, R. (1997) *Dominance without Hegemony: History and power in colonial India*, Cambridge, Mass., Harvard University Press.

Halasz, J. (1966) *The Socialist Concept of Human Rights*, Budapest, Akademiai Kiado.

Hallward, P. (2004) 'Haitian Inspiration: On the bicentenary of Haiti's independence' in *Radical Philosophy*, Commentaries January/February 2004, at http://www.radicalphilosophy.com/default.asp?channel_id=2187&editorial_id=14344, last accessed April 2007.

Hardt, M. and Negri, A, (2000) *Empire*, Cambridge, Mass., Harvard University Press.

Haugaard, M. (1997) *The Constitution of Power: A theoretical analysis of power, knowledge and structure*, Manchester, Manchester University Press.

Hay, C. (1995) 'Structure and Agency' in Marsh, D. and Stoker, G., *Theory and Methods in Political Science*, Basingstoke, Macmillan, pp.189–206.

Hegedus, Z. (1989) 'Social movements and social change in self-creative society' *International Sociology*, 4(1)19–36.

Held, D. (1995) *Democracy and the Global Order*, Cambridge, Polity Press.

Held, D., McGrew, A., Goldblatt, D. and Perraton, J. (1999) *Global Transformations*, Cambridge, Polity Press.

Herman, D. (1994) *Rights of Passage: Struggles for lesbian and gay equality*, Toronto, University of Toronto Press.

Heywood, A. (2007) *Political Ideologies: An Introduction*, 4th edition, Basingstoke, Palgrave Macmillan.

Hill, C. (1972) *The World Turned Upside Down*, London, Temple Smith.

Hinchman, L. (1984) 'The Origin of Human Rights: A Hegelian Perspective' in *Western Political Quarterly*, 37(1)7–31.

Hindess, B. (1996) *Discourses Of Power: From Hobbes to Foucault*, Oxford, Blackwell.

Hobsbawm, E. (1962) *The Age of Revolution 1789–1848*, London, Weidenfeld and Nicolson.

— (1967) *Labouring Men*, New York, Anchor Books.

— (1975) *The Age of Capital 1848–1875*, London, Weidenfeld and Nicolson.

— (1987) *The Age of Empire 1975–1914*, London, Weidenfeld and Nicolson.

— (1992) *Nations and Nationalism Since 1780: Programme, myth, reality*, 2nd edition, Cambridge, Cambridge University Press.

Holloway, J. and Pelaez, E. (1998) *Zapatista: Reinventing Revolution in Mexico*, London, Pluto Press.

Honneth, A. (1991) *The Critique of Power*, Cambridge, Mass., MIT Press.

— (1995) *The Struggle for Recognition: the moral grammar of social conflicts*, Cambridge, Polity Press.

Hopgood, S. (2000) 'Reading the Small Print in Global Civil Society: The Inexorable Hegemony of the Liberal Self' in *Millennium: Journal of International Studies*, 29(1)1–25.

Howarth, D. (2000) *Discourse*, Buckingham, Open University Press.

HREA (2007) Human Rights Education Association, *Study Guides: Sexual Orientation and Human Rights* at http://www.hrea.org/learn/guides/lgbt.html, last accessed April 2007.

Hulme, D. and Edwards, M. (1997) *NGOs, States and Donors: Too close for comfort*, Basingstoke, Macmillan.

Human Rights Watch (2007) web pages of Human Rights Watch at http://www.hrw.org/, last accessed April 2007.

Hunt, A. (1990) 'Rights and Social Movements: Counter-hegemonic strategies' in *Journal of Law and Society*, 17(3)309–28.

Hunt, L. (1986) *Politics, Culture and Class in the French Revolution*, London, Methuen.

— (1996) *The French Revolution and Human Rights: A brief documentary history*, Boston, Bedford/St Martin's Press.

Ignatieff, M. (2001) *Human Rights as Politics and Idolatry*, Princeton, New Jersey, Princeton University Press.

ILO (2007) 'Export Processing Zones' web pages at http://www.ilo.org/public/english/dialogue/sector/themes/epz.htm, last accessed October 2007.

Inglehart, R. (1977) *The Silent Revolution*, Princeton, New Jersey, Princeton University Press.

Ishay, M. (ed.) (1997) *The Human Rights Reader*, London/New York, Routledge.

— (2004) *The History of Human Rights*, Berkeley, University of California Press.

James, C.L.R. (1963) *The Black Jacobins*, 2nd edition, New York, Vintage.

Jones, P. (1994) *Rights*, Basingstoke, Macmillan.

Kabeer, N. (ed.) (2005) *Inclusive Citizenship: Meanings and Expressions*, London, Zed Books.

Kapur, R. (2006) 'Revisioning the Role of Law in Women's Human Rights Struggles' in Meckled-Garcia, S. and Cali, B (eds) *The Legalization of Human Rights*, London, Routledge, pp.101–16.

Kariithi, N. (2001) 'New Institutionalism' in Michie, J. (ed.) *Reader's Guide to the Social Sciences*, London: Fitzroy Dearborn Publishers, pp.373–7.

Kavada, A. (2005) 'Civil Society Organisations and the Internet: The case of Amnesty International, Oxfam and the World Development Movement' in de Jong, W., Shaw, M. and Stammers, N. (eds) *Global Activism, Global Media*, London, Pluto Press, pp.208–22.

Keane, J. (1996) *Tom Paine: A Political Life*, London, Bloomsbury.

Keck, M. and Sikkink, K. (1998) *Activists Beyond Borders: Advocacy networks in international politics*, Ithaca, Cornell University Press.

Kiss, E. (1997) 'Alchemy or Fool's Gold? Assessing Feminist Doubts About Rights' in Lyndon, M. and Narayan, U. *Reconstructing Political Theory: Feminist Perspectives*, Cambridge, Polity Press, pp.1–24.

Klein, N. (2001) 'The Unknown Icon' in *The Guardian,* 3rd March 2001, http://www.guardian.co.uk/Archive/Article/0,4273,4145255,00.html, last accessed May 2007.

Korey, W. (1998) *NGOs and the Universal Declaration of Human Rights: A curious grapevine*, Basingstoke, Macmillan.

Koskenniemi, M. (2004) *The Gentle Civilizer of Nations: The Rise and Fall of International Law 1870–1960*, Cambridge, Cambridge University Press.

Kuper, A. (2003) 'Return of the Native' in *New Humanist*, 18(3)22–5, September 2003.

Kuron, J. (1981) 'Not to Lure the Wolves Out of the Wood: An Interview with J. Kuron' in *Telos*, 47:93–7.

Labouchère, H. (1899) *The Brown Man's Burden* at http://www.swans. com/library/art8/xxx074.html, last accessed September 2008.

Laclau, E. and Mouffe, C. (1985) *Hegemony and Socialist Strategy*, London, Verso.

Langley, L.D. (1996) *The Americas in the Age of Revolution 1750–1850*, New Haven, Yale University Press.

Laslett, P. (1967) (ed.) *Locke's Two Treatises of Government*, 2nd edition, Cambridge, Cambridge University Press.

Laxer, G. and Halperin, S. (eds) (2003) *Global Civil Society and its Limits*, Basingstoke, Palgrave Macmillan.

Layder, D. (1994) *Understanding Social Theory*, London, Sage.

Levellers (1647) *Agreement of the People 1647* at http://www.constitution. org/lev/eng_lev_07.htm, last accessed April 2007.

Liebel, M. (2003) 'Working Children as Social Subjects: The contribution of working children's organizations to social transformations' in *Childhood*, 10(3)265–85.

Liebel, M., Overwien, B. and Recknagel, A. (eds) (2001) *Working Children's Protagonism: Social Movements and Empowerment in Latin America, Africa and India*, Frankfurt and London, IKO (Verlag für interkulturelle Kommunikation).

Linebaugh, P. and Rideker, M. (2000) *The Many Headed Hydra: Sailors, slaves, commoners and the hidden history of the revolutionary Atlantic*, Boston, Beacon Press.

Lukes, S. (1974) *Power: A Radical View*, Basingstoke, Macmillan.

— (1977) *Essays in Social Theory*, London, Macmillan.

— (1986) *Power*, Oxford, Blackwell.

— (2005) *Power: A Radical View*, 2nd expanded edition, Basingstoke, Palgrave Macmillan.

Mackinnon, C. (1993) 'Crimes of War, Crimes of Peace' in Shute, S. and Hurley, S. *On Human Rights: The Oxford Amnesty Lectures 1993*, New York, Basic Books, pp.83–109.

MacPherson, C.B. (1962) *The Political Theory Of Possessive Individualism*, Oxford, Clarendon Press.

— (1977) *The Life and Times of Liberal Democracy*, Oxford, Oxford University Press.

Maeckelbergh, M. (2007) *'Decentralized Network Democracy: Prefiguring Horizontality and Diversity in the Alterglobalization Movement'*, D.Phil. thesis, University of Sussex.

Mahoney, K.E. and Mahoney, P. (1993) *Human Rights in the Twenty-First Century: A Global Challenge*, London/Dordrecht, M. Nijhoff.

Maiguascha, B. (1994) 'The Transnational Indigenous Movement in a Changing World Order' in Sakamoto, Y. *Global Transformation: Challenges to the State System*, New York, United Nations University Press, pp.356–82.

Mamdani. M. (2000) *Beyond Rights Talk and Culture Talk*, New York, St. Martin's Press.

Mann, M. (1986) *The Sources of Social Power: V.1 History of power from the beginning to AD 1760*, Cambridge, Cambridge University Press.

Manning, B. (1996) *Aristocrats, Plebeians and Revolution in England 1640–1660*, London, Pluto Press.

Mayer, M., Ely, L. and Schatzschneider, M. (1998) *The German Greens: Paradox Between Movement and Party*, Philadelphia, Temple University Press.

McGrew, A. (ed.) (1997) *The Transformation of Democracy*, Cambridge, Polity Press.

— (1998) 'Human Rights in a Global Age' in Evans, T. (ed.) *Human Rights Fifty Years On: A Reappraisal*, Manchester, Manchester University Press, pp.188–210.

McLellan, D. (1977) *Karl Marx: Selected Writings*, Oxford, Oxford University Press.

McNay, L. (1992) *Foucault and Feminism*, Cambridge, Polity Press.

Meckled-Garcia, S. and Cali, B. (eds) (2006) *The Legalization of Human Rights*, London, Routledge.

Melucci, A.(1989) *Nomads of the Present*, London, Century Hutchinson.

— (1996) *Challenging Codes: Collective Action in the Information Age*, Cambridge, Cambridge University Press.

Mertes T. (ed.) (2004) *A Movement of Movements*, London, Verso.

Mertus, J.A. (2005) *The United Nations and Human Rights,* London, Routledge.

Meyer, D.S. and Tarrow, S. (eds) (1998) *The Social Movement Society: Contentious Politics for a New Century*, Lanham MA, Rowman and Littlefield.

Michels, R. (1962 [1915]) *Political Parties: A Sociological Study of the Oligarchical Tendencies of Modern Democracy*, Glencoe, The Free Press.

Microsoft Corporation (2004) *Encarta Premium Suite 2004*.

Mohanty, M., Mukherji, P.N., with Törnquist, O. (1998) *People's Rights: Social Movements and the State in the Third World*, New Delhi, Sage Publications.

Moran, M. (2006) 'Interdisciplinarity and Political Science' in *Politics*, 26(2)73–83.

Morsink, J. (2000) *The Universal Declaration of Human Rights: Origins, Drafting and Intent*, Philadelphia, University of Pennsylvania Press.

Nandy, A. (1994) *The Illegitimacy of Nationalism*, Delhi/Oxford, Oxford University Press.

Nelson, P.J. (2006) *Organizational Fields, Social Movements and the International Movement for Economic, Social and Cultural Rights*, unpublished manuscript.

Newell, P. and Wheeler, J. (eds) (2006) *Rights, Resources and the Politics of Accountability*, London, Zed Books.

Nightingale, V. and Ross, K. (2003) *Critical Readings: Media and Audiences*, Maidenhead, Open University Press.

Nye, J.S. (2002) *The Paradox of American Power*, Oxford, Oxford University Press.

O'Brien, R., Goetz, A.M., Scholte, J.A. and Williams, M. (2000) *Contesting Global Governance: Multilateral economic institutions and global social movements*, Cambridge, Cambridge University Press.

Offe, C. (1985) 'New Social Movements: Challenging the Boundaries of Institutional Politics' in *Social Research*, 52(4) Winter 1985.

— (1990) 'Reflections on the Institutional Self-transformation of Movement Politics' in Dalton, R., Kuechler, M. *Challenging the Political Order: New Social and Political Movements in Western Democracies*, Cambridge, Polity Press, pp.232–50.

OHCHR (2003) Office of the High Commissioner for Human Rights, 'Norms on the responsibilities of transnational corporations and other business enterprise with regard to human rights' at http://daccessdds.un.org/doc/UNDOC/GEN/G03/160/08/PDF/G0316008.pdf?OpenElement, last accessed September 2008.

OHCHR (2007) Office of the High Commissioner for Human Rights at http://www.ohchr.org/english/issues/indigenous/index.htm, last accessed May 2007.

Otto, D. (1996) 'Nongovernmental Organizations and the United Nations System: The Emerging Role of International Civil Society' in *Human Rights Quarterly* 18(1)107–41.

Page, E.C. (1999) 'The insider/outsider distinction: an empirical investigation' in *The British Journal of Politics and International Relations* 1(2)205–14.

Paine, T. ([1775] 2008) 'African Slavery in America' at http://www.thomaspaine.org/Archives/afri.html, last accessed November 2008.

Paine, T. ([1776] 1995) 'Common Sense' in Paine, T. (1995) *Rights of Man, Common Sense and Other Political Writings* edited by Mark Philip, Oxford, Oxford University Press.

Paine, T. ([1791,1792] 1995) 'Rights of Man' in Paine, T. (1995) *Rights of Man, Common Sense and Other Political Writings* edited by Mark Philip, Oxford, Oxford University Press.

Paine, T. ([1797] 1995) 'Agrarian Justice' in Paine, T. (1995) *Rights of Man, Common Sense and Other Political Writings* edited by Mark Philip, Oxford, Oxford University Press.

Parajuli, P. (1991) 'Power and knowledge in development discourse: new social movements and the state in India' in *International Social Science Journal*, 127:173–90.

Pasha, M.K. and Blaney, D.L. (1998) 'Elusive Paradise: The Promise and Peril of Global Civil Society' in *Alternatives* 23(4)417–50.

Petras, J. and Veltmeyer, H. (2001) *Globalization Unmasked: Imperialism in the 21st Century*, London, Zed Books.

Pinto, V. (1998) *Gandhi's Vision and Values*, London, Sage.

Plotke, D. (1995) 'What's so new about New Social Movements' in Lyman, S.M. *Social Movements: Critiques, Concepts, Case-Studies*, Basingstoke, Macmillan, pp.113–36.

Pogge, T. (2002) *World Poverty and Human Rights*, Cambridge, Polity Press.

Political Studies Association (2006) *Political Studies Review*, v.4.

Pollis, A. and Schwab, P. (1980) *Human Rights: Cultural and Ideological Perspectives* New York, Praeger.

Prasad, N. (1985) *Hind Swaraj: A fresh look*, New Delhi, Gandhi Peace Foundation.

Prothero, I. (1997) *Radical Artisans in England and France 1830–1870*, Cambridge, Cambridge University Press.

Rajagopal, B. (2003) *International Law From Below: Development, social movements and third world resistance*, Cambridge, Cambridge University Press.

Ramazanoglu, C. (1989) *Feminism and the Contradictions of Oppression*, London, Routledge.

Richardson, J.L. (1997) 'Contending Liberalisms: Past and Present' in *European Journal of International Relations*, 3(1)5–33.

Riles, A. (2006) 'Anthropology, Human Rights and Legal Knowledge: Culture in the Iron Cage' *American Anthropologist*, 108(1)52–65.

Risse, T., Ropp, S. and Sikkink, K. (eds) (1999) *The Power of Human Rights: International Norms and Domestic Change*, Cambridge, Cambridge University Press.

Robertson, R. (1992) *Globalization: Social Theory and Global Culture*, London, Sage.

Robinson, F. (2002) *Human Rights Discourse and Global Civil Society: Contesting Globalisation?* Paper for the 2002 Annual Meeting of the International Studies Association, New Orleans, Louisiana, March, 2002 at http://www.isanet.org/noarchive/robinson.html, last accessed April 2007.

Ronen, D. (1979) *The Quest for Self-Determination*, London/New Haven Conn., Yale University Press.

Rosenberg, J. (2000) *The Follies of Globalisation Theory*, London, Verso.

— (2005) 'Globalisation Theory: A Post Mortem', in *International Politics*, 42(1)2–74.

Rowbotham, S. and Linkogle, S. (2001) *Women Resist Globalization*, London, Zed Books.

Royle, E. (1996) *Chartism*, 3rd edition, London, Longman.

Santos, B. de Sousa (1995) *Towards a New Common Sense: Law, science and politics in the paradigmatic transition*, New York, Routledge.

— (1999) 'Towards a Multicultural Conception of Human Rights' in Featherstone, M. and Lash, S. *Spaces Of Culture: City, Nation, World*, London, Sage, pp.214–29.

— (2006) *The Rise of the Global Left: The World Social Forum and Beyond*, London, Zed Books.

Sarah, E. (ed.) (1983) *Reassessments of 'First Wave' Feminism*, Oxford, Pergamon.

Sassoon, D. (1997) *One Hundred Years of Socialism*, London, Fontana.

Sayer, A. (1992) *Method in Social Science: A Realist Approach*, 2nd edition, London, Routledge.

— (2000) *Realism and Social Science*, London, Sage.

— (2003) *Long live postdisciplinary studies! Sociology and the curse of disciplinary parochialism/imperialism*, published by the Department of Sociology, Lancaster University, at http://www.lancs.ac.uk/fass/sociology/papers/sayer-long-live-postdisciplinary-studies.pdf, last accessed November 2008

Scheingold, S.A. (2005) *The Politics of Rights: Lawyers, public policy and political change*, 2nd edition, Ann Arbor, University of Michigan Press.

Schumpeter, J.A. (1976) *Capitalism, Socialism and Democracy*, 5th edition, London, Allen and Unwin.

Scott, A. (1990) *Ideology and the New Social Movements*, London, Unwin Hyman.

Seidman, S. (2004) *Contested Knowledge: Social Theory Today*, 3rd edition, Oxford, Blackwell Publishing.

Sen, J., Anand, A., Escobar, A. and Waterman, P. (eds) (2004) *World Social Forum: Challenging Empires*, New Delhi, The Viveka Foundation.

Sheller, M. (2000) *Democracy After Slavery: Black publics and peasant rebels in Haiti and Jamaica,* Basingstoke, Macmillan.

Shivji, I.G. (1989) *The Concept of Human Rights in Africa*, London, Codesria.

Shue, H. (1980) *Basic Rights: Subsistence, Affluence and US Foreign Policy,* Princeton, New Jersey, Princeton University Press.

Sklair, L. (2002) *Globalization: Capitalism and its Alternatives*, Oxford, Oxford University Press.

Smith, J., Chatfield, C. and Pagnucco, R. (1997) *Transnational Social Movements and Global Politics: Solidarity Beyond the State*, Syracuse, New York: Syracuse University Press.

Smith, M. (1999) *Lesbian and Gay Rights in Canada,* Toronto, University of Toronto Press.

Smith, R. and van den Anker, C. (eds) (2005) *The Essentials of Human Rights*, London, Hodder Arnold.

Sorell, T. (2006) 'The UN Norms' in Dine, J. and Fagan, A. (eds) *Human Rights and Capitalism*, London, Edward Elgar, Ch.11.

Spivak, G.C. (2004) 'Righting Wrongs' in *South Atlantic Quarterly*, 103(2/3)523–81.

Stammers, N. (1995) 'A Critique of Social Approaches to Human Rights' in *Human Rights Quarterly*, 17(3)488–508.

— (1999a) 'Social Movements and the Social Construction of Human Rights' in *Human Rights Quarterly*, 21(4)980–1008.

— (1999b) 'Social Movements and the Challenge to Power' in Shaw, M., (ed.) *Politics and Globalisation: Knowledge, ethics and agency*, London, Routledge, pp.73–88.

— (2001a) 'Social Democracy and Global Governance' in Martell, L. et al. (eds) *Social Democracy: Global and National Perspectives*, Basingstoke, Palgrave Macmillan, pp.27–48.

— (2001b) (ed.) *Papers in Social Theory 6: Rights, Movements, Recognition*, Brighton, Warwick social theory centre/Sussex centre for critical social theory.

Stammers, N. and Eschle, C. (2005) 'Social Movements and Global Activism' in de Jong, W., Shaw, M. and Stammers, N. (eds) *Global Activism, Global Media*, London, Pluto Press, pp.50–67.

Steiner, H.J. and Alston, P. (2000) *International Human Rights in Context*, 2nd edition, Oxford, Oxford University Press.

Stewart, A. (2001) *Theories of Power and Domination*, London, Sage.

Swaraj Foundation (2007*) 'What is Swaraj?'* at http://www.swaraj.org/whatisswaraj.htm, last accessed December 2007.

Sztompka, P. (1990) 'Agency and Progress: the idea of progress and changing theories of change' in Alexander, J. and Sztompka, P. *Rethinking Progress*, London, Unwin Hyman, pp.247–63.

— (1993) *The Sociology of Social Change*, Oxford, Blackwell.

Tarrow, S. (2005) *The New Transnational Activism*, Cambridge, Cambridge University Press.

Thiele. L.P. (1993) 'Making Democracy Safe for the World: Social Movements and Global Politics' in *Alternatives,* 8(3)273–305.

Thompson, D. (ed.) (2001) *The Essential E. P. Thompson*, New York, The New Press

Thompson, E.P. (1978) *The Poverty of Theory and Other Essays*, London, The Merlin Press.

— (1980) *The Making of the English Working Class*, London, Penguin Books.

Thompson, N. (1998) *The Real Rights of Man*, London, Pluto Press.

Thompson, W. (2000) *What Happened to History?*, London, Pluto Press.

Tilly, C. (1986) *The Contentious French*, Cambridge, Mass., Belknap Press

— (1993) *European Revolutions 1492–1992*, Oxford, Blackwell.

— (2004) *Social Movements 1768–2004*, Boulder, Paradigm Publishers.

Touraine, A. (1977) *The Self-Production of Society*, Chicago, University of Chicago Press.

— (1981) *The Voice and the Eye*, Cambridge, Cambridge University Press.

Tuck, R. (1979) *Natural Rights Theories: Their origin and development*, Cambridge, Cambridge University Press.

Tucker, K. (1991) 'How New are the New Social Movements' in *Theory Culture and Society,* 8:75–98.

Tucker, K.H. (1998) *Anthony Giddens and Modern Social Theory*, London, Sage.

Turner, B.S. (2006) *Vulnerability and Human Rights*, Pennsylvania State University Press.

Tully, J. (1993) *An Approach to Political Philosophy: Locke in Contexts*, Cambridge, Cambridge University Press.

UNDP (2003) *Human Development Report 2003* at http://hdr.undp.org/en/reports/global/hdr2003/, last accessed November 2008.

— (2005) *Human Development Report 2005* at http://hdr.undp.org/en/reports/global/hdr2005/, last accessed November 2008.

UN Non-Governmental Liaison Service (1998) 'Roundup 30: Human Rights Approaches to Development', November 1998.

Van Kley, D. (ed.) (1994) The French Idea of Freedom: The Old Regime and the Declaration of Rights, Stanford, California, Stanford University Press.

Vincent, R.J. (1986) Human Rights and International Relations, Cambridge, Cambridge University Press.

Voltaire ([1763] 2000) Treatise on Tolerance, edited and translated by Simon Harvey, Cambridge, Cambridge University Press.

Waldron, J. (1984) Theories of Rights, Oxford, Oxford University Press.

— (ed.) (1987) Nonsense Upon Stilts: Bentham, Burke and Marx on the Rights of Man, London, Methuen.

Walker, R.B.J. (1988) One World, Many Worlds: Struggles for a Just World Peace, Boulder, Lynne Rienner/London, Zed Books.

— (1993) Inside/Outside: International relations as political theory, Cambridge, Cambridge University Press.

Waltz, S. (1999) 'On the Universality of Human Rights' in 'Journal of the International Institute', 6(3) at http://quod.lib.umich.edu/cgi/t/text/text-idx?c=jii;cc=jii;q1=waltz;rgn=main;view=text;idno=4750978.0006.302, last accessed November 2008.

Waterman, P. (2005) 'Between a political-institutional past and a communicational-networked future: Reflections on the Third World Social Forum, 2003' in de Jong, W., Shaw, M. and Stammers, N. (eds) Global Activism, Global Media, London, Pluto Press, pp.68–79.

Weiss, T.G. and Gordenker, L. (eds) (1996) NGOs, The UN and Global Governance, Boulder, Lynne Rienner.

Welch, C. (2000) NGOs and Human Rights: Promise and Performance, Philadelphia, University of Pennsylvania Press.

Wendt, A. (1987) 'The Agent–Structure Problem in International Relations' in International Organisation, 41(3)335–70.

Weston, B.H. (1992) 'Human Rights' in Claude, R.P. and Weston, B.H. Human Rights in the World Community: Issues and Action, 2nd edition, Philadelphia, Pennsylvania, University of Pennsylvania Press, pp.14–30.

Wignaraja, P. (ed.) (1993) New Social Movements in the South London, Zed Books.

Williams, G.A. (1989) Artisans and Sans-Culottes: Popular Movements in France and Britain During the French Revolution, 2nd edition, London, Libris.

Williams, G. (2005) The Voice of the Street: Protest and Power in Southern France, PhD thesis, Dept. of Social Anthropology, Kings College, University of Cambridge.

Williams, P. (1993) *The Alchemy of Race and Rights*, London, Virago Press.

Wilson, R. (ed.) (1997) *Human Rights, Culture and Context: Anthropological Perspectives*, London, Pluto Press.

Winston, M. (2007) 'Human Rights as Moral Rebellion and Social Construction' in *Journal of Human Rights*, 6:279–305.

Wolpert, S. (1993) *A New History of India*, 4th edition, New York, Oxford University Press.

Wood, E.M. (2002) *The Origin of Capitalism: a longer view*, London, Verso.

Wootton, D. (1991) 'Leveller Democracy and the Puritan Revolution' in Burns, J.H. *The Cambridge History of Political Thought 1450–1700*, Cambridge, Cambridge University Press, pp. 412–42.

— (1992) 'The Levellers' in Dunn, J., *Democracy: The Unfinished Journey 508BC to AD 1993*, Oxford, Oxford University Press.

INDEX

Compiled by Sue Carlton